AMERICAN AUTHORS
AND CRITICS SERIES

GENERAL EDITOR
JOHN MAHONEY, University of Detroit

ABOUT THE AUTHOR

LAWRANCE THOMPSON, former Guggenheim Fellow and Ford
Foundation Fellow, is a Professor of English and American
Literature at Princeton University. He has lectured at the
Salzburg (Austria) Seminar in American Studies; at the uni-
versities of Ljubljana, Zagreb, and Belgrade (Yugoslavia); at
the University of Oslo (Norway); and at the Hebrew University of Jerusalem (Israel). His writings include *Young Long-
fellow; Fire and Ice: The Art and Thought of Robert Frost;
A Comic Principle in Sterne, Meredith, and Joyce; Melville's
Quarrel With God;* and an edition of Edwin Arlington Robin-
son's *Tilbury Town* poems.

ISSETIBBEHA'S

Hunting & fishing camp where Wash Jones killed Sutpen. Later owned by Major De Spain

TALLAHATCHIE RIVER

GO DOWN, MOSES

McCaslin Edmonds

WAS

WASH
THE BEAR
A JUSTICE
RED LEAVES

Sutpen's Hundred

John Sartoris' Railroad

CHICKASAW

ABSALOM, ABSALOM!

Where by 1820 his people had learned to call it "The Plantation" just like the white men did

RAID
AN ODOR OF VERBENA
A ROSE FOR EMILY

Sartoris

THE UNVANQUISHED

PATENT

Grierson
Burden

SANCTUARY

Where Lee Goodwin was jailed tried & lynched

THE SOUND

PERCY GRIMM

LIGHT IN AUGUST

Airport

Compson's Mile

THAT EVENING SUN

DEATH DRAG

AND THE FURY

for which Jason I swapped Ikkemotubbe a race horse & the last fragment of which Jason IV sold in order to become free

JEFFERSON
and
YOKNAPATAWPHA
COUNTY
Mississippi
1945

SPOTTED HORSES

THE HAMLET

Varner's Crossroads

Old Frenchman Place

where Popeye murdered Tommy

YOKNAPATAWPHA RIVER

OLD MAN

Here was born the convict & grew a man & sinned & was transported for the rest of his life to pay for it

Surveyed & mapped for this volume by
WILLIAM FAULKNER

MAP OF YOKNAPATAWPHA COUNTY

WILLIAM
FAULKNER

An Introduction and Interpretation

LAWRANCE THOMPSON
Princeton University

Barnes & Noble, Inc.　　New York

Publishers　　Booksellers　　Since 1873

ACKNOWLEDGMENTS:

From *Absalom, Absalom!*, by William Faulkner. Copyright 1936 by William Faulkner. Reprinted by permission of Random House, Inc.; and by permission of Chatto & Windus Ltd.

From *Go Down, Moses*, by William Faulkner. Copyright 1942 by William Faulkner. Reprinted by permission of Random House, Inc.; and by permission of Chatto & Windus Ltd.

From *The Hamlet*, by William Faulkner. Copyright 1940 by William Faulkner. Reprinted by permission of Random House, Inc.; and by permission of Chatto & Windus Ltd.

From *Light in August*, by William Faulkner. Copyright 1932 and renewed 1959 by William Faulkner. Reprinted by permission of Random House, Inc.; and by permission of Chatto & Windus Ltd.

From *Requiem for a Nun*, by William Faulkner. Copyright 1940, 1951 by William Faulkner. Reprinted by permission of Random House, Inc.; and by permission of Chatto & Windus Ltd.

From *Sanctuary*, by William Faulkner. Copyright 1931 and renewed 1958 by William Faulkner. Reprinted by permission of Random House, Inc.; and by permission of Chatto & Windus Ltd.

From *The Sound and the Fury*, by William Faulkner. Copyright 1929 and renewed 1956 by William Faulkner. Reprinted by permission of Random House, Inc.; and by permission of Chatto & Windus Ltd.

From *The Town*, by William Faulkner. © Copyright 1957 by William Faulkner. Reprinted by permission of Random House, Inc.; and by permission of Chatto & Windus Ltd.

From *The American Novel and Its Tradition*, by Richard Chase. Copyright © 1957 by Richard Chase. Reprinted by permission of Doubleday & Company, Inc.; and by permission of G. Bell & Sons, Ltd.

From "Faulkner's Mythology," by George Marion O'Donnell, in *The Kenyon Review*, Summer 1939. Reprinted by permission of *The Kenyon Review*.

CONTENTS

ILLUSTRATIONS

CHRONOLOGY

1897 William Falkner born September 25, in New Albany, Mississippi. The eldest of four sons of Murray Charles and Maud Butler Falkner. Named after his great-grandfather, Colonel William Falkner, who fought in the Civil War, built railroads, and wrote a popular novel, *The White Rose of Memphis*. (The discrepancy in the spelling of the family name did not occur until 1924, when the title page of *The Marble Faun* carried "by William Faulkner." Thereafter, he continued to use that spelling.)

1901–18 Moved with family from New Albany to Oxford, Mississippi, where Murray Charles Falkner first operated a livery stable, then went into the hardware business, and finally became business manager of the University of Mississippi. Attended public schools in Oxford, but left high school without graduating, and worked in grandfather's bank. Friendship with Phil Stone, a young lawyer, encouraged his interest in writing.

1918 Went to Canada, enlisted in Royal Canadian Flying Corps, and was in training as a pilot at the time of the World War I Armistice.

1919–21 Special student at the University of Mississippi. Published poetry and prose in *The Mississippian*.

1922–24 Worked at a book store in New York (where he met Elizabeth Pratt, later the wife of Sherwood Anderson) and then returned to Oxford to become Postmaster at the University of Mississippi, where he neglected his duties and was dismissed.

1924 *The Marble Faun,* first volume of poems, published December 15.

1925 In New Orleans, from January to June, lived in Pirates' Alley and became acquainted with Sherwood Anderson through Elizabeth Pratt (Mrs. Sherwood Anderson). Published poems, sketches, and essays in the *Times-Picayune* and *Double Dealer*. Wrote his first novel, *Soldiers' Pay*, in six weeks during this period. In June, went to New York, and from there shipped aboard a freighter bound for Milan, Italy, working his way in engine room and on deck. Traveled on bicycle and on foot through Italy and France. Returned to the United States in November.

1926 *Soldiers' Pay* published February 25. Settled briefly in Pascagoula, Mississippi, to finish second novel, *Mosquitoes*, then returned to Oxford and made his home there permanently. Worked as carpenter, painter, paper hanger, and coal-heaver in Oxford power plant.

1927   *Mosquitoes* published April 30.

1929   *Sartoris,* first novel in the saga of Yoknapatawpha County, published January 31. Married Estelle Oldham Franklin, in Oxford, June 30. *The Sound and the Fury* published October 7.

1930   *As I Lay Dying* published October 6.

1931   *Sanctuary* published February 9: a best seller which was also made into a motion picture entitled "The Story of Temple Drake." First collection of short stories, *These Thirteen,* published September 21.

1932   Motion picture rights to a short story entitled "Turnabout" (published in *The Saturday Evening Post* on March 5) were bought. Worked in Hollywood writing screen play adaptation of "Turnabout" under title, "Today We Live." (Made frequent visits to Hollywood in 1936, 1939, 1944, and 1946 to work on other screen plays.) *Light in August* published October 6.

1933   *A Green Bough,* volume of poetry, published April 20. Birth of daughter, Jill.

1934   *Doctor Martino and Other Stories* published April 16.

1935   *Pylon* published March 25.

1936   *Absalom, Absalom!* published October 26.

1938   *The Unvanquished* published February 15.

1939   *The Wild Palms* published January 19.

1940   *The Hamlet* published April 1.

1942   *Go Down, Moses and Other Stories* published May 11.

1948   *Intruder in the Dust* published September 27. A motion picture based on this novel was made later in Oxford.

1949   *Knight's Gambit,* volume of short stories, published November 7.

1950   *Collected Stories of William Faulkner* published August 21. In December, accompanied by daughter Jill, went by plane to Sweden to accept award of Nobel Prize for Literature. Made Speech of Acceptance in Stockholm, December 10.

1951   *Requiem for a Nun,* a play, published September 27. (Later, 1958, presented by The Theatre Guild in New York City.) Made an Officer of the French Legion of Honor, October 26.

1954   *A Fable* published August 2. Visited Brazil, in August, on invitation of the Exchange of Persons Branch of the State Department, and attended International Writers' Conference in São Paulo as a United States delegate.

1955   Received National Book Award for Fiction, in New York City, January 25, and delivered Acceptance Address. The Pulitzer Prize for Fiction was awarded to *A Fable* on May 1. Visited Japan, in August, on invitation of the Exchange of Persons Branch of the State Department, and took part in the Nagano Seminar.

1957   Began an association with the University of Virginia, Charlottesville, Virginia, as Writer-in-Residence, which lasted from February to June during each of the following five years. Under the auspices of the State Department, visited Greece, in March, where he was awarded the Silver Medal of the Athens Academy. *The Town* published May 1.

1959 *The Mansion* published November 13.

1962 *The Reivers* published June 4. Died of a heart attack on July 6 in Oxford, Mississippi, where he is buried.

◁ၭ INTRODUCTION

F ROM THE beginning to the end of his literary career, William
Faulkner had difficulty in winning his right to be regarded as a
major American author. The controversy over his artistic merits and
defects, which began with the publication of his first novel, had not
ended by the time of his death and shows no immediate sign of abate-
ment. At one extreme, the most fanatical among his admirers are so
positive that Faulkner is by far the best writer of prose fiction America
has ever produced that they resent any faultfinding. At the other
extreme, some equally fanatical detractors continue the old condemna-
tion of Faulkner as an illiterate who liked to wallow in psychopathic
horrors while keening his laments over the Northern rape of the South
in "labyrinthine prolixities of verbal obfuscation."

The average reader, initially puzzled by the undeniable eccentricities
in Faulkner's style, and then infuriated by the apparent perversity in
his ways of telling a story, very largely ignored him during the years
when he was doing his best work. As late as 1945, after he had published fifteen volumes of novels and short stories, his only novel easily
available was the notorious *Sanctuary*. Most of his other stories were
then out-of-print. At the same time, by contrast, European critics
were praising Faulkner as a major novelist of the twentieth century,
and translators had already begun to make his works well known
in many European countries. French readers in particular seemed
so comfortably familiar with experimental trends and innovations
throughout modern poetry and prose that they found Faulkner's bold
idiom understandable and even fascinating. But many Americans who
noticed the glowing tributes sent from Paris to New York concerning
Faulkner's art, were either annoyed or indifferent: if the French liked
Faulkner, they could have him.

A sense of shock and bewilderment was therefore conveyed to most
American readers, by the announcement that the Nobel Prize for
Literature, in 1949, had been awarded to the Chronicles of Yoknapa-
tawpha County written by Faulkner in a steadily growing series of

I

novels and short stories. That bewilderment was further heightened by the discovery that Faulkner's Acceptance Address, given in Stockholm and widely quoted in American newspapers, did something more than make sense. It implied that Faulkner was not a "determinist" or a "cosmic pessimist," as many had claimed. Instead, that Acceptance Address made it apparent that Faulkner had used that occasion for purposes of taking issue with those European and American existentialist writers, either of fiction or philosophy, who seemed willing and eager to predict the approaching end of the human race, doomed by the bomb. "I decline to accept the end of man," said Faulkner in Stockholm. "I believe that man will not merely endure: he will prevail. . . . because he has a soul, a spirit capable of compassion and sacrifice and endurance."

The impact of Faulkner's Nobel Prize Address gave pause to many serious critics. It made them wonder whether he had suddenly changed his tune or whether, in even his most horrific narratives he had possibly been trying, all the time, to illuminate unnecessary causes of human self-betrayals. Of course he had not changed his tune. The more enlightened of Faulkner's readers and critics had been attempting for years to make the doubtful ones see that Faulkner's thematic coin had always been two-sided, even when he defined his positive idealism in terms of negatives, and that the artistic logic behind Faulkner's difficult ways of unfolding a narrative had been calculated by Faulkner to throw indirect light on his own persistent and yet cautiously qualified affirmations.

Gradually, in the wake of that Nobel Prize Address, some of Faulkner's most hostile critics began to discover the good sense, or at least the expediency, of granting that there might be some merit in Faulkner's art, and even in Faulkner's themes, in spite of his faults and shortcomings. Unfortunately, however, some of those fumbling attempts to recover, and to correct earlier mistakes in judgment, created a new variety of errors. During the 1950's, when Faulkner's literary powers were in obvious decline, some of his least important work was singled out for loudest praise. An ironic example occurred when the Pulitzer Prize Committee for the first time awarded honors to Faulkner, in 1954, and for one of his most gallant literary failures, the allegorical novel entitled *A Fable*. But the ultimate irony took place when Faulkner's last full-length narrative, *The Reivers*, was praised so highly by so many critics, as being "one of the best novels Mr. Faulkner has written," that their misjudgment helped to lift *The Reivers* high up on the best-seller list.

Now that Faulkner has completed his work, the time is right for attempting a detached and objective reassessment of his many strengths and weaknesses, and the following essays try to make such a reassessment. They are addressed not only to mature readers who have already acknowledged difficulty in appreciating Faulkner's best, but also to younger and less experienced readers who may find useful orientations in this introduction. The structural arrangement of these essays has a calculated continuity. Chapter one briefly surveys and evaluates all of Faulkner's major writings, not merely to give an over-all chronological view of the whole but also to sort out Faulkner's artistic failures from his artistic successes, granting the risk in such oversimplification. Chapter two makes preparatory uses of certain early twentieth-century literary trends and innovations, and calls particular attention to those experimental techniques of Joyce and Eliot which prepared the way for some of Faulkner's most difficult and troublesome storytelling strategies. The naming and describing of those strategies, in chapter two, is designed to assist the reader in handling more detailed and incisive analyses and interpretations which follow. In each of the next eight chapters, separate treatment is given to one of Faulkner's most significant prose works. An attempt is made, in each case, to differentiate significances, for purposes of identifying all the major colors in the Faulknerian spectrum. Another goal, in each of those chapters, is to explain and correlate the "how" and the "what" of inextricable form-and-content relationships, and to show how Faulkner's telling of a particular narrative has its own indirect ways of illuminating and dramatizing ideas which are centrally cumulative within the story itself. The first detailed analysis and interpretation is devoted to *The Sound and the Fury*, for several reasons. It happens to be one of Faulkner's best, but it also happens to permit considerations, within a relatively brief compass, of many technical elements first used there by Faulkner and diluted in subsequent adaptations. So it provides an excellent place for any reader to take preliminary bearings.

Throughout this introductory study, attempts are constantly made to urge the validity of one basic suggestion: whenever a reader pays careful attention to Faulkner's formal principles of ordering, such an act of collaboration between reader and author increases the reader's enjoyment of the story and of the ideas illuminated by that story. But more than that, some of the underlying ideas do not even become apparent or available to the reader until they are consciously approached through the artistic indirections which implicitly formulate those ideas. As a corollary, the assumption is also made, throughout, that the ultimate value of an artistically ordered narrative depends first on its power, as story, to hold the attention and interest of the reader; then ultimately on its power to move (in Faulkner's case, frequently, to move by hurting) the emotional and intellectual sensibilities of the reader. In the collaborative act of reading, of course, the extra efforts required of the reader by a difficult storyteller like Faulkner, must always be rewarded ultimately by the power to move the reader profoundly. In the concluding chapter, a summary correlation of techniques and ideas is made, in an attempt to demonstrate continuities in Faulkner's moral vision.

These introductory remarks should make it clear that these essays aim at several other goals beyond that of temporarily reassessing and re-evaluating Faulkner's work. One other goal is to enable any serious reader to use these essays as steppingstones, beyond which the reader may proceed independently to become well-acquainted with all of Faulkner's writings, and thus to make his own judgments as to which are the best. Or perhaps it would be better to offer these essays as whetstones, against which any reader may sharpen his own capacities for independent judgment. The interpretive insights and critical evaluations here tentatively and provisionally made, are thus conceived as having a serviceable function if they serve primarily as provocations. Any sensible critic expects to be challenged, corrected, and eventually superseded. Nevertheless, one claim on which these essays willingly stand or fall is that anyone who becomes well-acquainted with the impressive range, depth, and quality of Faulkner's art should become self-convinced that Faulkner's best work entitles him to a permanent place, nationally and internationally, as a major twentieth-century novelist and short-story writer.

1

⤑ LITERARY CAREER

THE SHEER bulk of William Faulkner's life-work is impressive. His publications include approximately fifty poems, ninety short stories, seventeen novels, and a three-act drama which was produced on Broadway. But the discrepancy between quantity and quality in his work is enormous. The unmistakable genius of his artistic talent was marred from start to finish by a curiously arrogant and self-indulgent contempt not only for the reader but also for self-discipline and revision. As a result, the best and the worst of his accomplishments may often be found intermingled within the same work, so that any fastidious reader must make discriminations from page to page. The following brief survey of his literary career can not cope with such discriminations; it is designed merely to provide an initial perspective of the whole.

After the manner of so many other authors who have achieved their greatest distinction as writers of prose narratives, Faulkner began his literary career as a poet, and that fact colored all his later writing of prose. He said repeatedly that he thought of himself as a "failed poet" who had turned to the writing of poetic prose narratives as "the next best thing." Fourteen of his derivative and early poems appeared in the weekly student newspaper, *The Mississippian*, from October of 1919 to May of 1921, while he was taking courses at the University of Mississippi. His first published volume was a collection of nineteen lyrics: *The Marble Faun* (1924). Soon after the publication of *The Marble Faun*, he turned primarily to the writing of prose sketches, short stories, and novels. Later he demonstrated his continuous attempts to achieve valid lyric utterance: in 1933 he published forty-five poems, largely lyrics, under the title, *A Green Bough*. None of them merits particular praise.

Another phase of literary apprenticeship began for Faulkner when he moved from Oxford to New Orleans near the beginning of 1925. He found in the French Quarter considerable inspiration for writing brief sketches of picturesque characters and fragmentary incidents, and sixteen of those sketches were published in the *Times-Picayune* during 1925. The limpid style of those little narratives and the oblique handlings of themes provide hints that Faulkner had already come under the influence of Joyce's *Dubliners*. But they lack Joyce's bitterly incisive treatment of moral paralysis—a theme which later attracted Faulkner.

While still in New Orleans, adjusting himself more or less comfortably to the Bohemian life of painters and writers there, Faulkner continued his apprentice period by writing his first novel, *Soldiers' Pay* (1926). The title was ironically intended, and Faulkner poured into that narrative his own postwar disillusionments. The plot is built around the return of an American boy, from the war, to his home in Georgia, to die from wounds received while serving with the British Air Force. The plight of the boy is completely misunderstood by his former friends and even by his family. Faulkner's anguished and embittered involvement with the dying airman is genuine enough; but it is injurious to his control of the story. The style is clumsy and turgid, the attempt to braid three plots is awkward, and the handling of characterizations is wooden. Yet the narrative foreshadows the later Faulknerian idiom through its crude capacity for hurting and shocking the reader.

By contrast, Faulkner's second novel, *Mosquitoes* (1927), eschews the tragic and attempts the satirically comic. It is a slight and flippant treatment of those artistic and social circles in New Orleans which had aroused Faulkner's distaste while he was there. The poetic influence of Eliot, rather than the stylistic influence of Joyce, is here apparent. Most of the characters are represented as bloodless and bloodsucking insects who are not unrelated to Eliot's Hollow Men, Prufrocks, Nightingales, and Sweeneys. The plot is almost nonexistent, and most of the narrative is comprised of hollow talk. One character in *Mosquitoes*, a novelist named Dawson Fairchild, seems to be an unflattering fictional portrait of Faulkner's friend and enemy of those New Orleans days, Sherwood Anderson.

As it happened, Sherwood Anderson in New Orleans gave Faulkner a casual piece of advice which eventually started him toward his major literary achievements. "You're a country boy," Anderson reminded him. "All you know is that little patch up there in Mississippi where you started from. But that's all right too." Years later, Faulkner remembered and liked to quote that remark as the initial stimulus which indirectly drove him home; the stimulus which helped him give literary transformation of his Mississippi home town, Oxford, and his home county of Lafayette, into the fictional town of Jefferson and the fictional county of Yoknapatawpha. But he went home by way of New York and Paris and Rome, thus managing to knock around just long enough to get the wanderlust out of his blood. Even Anderson's very sensible advice did not immediately open his eyes to literary possibilities which existed for Faulkner in a region so painfully familiar to him that for a time he had been glad to turn his back on it.

The town and environs of Oxford did indeed contain abundant materials for storytelling, as Faulkner had been learning ever since childhood. Nurtured on a typical Southern diet of legend, history, folklore, gossip, tall tales, and wry humor, he gradually found that he possessed in his own memory and knowledge all the subject matter and settings needed for his creative imagination. Given fictional handling, Oxford could serve as a microcosm of the Deep South, and Faulkner's own family history could provide the makings of a saga. Pertinent regional yarns reached back to the early years of the nineteenth century, when sober pioneers mingled with intoxicated adventurers in the migration across the coastal plains of the Carolinas and Virginia, over the mountains, and on down toward the lower Mississippi Valley. Those pioneers and adventurers had vied with each other in their bargaining for Chickasaw Indian land. Trading posts had appeared in that region years before anyone began to hack plantations out of semitropical bottomland woods and jungles. Among those pioneers, Faulkner's own ancestors had played their parts, and had managed well enough, in Mississippi, throughout the early decades of settlement and development. Some of them later distinguished themselves in the fighting and suffering which came with and after that never-to-be-forgotten War Between the States; that war which had translated so many Southern triumphs and hopes into failures and illusions. William Faulkner, because of his enriched historical heritage, thus encompassed in his own consciousness not only the anguish of that war but also the predatory injustices and inhumanities of the Reconstruction Era. He grew up knowing that the word "failure" possessed a special legacy of meaning for the South and for himself. When he returned to Oxford, at the end of World War I, after his own disappointing adventures in Canada and after his postwar wanderings in Europe, he brought home a disillusioned perspective concerning Southern history. Tending to view himself as a rebel among the rebels, he began his Yoknapatawpha saga in a way which permitted him to treat critically, ironically, sardonically, and yet compassionately, a great many Southern postures, codes, illusions, and myths. As he continued to build that saga, one theme which inevitably occurred was his ambiguous treatment of Southern gallantry, past

7

and present—either the actual or the pretended gallantries, but particularly those well-intentioned human efforts which lacked moral fibre and therefore brought failure.

Sartoris (1929), the foundation stone for the construction of the Yoknapatawpha saga, was given a setting in the fictitious town of Jefferson, so much like the actual Oxford, in the fictitious Mississippi county of Yoknapatawpha, the old Indian name of an actual river which flows through Lafayette County. In *Sartoris*, Faulkner dramatized the decay of a proud Southern family, very much like his own; dramatized it in ways which permitted him to explore and probe historical perspectives unflatteringly and yet sympathetically. There, for the first time, the Sartoris family was represented as coming to grips with the unpleasant amoralities of the Snopes clan. Viewed in retrospect, after all the other parts of the Yoknapatawpha saga have been put in place, *Sartoris* has a primary importance. But if it is evaluated merely on its own merits, it stands only as another apprentice novel, not far removed from *Soldiers' Pay*. The central character is once again an aviator, home from the war, embittered, isolated, and compulsively driven to self-destruction. This time, his name is Bayard Sartoris. Occasional passages have the ring of authentic Faulknerian metal, as for example the episode in which Bayard Sartoris visits and lingers with a backwoods Negro family, long familiar to him. But the total effect is disappointing and poor.

The end of Faulkner's apprentice period, and the beginning of the most important eight-year phase in his entire literary career, was marked by the writing and publishing of *The Sound and the Fury* (1929). A deliberate and bold tour de force, in which Faulkner brilliantly adapted from James Joyce's *Ulysses* three stream-of-consciousness styles, *The Sound and the Fury* deserves to stand as Faulkner's first major literary triumph, and perhaps his greatest. In subject matter, it has this much in common with *Sartoris:* it is another fictional study of the collapse of a proud and once distinguished Southern family; this time, the Compson family.

Throughout his career, Faulkner continued to make intensive uses of the stream-of-consciousness mode. But his next novel, *Sanctuary*, represented a brief return to traditional techniques for reasons which were sardonic enough. *Sanctuary* seems to have been inspired primarily by Faulkner's disappointing and disillusioning lack of success in finding an immediate publisher for the manuscript of *The Sound and the Fury*. If publishers who pandered to low tastes of common readers could scorn his best efforts, Faulkner seemed to feel that he might return scorn for scorn, vengefully. Why not feed those tastes whatever was popularly palatable. Quickly, and with indignant fury, he tossed off *Sanctuary* as a shilling shocker, and soon found a publisher for it. The insult worked, and even turned a nice profit for Faulkner. Unsuspecting common readers bought *Sanctuary* so fast that it became a best-seller, and then Hollywood made it into a soap-opera film entitled "The Story of Temple Drake." Faulkner later deprecated *Sanctuary* by granting that a "cheap idea" had motivated the writing of it. But a case can be made to demonstrate that *Sanctuary* deserves a higher position among Faulkner's literary accomplishments than is usually given it. Incidentally, *Sanctuary* may be viewed as a sequel to *Sartoris* in the sense that several of the Jefferson characters who previously appeared in *Sartoris* become involved in the tribulations of Temple Drake.

After Faulkner had sardonically unburdened himself through the writing of *Sanctuary*, and before he had found a publisher for it, he turned back from the relatively traditional style of *Sanctuary* to the stream-of-consciousness innovations he had used for the first time in *The Sound and the Fury*. Experimenting even more boldly in *As I Lay Dying* (1930), he created an extreme tour de force in which the story is obliquely unfolded through sixty separate soliloquies, distributed among eight characters in the action. The result is a brief mock-epic which represents the labors of a poor-white family named Bundren, primarily engaged in carrying out the dying wish of the mother-wife, Addie Bundren, that her body be taken for burial to her distant home town of Jefferson. Artistically considered, this sleight-of-words might bring to mind Doctor Johnson's comment on the lady preacher's sermon, which he compared to the act of a dog walking on its hind legs: it was not done well, but one was surprised to see it done at all. After the reader has marveled at Faulkner's experimentations in *As I Lay Dying*, there is no need to be stricken into critical silence by it. The total effect is disappointing; the inadequacy of the characterizations fails to arouse our sympathies and compassions; the ending makes us feel as though we had been tricked into caring at all; the artistry seems glib when compared with the uses of the same technical procedures in *The Sound and the Fury;* and the total idea moves us even less than the total action. But so much adoration has been spent on *As I Lay Dying* by other critics of Faulkner that the general acclaim given it must be mentioned; nevertheless, the position here taken is that *As I Lay Dying* has been too highly praised by too many critics.

So far, in this brief survey of Faulkner's literary career, nothing has been said about his very successful venture into the field of short-story writing. That venture began very ingeniously with the publication of a very successful Faulknerian shocker entitled "A Rose for Emily," which appeared in the *Forum* magazine for April 1930. During the next few months thereafter, Faulkner's brief concentration on short-story writing resulted in the appearance of several more stories in leading magazines. Then a baker's dozen of them were gathered and published as *These Thirteen*, late in 1931. Subsequently, the stories in that volume were supplemented by two new collections, *Doctor Martino and Other Stories* (1934) and *Knight's Gambit* (1949). Many of those stories fit into the framework of the Yoknapatawpha saga, and some of them were later revised for inclusion as parts of novels. Good arguments have been marshaled to support the claim that Faulkner did his best literary work as a writer of short stories rather than as a novelist; but the present study is not in accord with such arguments. Although the best of his short stories are indeed so excellent that they leave an indelible and almost searing hurt, the assumption here made is that any reader who learns to handle Faulkner's difficult idiom, as it operates in his far more elaborate novels here considered, can transfer from that experience the wherewithal for handling the short stories. Forty-two of his best are available in a volume entitle *Collected Stories of William Faulkner* (1950).

The Yoknapatawpha series of novels was given splendid enrichment with the publication of *Light in August* (1932). There for the first time Faulkner chose to build a long narrative around the subject matter of relationships between Negroes and whites in the South and around certain social, psychological, and religious attitudes towards Negro blood, either pure or defiled. The central character in *Light in August* is a foundling named Joe Christmas who, in spite of gossip to the effect that there is some Negro blood beneath his white skin, never finds out whether the gossip is true or false, and the reader is never told. But the carefully instilled prejudices of guilt by association are enough to poison the responses of Joe Christmas and the responses of others, in ways which help to ruin his life. Certainly one of Faulkner's best novels, *Light in August* belongs in a special class with only two others: *The Sound and the Fury* and *Absalom, Absalom!*

Faulkner's eighth novel, *Pylon* (1935), happens to be one of his worst. The plot is built around the clumsy and yet sympathetic attempts of a New Orleans newspaper reporter to understand the compulsive and bizarre activities of a pair of barnstorming stunt aviators (and their shared wife and child), just as they are climactically caught up in a fatal web of events during a five-day Mardi gras carnival. As in *Soldiers' Pay* and *Sartoris*, Faulkner's wartime training seems to have given him particular sympathy for returned airmen; but here again his characters are not adequately motivated, and the plot falls apart from too much melodrama.

Another unit of construction was added to the Yoknapatawpha series in Faulkner's next novel, *The Unvanquished* (1938). Because the action therein represents the vicissitudes of the Sartoris family during and immediately after the War Between the States, the earlier novel named *Sartoris* might make more sense if read as a sequel to *The Unvanquished*. It deserves to be considered as yet another typically Faulknerian literary experiment. The structural units are seven well-integrated short stories, six of which were published separately before they were revised and thus integrated. The center of consciousness, throughout, is a young man, who later became the grandfather for whom the hero of *Sartoris* was named. This earlier Bayard, growing up through the trying wartime experiences of 1861–65, is educated not only by Southern codes and traditions but also by conflicts among Southerners themselves. He reaches his maturity, and the narrative reaches its crisis, only when he governs his own actions by certain forms of morality and honor which transcend the letter of the laws laid down in the ancient codes. *The Unvanquished* is one of Faulkner's many good novels, but it reaches past that level and attains first-rate quality in the crucial chapter (or story) entitled "An Odor of Verbena."

In writing *The Wild Palms* (1939), Faulkner tried another experimental innovation—another difficult manipulation of literary counterpoint. He attempted to establish and maintain polarities which would acquire cumulative thematic significance, by playing off the title narrative against a subordinate story entitled "Old Man." The plots of the two stories are entirely separate; they do not share any characters. But the process of alternating separate chapters of each, throughout, establishes a literary pattern of thesis and antithesis which helps to sharpen the significance of images and characters and actions. The total effect of the experiment is not successful. The subordinate story, "Old Man," is much the better of the two, and has frequently been reprinted successfully as a separate unit. Yet any patient and sympathetic reader of Faulkner will find much to admire in the literary counterpoint of *The Wild Palms*, notwithstanding the fact that this novel has to be included among Faulkner's gallant failures.

The Hamlet was published in 1940 without any indication that it would eventually constitute the first volume in a trilogy devoted to the grotesque and tragicomic affairs of that Snopes family which had first been mentioned in *Sartoris*. Faulkner later admitted that he had conceived and had begun to work on that trilogy (*The Hamlet, The Town, The Mansion*) as far back as 1925, and that admission finds at least partial corroboration when it is noticed that the references to Flem Snopes in *Sartoris* are all of a piece with Flem's activities in *The Hamlet* and in *The Town*. Further evidence concerning the slow growth of the Snopes trilogy may be found in early magazine publications of four Snopes stories which were later revised and expanded for inclusion as parts of *The Hamlet*. Although evaluative judgments on *The Hamlet* differ sharply, it surely deserves a place among Faulkner's good novels.

Go Down, Moses (1942) enabled Faulkner to achieve a new structural pattern, experimentally, and an entirely new set of characters for purposes of exploring relationships between Negroes and whites in Yoknapatawpha County. This time several generations of the McCaslin clan provide the central social group: three lines of descent (male, female, and Negro) are dramatically traced from the "old Abraham" of the family, the pioneer Carothers McCaslin. Conflicts among all three branches of this family tree provide Faulkner with opportunities to place the miscegenation theme in contexts quite distinct from those found in *Absalom, Absalom!* and *Light in August*. Here again, however, even as in *The Unvanquished*, the structural units of the narrative are seven closely related short stories; and here also, six of these seven had previously been published separately before they were integrated by means of revisions. One major unification was achieved in those revisions by representing as the center of consciousness old Isaac McCaslin, here represented as retrospectively viewing the history of his clan. Unevenness of qualities in style and plot spoil the possibility of including this work among Faulkner's best. But the units entitled "Pantaloon in Black," "The Old People," "Delta Autumn," and especially "The Bear" (each enriched by the larger context) raise *Go Down, Moses* to a topmost position among Faulkner's good works. After *Go Down, Moses*, Faulkner's literary skill began to weaken.

Intruder in the Dust (1948) may be considered as a sequel to *Go Down, Moses*, at least to the extent that the central character, Lucas Beauchamp, plays an important role in both narratives. A Negro grandson of old Carothers McCaslin, Lucas Beauchamp is here represented as being unjustly accused of murder and in danger of a death sentence. After plenty of action salted by detective-story suspense, a fast motion of events, and some spine-tingling melodrama, Lucas is rescued by the combined efforts of a white boy and a white woman. Considered as a murder mystery, or merely as an adventure story,

Intruder in the Dust makes good reading for those familiar with Faulkner's idiom. (The story was also made into an excellent motion picture.) But this example of a facet of Faulkner's virtuosity which might be called his *Saturday Evening Post* style is marred by too many propagandistic preachments placed in the mouth of that familiar all-purpose, heavy-duty character named Gavin Stevens.

New and difficult experiments in literary counterpoint were employed by Faulkner in writing *Requiem for a Nun* (1951), which is a genuine sequel to *Sanctuary*. Three formal acts of drama are constructed around some very melodramatic happenings in the home of Temple Drake, after her marriage. Each of these three acts, in turn, is prefaced by a prose narrative or prologue, and each prologue deals with a unit of events in the early history of Yoknapatawpha County. Thematic and symbolic counterpoints between each prologue and each accompanying act of drama are made to operate very effectively. Nevertheless, whether taken separately, or as making up a whole, these two different elements do not achieve artistic success. The prologues do not jell as narratives, and the three acts are not sufficiently dramatic to make good theatre. Too much of the dialogue is devoted to retrospective summaries of what happened to Temple Drake in *Sanctuary*. Although *Requiem for a Nun* therefore adds another title to Faulkner's ambitious failures, it is given a chapter of interpretation here for special reasons. Some of the very factors therein which must be measured as poor art, or at least as faulty art, provide overt statements of some aspects of Faulkner's all-pervading moral vision; aspects which are handled more covertly and more artistically in Faulkner's three best works and elsewhere. So any reader who is seriously trying to understand continuities in Faulkner's moral vision may profitably overlook the artistic weaknesses of *Requiem for a Nun* long enough to examine it closely for its central ideas.

Among Faulkner's failures, the most ambitious and the most elaborately contrived is *A Fable* (1954). The major action takes place during the False Armistice, in France, at the end of World War I. Perhaps the worst artistic fault is that the allegorical skeleton sticks through the flesh unpleasantly, and the characters come too near to being types who seem created too largely for purposes of illuminating the thinly-concealed allegorical meaning. Mistakenly puffed by Faulkner's publisher as "the crowning achievement" of his career, and then mistakenly awarded a Pulitzer Prize, *A Fable* very soon found its way down near the bottom of the barrel.

The second novel in the Snopes trilogy, *The Town* (1957), continued the action of *The Hamlet* as a direct sequel by representing the devious processes by which Flem Snopes and his relatives moved in on Jefferson from Frenchman's Bend to match amoral cunning against the wits of certain well-intended upholders of Southern gentility and idealism there. The leader of the opposition, during this phase of warfare against Snopesism, is the quixotic Gavin Stevens. But at the end of this tragicomedy, Flem Snopes has triumphed once more. One of Faulkner's good novels, *The Town* has much to recommend it.

The undeniably poor novel in the Snopes trilogy is the last, entitled *The Mansion* (1959). It contains a curious prefatory note in which Faulkner advised the reader that certain discrepancies and contradictions could be found between his earlier and this his last treatment of these characters. But he asked that these discrepancies be accepted as proof that the author had learned more about Snopesism than he knew when he first began to write about it. Some such excuse had to be made, because Faulkner gave *The Mansion* a questionable hero-villain named Mink Snopes; the same Mink Snopes who was jailed for petty murder in *The Hamlet* and who became infuriated because his kinsman Flem Snopes had made no effort to buy off the court which sentenced Mink to imprisonment. In *The Mansion*, Mink is betrayed far more culpably by Flem Snopes, with the result that Mink devotes much of his prison life to plotting vengeance. The reader's interest in all this baseness might be expected to increase as soon as Mink gets out of jail and starts his epic journey for the far-off mansion of Flem Snopes in Jefferson. But the end is more than foreseen: the life has gone out of Flem Snopes, as a character in a fiction, long before he is shot and killed by his kinsman. Even worse, there is too much listlessness in all the supporting cast of characters who had been driven into engrossing and tragicomic actions by complicated motives throughout the first two novels of the Snopes trilogy. As a result of these weaknesses, and others, the entire action of *The Mansion* is boring. To heighten the reader's discomfort, Faulkner's style in *The Mansion* reads like a parody or burlesque of his earlier mannerisms. Even Faulkner seems bored, as he clumsily contrives characters and situations. Perhaps he discomforted himself with his erroneous decision to conclude the trilogy with the falsehood that Snopesism will always destroy itself, even as it does here. He knew better than that.

Faulkner's last novel, *The Reivers* (1962), is neither one of his best nor one of his worst; but it is disappointing. Apparently designed as a comic postlude for the Yoknapatawpha saga, it provides the reader with only trivial forms of amusement. The plot seems to be made up of literary remnants or sweepings. The central action turns on a well-intended prank which gets out of hand during the five-day action.

Back in 1905, one of the first automobiles bought in Jefferson was "borrowed" and used for a joy ride to Memphis by three well-meaning characters. One is a part-Indian livery stable attendant, Boon Hoggan-beck (sacred to the memory of "The Bear" in *Go Down, Moses*). Another is a shrewd part-Negro operator, Ned McCaslin (descended from old Carothers McCaslin). The third is an eleven-year-old boy, Lucius Priest (also a descendant from old Carothers McCaslin, on the distaff side). No important complications occurred in this mildly amusing yarn until the trio reached Memphis and settled in at the "house" of Miss Reba Rivers (landlady to Temple Drake, Popeye, and Red, in *Sanctuary*). While Boon and Lucius enjoyed one alterca-tion after another among the touchy members of the brothel, Ned surprised them. He traded the borrowed automobile for a borrowed horse. As might be guessed, the rest of the story turns primarily on a series of horse races, unsuccessfully arranged by Ned for purposes of winning back the borrowed car. Throughout *The Reivers*, Faulkner's tired thematic interests are preoccupied with the gradual education of the boy, Lucius, concerning the intermixture of good and evil in everyone, including the boy himself. Lucius further represents a kind of virtue rewarded. He manages to acquire his five-day education without losing his idealism, and he even finds that his idealism reawak-ens a sense of human decency among several disillusioned characters, including a prostitute who finally becomes a decent woman after Boon marries her. Artistically, Faulkner arranged to have this story told as a "reminiscence" by the boy, after he had become a grand-father. Such an arrangement might provide an artistic excuse for Lucius-the-narrator to become sentimental in his review of McCaslin clan relationships. But the garrulousness of the boy-turned-grand-father does not conceal the garrulousness of grandfather Faulkner, particularly for readers who have gone over much the same ground of McCaslin clan relationships, far more meaningfully, in *Go Down, Moses*. In a sense, of course, the peripheral reminiscences in *The Reivers* do tie a nice big bowknot on the Yoknapatawpha saga. But that bowknot has the spurious quality of something gotten up be-latedly for a costume-party charade. As a result, *The Reivers* brings the Yoknapatawpha saga to a close on a note which is more garrulously sentimental and tricksy than comic. As might be expected by readers of Faulkner, the best parts of this narrative are the horse races.

In summary, Faulkner's most significant literary accomplishment has to be seen as his Chronicles of Yoknapatawpha County. Malcolm Cowley has well-summarized that accomplishment as "a labor of imagination that has not been equaled in our time, and a double labor:

first to invent a Mississippi county that was like a mythical kingdom, but was complete and living in all its details; second to make his story of Yoknapatawpha County stand as a parable or legend of all the Deep South." But Faulkner did more than that. He did more than recreate his own Southern heritage in fictional forms for purposes of reinterpreting the significance of a local past to a local present. His best themes always have universal applications. For example, his narratives repeatedly start out with the typical Southern view of a close-knit family relationship as providing the basic social unit in a community. Then such narratives consistently develop dramatic conflicts between blood relatives, even between Negroes and whites. But by the time Faulkner finishes any of his best narratives, he has managed to probe very deeply into various phases of man's calculated injustice and inhumanities to man, throughout the entire human family.

There should be the double pleasure and pain, then, for any reader to contemplate Faulkner's narratives not merely as narratives but also as vehicles which, at their best, move us to profound meditations. But we are not adequately qualified to appreciate that double value until we have increased our understanding of how Faulkner's bold idiom employed technical innovations to make his storytelling forms become his meanings.

2

⋖⋗ TECHNICAL INNOVATIONS

T HERE IS no possible way of determining the degree of deliberate and conscious intent with which an author like William Faulkner handles his techniques of storytelling. But that mystery creates no crisis. It does not even matter that Faulkner liked to insist, with a sly thickening of his very Southern drawl, that he just didn't know anything about literary art, and that he was just a little old Mississippi farmer who liked to tell stories. If he had carried that deception one step further, and had claimed that all his technical innovations which provided him different ways of unfolding narratives came to him unconsciously and instinctively, thus providing him with a form of automatic writing, even that claim could be tolerated. The important fact would still remain: his techniques of ordering, whether conscious or unconscious, whether original or borrowed or adapted, did create effects which (when noticed) help to guide and control the reader's awareness of relationships between how he told a story and what he made that story mean.

There were times when Faulkner's handling of style and plot and characterization and setting and symbolism and structure were comfortably conventional. But his most unconventional strategies and his most troublesome techniques are best understood as adaptations and extensions of certain artistic experiments and innovations first employed in prose by James Joyce and first employed in poetry by T. S. Eliot. By way of brief review and preparation, it may be worthwhile to consider here some of the most important innovations which Faulkner inherited from Joyce and Eliot.

Because *Ulysses* and *The Waste Land* were both published in 1922, it is easy to understand Eliot's sympathetic defense of Joyce and his praise of Joyce for having introduced new literary techniques which, said Eliot, "psychology (such as it is, and whether our reaction to it be comic or serious), ethnology, and *The Golden Bough* have concurred to make possible." Eliot's defense of Joyce may have been a form of self-defense. He might have added that his own independent development of original and yet closely related techniques, in *The Waste Land*, had also been made possible by new theories and findings in related fields of psychology, ethnology, and mythology.

In the field of psychology, the theories and findings of Freud seem to have had the most profound effect on literature, and on literary adaptations from ethnology and mythology. Faulkner, like Eliot and Joyce, resisted many implications of Freudian theories, while making use of whatever seemed suitable to literary needs. So there is particular pertinence in recalling, here, a few Freudian concepts which helped to stimulate so many literary innovations during the first half of the twentieth century. Perhaps Freud's most provocative effect on literature (and on psychology) was achieved by his provision of new insights concerning the dynamics of nervous energy operative in any human being, and operative particularly in determining interior drives. Indirectly, Freud thus refreshed the significance of free associations in the stream of consciousness. He assigned new meanings to unconscious and subconscious motivations. He provided new interpretations as to the workings and the significances of reveries and dreams. He placed particular emphasis on a reinterpretation of tensions between the child and its parents in his theory of the Oedipus complex. In all these ways he threw new light on neurosis and so-called madness.

The literary innovations made possible by these theories were so many that even when authors like Joyce, Eliot, and Faulkner wrote with only a limited approval of Freud, they found much they could adapt. Freud's theories particularly enriched the literary possibilities which involved the manner and the matter of symbolic statements and symbolic actions. Radical changes in emphasis, thus made available, affected traditional concepts of characterization and setting and plot. Meaningful distortions of conventions in style and language and syntax began to be used to suggest poetic ambivalences through fragmentary associations in the stream-of-consciousness mode. Plot innovations could now be achieved, meaningfully, by beginning with effects which might seem to be meaningless; then by working backwards and forwards through fragments of action, to clarify initial causes and ultimate consequences. Within such a plot, the conventional unfolding of dramatic actions through a smooth narration of cause-and-effect might be displaced by a scrambling of past and present impressions which would at first seem chaotic until the reader noticed that meanings were controlled by an artistically manipulated use of seemingly free associations. Users of these innovations soon found that the conventional portrayal of personality through a mere representation of outward evidence as to what a character might do or say, became an inadequate form of characterization. Now that conventional procedure could be amplified, not merely by representing such a character's unspoken thoughts but also by representing reveries, dreams, hallucinations which might provide the reader with insights not available to the character. The new concern for unconscious motivations gave greater importance to what might be represented as happening within character, to provide implicit explanations of even more than the character might understand concerning his or her own thoughts and utterances and actions. Hence the most important stage for dramatic action might at times be transferred from a physical setting, in time and space, to a metaphysical-psychological setting.

From the start, these innovations were discussed at length by critics, and even by authors who used them. After Joyce had paid his own tribute to the French author, Edouard Dujardin, by acknowledging indebtedness to *Les Lauriers sont Coupés*, for example, Dujardin provided some helpful afterthoughts concerning the interior monologue and the gains he thought he derived from using the interior monologue. Some of his remarks are pertinent to an understanding of Faulkner's adaptations of that mode from Joyce. Dujardin described the artistic representation of reverie as

> . . . the speech of a character in a scene, having for its object the direct introduction of the reader into the interior life of the character, without any interventions in the way of explanations or commentary on the part of the author; like other monologues, it has theoretically no hearers and is not spoken. But it differs from the traditional monologue in these respects: in the matter of content, it is the expression of the most intimate thoughts, those which lie nearest the unconscious; in its nature it is a speech which precedes logical organization, reproducing the intimate thoughts just as they are born and just as they come; as for form, it employs direct sentences reduced to the syntactical minimum; thus in general it fulfills the same requirements which we make today for poetry.

Although Dujardin's explanation can serve as a fairly accurate description of ways in which both Joyce and Faulkner intermittently handled the stream-of-consciousness mode, it does not suggest Faulkner's particular pleasure in interweaving past and present impressions, meaningfully, through conscious and subconscious associations.

To illustrate Faulkner's adaptations from these innovations previously introduced by Dujardin and Joyce, some pertinent peculiarities of *The Sound and the Fury* may be described here. The text of *The Sound and the Fury* is divided into only four parts, and in the first three of those four parts Faulkner completely removes himself from the traditional role of narrator. Strictly speaking, there is no narrator. Instead, each of those first three parts is represented as a separate soliloquy. Thus the reader is given the artistic illusion of eavesdropping on the impressions and rememberings of three separate soliloquizers who are brothers in the Compson family: Ben, Quentin, and Jason. Each of the brothers makes his soliloquy at the end of a separate day —a day which has particular importance in the life of that character. Each reverie takes the form of recollections concerning the events of that immediate day, and then, through seemingly free associations (which are of course carefully ordered by Faulkner), "flashbacks" give us recollections of events which occurred earlier—days or weeks or months or years earlier. The style, in each of these three soliloquies, is made by Faulkner to reflect very striking differences between the personalities of the three brothers; their verbal mannerisms give the artistic illusion that each is unselfconsciously characterizing himself. The repeated interruptions of immediate impressions, thrust aside by past impressions associationally invoked, is initially confusing to the reader. But the reader gradually becomes aware that the analogies, thus established, between past and present actions or images, are made highly meaningful by the larger context. Artistically considered, this Faulknerian tour de force becomes justified when it releases far more overtones of meaning than could be achieved with the same verbal economy in any other form of literary ordering except poetry.

Indeed, as Dujardin suggested, all these modifications of earlier literary conventions are essentially poetic, or at least essentially dramatic. But these innovations require the reader to modify conventional reading responses, through intensified acts of collaboration. When so many different kinds of meaning are implied, in so many different ways, there is more for the reader to do, by way of active collaboration with the author, than is required in the reading of a conventional narrative. The danger of over-collaboration should be obvious, and a simple corrective may be worth offering. This is nothing more than the common-sense principle employed by the reader of any highly wrought novel of the nineteenth century: the reader's imagination is alert to entertain innumerable possibilities; but those possibilities are held cautiously, tentatively, provisionally, until the further unfolding of the narrative tends to focus attention on the most pertinent of those possibilities. In *The Sound and the Fury*, for example, Faulkner himself encourages the reader to play that collaborative game of possibilities. He permits a character to make associations which are not immediately meaningful; but sooner or later Faulkner himself suggests more than one possibility of meaning; then finally he permits the story to close in on one possibility which becomes an actuality, and thus dominates the others.

There is another important technical innovation which Faulkner derived in part from reading Freud but probably in larger part from reading Joyce and Eliot. No single term can represent that innovation, which is achieved through the uses of free association to enrich the viability of a very old literary convention: the implying of analogies. Because Faulkner began his literary career as a poet, he was naturally inclined to make heavy uses of analogies, metaphors, and symbols, in even conventional ways, as soon as he began writing prose narratives. His interest in Shelley may have helped him to extend his pleasure in analogies by providing him with reminders of what Plato said the worldly images were "like unto." But if the various categories of analogizing, as in Faulkner's works, could be sorted out and arranged to suggest a Faulknerian version of a Platonic ladder, such an arrangement should place one favorite Faulknerian category of analogizing at the very top. It is the poetic process of implying analogies between the configuration of an immediate set of actions, in one of his own stories, and the configuration of an ancient set of actions, in a familiar mythic narrative. There are conventional ways of implying such analogies, but Joyce and Eliot would seem to have taught Faulkner some innovations.

Joyce provided the most influential of these innovations, in the handling of mythic analogies, when he gave to his celebrated narrative of one day's life in dear dirty Dublin the seemingly irrelevant title, *Ulysses*. Of course that title gradually becomes a gathering metaphor, as the reader notices various analogies implied between the ancient Greek epic and Joyce's modern Irish mock-epic—analogies implied between the classical patterns of action, dramatized in the Homeric epic by Ulysses, Penelope, and Telemachus, and the modern patterns of action dramatized in the Dublin story by Bloom, Molly, and Stephen. The meaning? The significance of these elaborately accumulated analogies? Because no immediate answer is available, the reader is forced by Joyce to play the collaborative game, to entertain many different possibilities, and to hold those possibilities tentatively, provisionally, until the action of the story provides an answer. As it happens, however, any single answer made to those questions will touch on a sore spot in Joyce criticism and interpretation. But Eliot's defense of *Ulysses* contains one answer which is cryptically pertinent:

> In using the myth, in manipulating a continuous parallel between contemporaneity and antiquity, Mr. Joyce is pursuing a method which others must pursue after him. . . . No one else has built a novel

upon such a foundation before: it has never before been necessary. I am not begging the question in calling *Ulysses* a 'novel'; and if you call it an epic it will not matter. If it is not a novel, that is simply because the novel is a form which will no longer serve; it is because the novel, instead of being a form, was simply the expression of an age which had not sufficiently lost all form to feel the need of something stricter. . . . It is simply a way of controlling, of ordering, of giving a shape and a significance to the immense panorama of futility and anarchy which is contemporary history. . . . It is a method for which the horoscope is auspicious. . . . Instead of narrative method, we may now use the mythical method.

In those cryptic remarks, Eliot did not say how the so-called mythical method can be made to work artistically to control and order and give shape to either a prose narrative like *Ulysses* or a poem like *The Waste Land*. Perhaps he did not say because he knew that the "mythical method" could be made to work in so many different ways, and with so many different permutations and combinations. He had demonstrated that fact, uniquely, in *The Waste Land*, where he implied that it should be the pleasure of careful readers to see how he made the "mythical method" work in several ways, simultaneously.

Anyone who begins his reading of Faulkner after reading Joyce and Eliot is not likely to need guidance on the workings of the "mythical method." But before we consider any of those ways, we need to pin down a few pertinent meanings for that much abused and slippery word, "myth." As Eliot implied, anthropologists and ethnologists have continued to provide abundant evidence that various primitive cultures seem to have performed analogous rituals, even back in prehistoric times, to propitiate those bodiless forces in nature (or behind nature) which those primitive peoples viewed as either granting or denying life; as either helping or hindering the different phases and processes of growth in plants, animals, and human beings. When these natural forces became personified, in those primitive rituals, and then were given personal representation in ritualistic narratives which expressed the primitive man's wonder, fear, hope, and awe, at that moment one form of "myth" had been created. Those "mythic" narratives hint at various ways in which human beings were thought capable of placing themselves in accord with, or in opposition to, such life-forces as the makers of those narratives thought they understood. Their stories thus served to provide poetic illuminations concerning certain generally accepted beliefs as to causes and consequences, origins and destinies, together with particular suggestions as to how human goals or ideals were either honored or betrayed by human actions. One basic definition for the term "myth" is thus provided by that set of usages. By extension, the same term may be applied to any later forms of narrative which serve related functions. Eliot implies as much when he refers to the Homeric epic as a "mythic" narrative. He implies as much when he employs his own "mythical method" in *The Waste Land*.

Eliot's essential procedure, in adapting the "mythical method" to his own needs in *The Waste Land*, is to invoke a cluster of myths, referentially, so that he may imply analogies or parallels or correspondences between certain elements of primitivistic, pagan, medieval, and Christian myths. Indirectly, he arranges to let that cluster or grouping or sequence of parallel values (moral and religious) serve as a yardstick which implicitly measures the actions of those subhuman beings who inhabit his modern land of waste; measures, in such a way as to suggest the causes and consequences of their moral shortcomings, and then implies possible correctives.

Faulkner seems to have learned much from his reading of Eliot's early works, but he seems to have learned even more from Joyce. So there may be justification for returning briefly to the previously mentioned sore spot in Joyce's criticism: the question of how Joyce used Homeric correspondences, and the related question of what meanings Joyce thus implied. When Eliot said that the term "mythic" might be used to characterize the Joycean handling of those Homeric correspondences, he suggested a set of familiar facts. During many centuries, and even today, and in many countries of the world, the name "Penelope" passes current as a type or symbol of the faithful wife. Similarly, the name "Ulysses" is repeatedly used as a type or symbol of a noble and yet human and therefore imperfect man who sets his heart on achieving a worthy goal through dignified action, asserts his will, overcomes many obstacles, and thus gets there. Less frequently, the name "Telemachus" is used as a type or symbol of the young man who, harrassed and distracted by the difficulties of adolescence, courageously struggles to overcome his own difficulties, and succeeds. In those usages, those names and the Homeric story have a "mythic" viability. Joyce, in his Dublin narrative, created initial and cumulative tensions of interest for the reader by implying analogies or correspondences between the actions of Molly Bloom and the "mythic" Penelope, between Leopold Bloom and the "mythic" Ulysses, even between Stephen Dedalus and the "mythic" Telemachus. Tendentiously, Joyce thus encouraged the reader to anticipate the possibility that the predicaments of these three modern Dublin characters might be resolved in ways quite similar to those of the Homeric characters.

Consider a few basic Homeric analogies in Joyce's *Ulysses*, in order to notice what they seem to foreshadow. Although Bloom and Molly live together in their own home, they are separated by various kinds of estrangement. In a sense, Bloom may be considered a husband seeking a "return" to his wife, even as Molly may be considered a wife awaiting the "return" of her husband. They have lost a son through death, and therefore in a sense they are a mother and father in search of a son. However, Stephen Dedalus is "homeless" in more senses than one. His mother is dead and his father is no father to him. Thus he is, in a sense, a son in search of a father, a mother, a home.

Those dramatic tensions, brought into sharper focus by the implied Homeric analogies, encourage the reader to anticipate a happy resolution. Stephen may find Bloom, even as Telemachus did find Ulysses. If so, they may return together to Bloom's home, and may clear out Molly's suitors, permanently. Such possibilities would enable Bloom and Molly to become reunited even as Ulysses and Penelope did become reunited, and would also permit the homeless Stephen to find a new home with these foster parents.

But Joyce does not resolve his narrative in that way. Eventually he inverts the Homeric correspondences. He thus combines a "comical method" with his "mythical method" to illuminate his meanings. After building his action to three outrageously ridiculous non-recognition scenes (which displace the recognition scenes anticipated by the reader), Joyce provides a climactic epitome-epiphany, in a touching Homeric tableau: he represents Molly and Bloom, alone at last, and in bed together. Like Odysseus and Penelope? Not exactly, because Molly and Bloom lie head-to-foot and back-to-back. This comic peripeteia, thus effected in that ridiculous tableau, almost completes the cumulative unmasking of Bloom, Molly, and Stephen. In the end, they remain still separate, still immersed in different forms of self-pity and self-deception. Joyce finally permits the collaborative reader to measure these Dublin characters against the generally accepted moral values represented by Ulysses, Penelope, and Telemachus; permits the reader to recognize the discrepancy between ideal and actual moral values; permits his narrative to serve as a tragicomic still-life study in modern forms of moral perversion, inversion, and paralysis. Like Eliot, Joyce thus implicitly suggests the causes and consequences of certain moral shortcomings, and then implies possible correctives.

In similar ways, always less elaborate, Faulkner repeatedly combines comic, tragicomic, and "mythic" modes to illuminate his meanings. He frequently permits his own contrapuntal arrangements of implied "mythic" analogies and antitheses to point up similarities and differences. Like Joyce and Eliot, he often arranges to invoke several different "mythic" narratives in one work so that all of them may serve implicitly as backdrops, or as yardsticks, against which the reader may measure Faulkner's modern characters.

For example, in *The Sound and the Fury*, the modern actions of the Compson family are dramatized against three mythic backdrops which are established through oblique forms of hinting: an element of Christian myth, several elements of primitivistic ritual, and what might be called "mythic" elements in Macbeth's celebrated fifth-act negations concerning life-time-death. The first of these three backdrops becomes established as soon as the text casually reveals that most of the action takes place during three days which fall on Good Friday, Holy Saturday, and Easter Sunday. The moral significances conventionally associated with the self-sacrificial love and death and resurrection of Jesus are frequently brought to mind, merely by passing references to one or all of those ritualistically meaningful days; but those moral significances are repeatedly ignored or betrayed or rejected by most of the Compsons. One striking exception is provided by the total action of the Negro servant woman, Dilsey. The second of these three backdrops, involving several elements of primitivism, is implied by the actions of the abnormal and (poetically speaking) "primitive" character, Benjamin Compson. That second mythic framework becomes operative as an artistic control-factor, intermittently, when Ben and his older sister Candace and the Negro servant Dilsey are repeatedly represented as performing certain actions which place them in accord with positive elements of primitivistic ritual. The third of these three backdrops is implicitly established and made operative as soon as Quentin and Jason and their parents begin to utter negations which echo the soliloquy of Macbeth—the soliloquy from which Faulkner pertinently adapted his title, *The Sound and the Fury*. That threefold manipulation of mythic analogies and antitheses helps to illuminate and to dramatize meanings which are central to Faulkner's thematic concerns, and yet simultaneously helps to release Faulkner from the need to assign any explicit thematic values.

These brief descriptions of how Faulkner handles the "mythical method" in *The Sound and the Fury* are intended to serve merely as preliminary forms of guidance. It is important to point out that Faulkner makes related uses of the "mythical method" (of course with varying degrees of emphasis) in the works treated here.

By way of further introduction, another important usage of analogies, albeit non-mythic analogies, should be described. At times, Faulkner implicitly orders and controls important central meanings in a narrative by merely hinting at analogies or antitheses between some of his own modern characters—analogies or antitheses between the patterns of action performed by these characters. For example, the apparent protagonist in *Light in August* is Joe Christmas. But he is figuratively encircled or surrounded by five characters whose actions deeply affect different phases of his life. At first glance, those five characters seem to be, and actually are, strikingly different kinds of people. Yet Faulkner has arranged to let the reader notice that there is one particular way in which all five of these characters are strikingly analogous. It is no artistic accident that one factor of analogy is differently brought to bear on Joe Christmas by each of these five characters. As a result, the total action of Joe Christmas is very strongly determined by these five characters. In a sense, then, the ultimate protagonist is not Joe Christmas. For the moment, no more need be said concerning that use of analogies between characters for purposes of illuminating implied meanings.

But *Light in August* may be used to provide an example of how Faulkner implies meanings through establishing antitheses or polarities or literary forms of musical counterpoint, between two characters: Joe Christmas and Lena Grove. The story of what happened to Joe Christmas is implicitly contrasted with the story of what happened to Lena Grove, and the antithesis or polarity or counterpoint thus established and continued, from beginning to end of *Light in August*, tends to reinforce and corroborate certain thematic meanings otherwise implied by the dramatic action. As will be shown in later chapters, whenever Faulkner arranged to let two characters thus serve dramatically as foils, he liked to heighten awareness of themes thereby.

Such a usage of foils is of course a traditional strategy of the dramatist or of the novelist; but it is the Faulknerian combination of these traditional elements with his experimental elements which provides the innovations. Similarly, it might be said that the Faulknerian techniques for implying analogies and antitheses are not far removed from the conventional forms of poetic and metaphorical statement; even in everyday life human beings have non-artistic needs to define one thing in terms of another, or in terms of opposites. Nevertheless, Faulkner's ultimate innovations, in his handling of analogies, made a paradoxical combination of what Freud referred to in his interpretation of dreams as the relationship between "manifest" meanings and "latent" meanings, and of what Plato referred to as the power of visible objects or images to "mirror" different aspects of the invisible, or the metaphysical. Strictly speaking, Faulkner was neither a Freudian nor a Platonist. Yet in an ulterior and ultimate sense, his writing of fiction seems calculated to reveal psychoanalytical and metaphysical and mystical preoccupations which do indeed make a paradoxical blend of what might be called Freudian and Platonic myths. Perhaps neither Freud nor Plato would have approved of the way in which Faulkner's poetic eye doth glance from earth to heaven, from heaven to earth, at the very moment when his technical innovations are helping him probe beneath surfaces for conflicts between conscious and subconscious motivations. Nevertheless, any careful reader should enjoy noticing that the ultimate Faulknerian versions and inversions of analogizing have an almost compulsive way of invoking and adapting certain mirror-principles which reconcile Platonic and Freudian elements. Consequently, whenever a reader notices that Faulkner has made elaborate uses of actual mirrors, as he has done in *The Sound and the Fury*, such usages are particularly worth watching. Poetically considered, such passages provide the reader with indirect glimpses of peculiar depths in Faulkner's equally peculiar moral vision, concerning proper relationships between the human and the divine. The ultimate innovation to be enjoyed, in any sustained Faulkner narrative, is the private and independent and heretical angle from which he assigns values.

Closely related to what has been described as the Faulknerian blending of Freudian and Platonic elements is his inveterate habit of blending realism and symbolism. Many readers who prefer the realistic mode are inclined to insist that Faulkner is at his artistic best when he restricts himself to a vivid and crisp narrative which is strongly realistic. By contrast, readers who are poetically inclined may prefer the symbolic mode to such an extent that they tend to press Faulkner's symbolism too far, and thus tend to make allegories out of all his stories. Those two possible forms of response are useful in noticing how Faulkner's own ambivalent interests forced him to take risks in both of those directions, and not always with success. It frequently happens, however, that some of his most dramatic actions, and some of his most crisp narrative passages, occur within contexts which validly endow them with symbolic overtones of meaning. It also happens, at times, that his myth-making tendencies can be seen as dangerously seducing him too far away from the realistic mode and too close to allegory. *A Fable* fails, as a work of narrative art, partly because Faulkner there lost the balance between the two modes. But when he was at his best, Faulkner preserved that balance and achieved very successful blends of realism and symbolism. On the other hand, if anyone doubts that the ultimate reaches of his myth-making tendencies were consciously and deliberately metaphysical, there is abundant textual evidence to correct those doubts—as, for example, in the stage directions (quoted in chapter eight) which Faulkner gave for the first and second acts of *Requiem for a Nun*.

By way of concluding these introductory remarks on technical innovations which usually cause the most trouble, a previously mentioned point needs to be extended. Dujardin was quoted to the effect that his innovations enabled him to present interior monologues "without any interventions in the way of explanations or commentary on the part of the author." Many readers are particularly perplexed by the problem of how such modern authors as Dujardin, Joyce, Eliot, and Faulkner could expect to convey thematic meanings through techniques which imply such detached and seemingly indifferent attitudes toward what their created characters do and say. But the language of indirect statement has always been the hallmark of highly wrought literary art, and the only problem here is to become familiar with innovations such as those considered in this chapter—innovations designed and calculated to provide, as Eliot said, "a way of controlling, of ordering, of giving a shape and significance" to the materials used. Joyce was more explicit. So it is possible that when Faulkner became interested in searching for useful aesthetic theories of artistic indirection he found helpful suggestions in *A Portrait of the Artist as a Young Man*. It will be remembered that Stephen Dedalus was there permitted to explain the Flaubertian notion that the dramatic mode is superior to either the lyric or the epic, because it enables an author to thrust his characters on stage, so to speak, even in prose fiction, and thus to let his characters act out meanings, even while the author achieves the illusion of having disappeared within or behind or above his work. Stephen Dedalus again echoes Flaubert in saying that, like the God of creation, any author can and does thus seem to be completely indifferent to whatever his created characters do and say. But, he goes on to say, the arrangement of the parts is the factor which orders and controls and implies meanings; the arrangement of the parts indirectly assigns evaluations and judgments. As we have seen, the arrangements of traditional analogies or of newly manipulated mythic analogies, may provide one way of implying meanings or of assigning evaluations. But always, Stephen concludes, the active and alert and imaginative collaboration of the reader is required, so that after these technical arrangements have produced the necessary moments of illumination and revelation and epiphany, the quick intelligence of the reader is able to see beneath surfaces and to recognize "their meaning which is still unuttered." Faulkner, at his best, repeatedly adapted and applied that aspect of the Joycean aesthetic.

3

✺§ THE SOUND AND THE FURY

O⸻F THE eight works here selected to represent various aspects of
Faulkner's art, *The Sound and the Fury* is considered first because
it combines so many important Faulknerian techniques which will be
found operative in different ways throughout his later novels. Any
reader who has been initiated into the mysteries by way of *The Sound
and the Fury* should be able to avoid getting lost in some of the elaborate Faulknerian labyrinths which occur in *Absalom, Absalom!* and
even in *Light in August.*

Faulkner admitted that when he first began writing *The Sound and
the Fury* he thought he was writing a short story which would center
around one image: "the muddy seat of a little girl's drawers in a pear
tree, where she could see through a window where her grandmother's
funeral was taking place and report what was happening to her brothers on the ground below." At another time, Faulkner added, ". . . the
girl was the only one that was brave enough to climb that tree to look
in the forbidden window to see what was going on . . . and it took
the rest of four hundred pages to explain why she was brave enough
to climb the tree and look in the window." That passage illustrates
the characteristically self-deprecatory and scarcely accurate way in
which Faulkner frequently talked about his art. Nevertheless, both
of these passages confirm one important point which the reader should
notice in the narrative itself: the central character in the action is
the Compson girl named Candace and nicknamed Caddy.

Faulkner also commented on another important point which the
reader should make much of. He said that he had attempted, while
writing the first draft of that story, to present the entire action through
the eyes of a child. Why? Because it then seemed to him that the
desired artistic effect could thus be achieved by giving the illusion that
the child-narrator was capable of knowing only what was happening,
without understanding anything about the motives or the significances
behind the events. Faulkner went on to say that when he found himself
dissatisfied with the results of that first draft he had tried telling the

29

same story again from the viewpoint of another character in the action; still dissatisfied, he had written the story again, from the viewpoint of a third character; still dissatisfied, he had let those first three parts stand, and then had tried serving as narrator, himself, in gathering leftover pieces of his narrative to fill in the gaps. Although he still felt that he had failed to achieve his hopes, he had nevertheless published those four separate parts as a unit under the title, *The Sound and the Fury.*

Again the self-deprecatory tone dominates those by no means satisfactory remarks, and suggests that any author's retrospective description of what he can remember about his own motives and procedures, during a particular act of literary creation, is likely to omit or distort far more than it clarifies. In the present case, it will be noticed that Faulkner there gave no hint as to how he happened to experiment for the first time with the Joycean stream-of-consciousness mode, and with fragmentary associational flashbacks. Moreover, those comments did not even suggest that Faulkner must have made meticulous revisions of all four parts, in order to achieve the ultimately intricate and brilliant counterpoint effects. As will be explained below, those four parts do talk back and forth to each other, poetically, in ways which greatly extend and complicate (and ultimately clarify) meanings which remain unuttered.

Faulkner's remarks about the brave girl in the tree for knowledge did not even hint that she appears in the story only through the memories of her three brothers. Nor did those remarks hint that the soliloquy which comprizes Part One is provided by the edge-of-sleep reveries of a character who has the emotional and mental faculties of a child who has not yet learned to talk, even though that character has just completed the celebration of his thirty-third birthday. Although Benjamin Compson is endowed by his literary creator with faculties of total recall, he is indeed represented as lacking even the slightest awareness of conventional meanings. Ben's version of the story does give us at least a fragmentary or impressionistic outline of the entire narrative, but it also gives us a first meaning for the title because Ben's version is indeed a tour de force "tale told by an idiot, full of sound and fury." But if the reader joins with those would-be wits who disparagingly observe that Ben's tale ends by "signifying nothing," such perversity of judgment ignores the many artistic gains which Faulkner made throughout this odd handling of Part One. Consider, for the moment, only a few of the initial gains.

Ben's unexplained and impulsive interweaving of events past and present, throughout his impressionistic psychological associations of

WILLIAM FAULKNER IN 1934

31

images and actions, might be said to provide the reader with a series of effects-without-causes. As a result, the reader's own associational responses are stimulated to imagine various possible causes. Thus invited to collaborate, the reader needs and wants certain narrative facts, not given in Ben's soliloquy, about Caddy. This foreshadows a typical Faulknerian strategy. He liked to withhold certain crucial narrative facts, as though to make the reader want precisely those elements of narrative which will be given; but given belatedly, at such times and in such contexts that they may acquire far more meaning than they could have had if given earlier. In other words, Faulkner liked to start with effects so that he could postpone the indirect presentation of causes until a moment when the larger context might endow with extra significance the facts initially withheld.

This artistic heightening of interest can be suggested merely by reviewing a few of the major facts given in Part One. We gather from Ben's fragments of impressions and rememberings that the Compson family has already suffered through all phases of decline and fall except the last, even before that thirty-third birthday which the idiot Ben spends aimlessly, under the teasing and insolent supervision of the Negro boy named Luster who is supposedly caring for him. Ben's one obsession, throughout that day, is provided by his hopeless and of course unreasoning search for his long lost sister Caddy. Unable to differentiate between impressions past and present, he consoles himself as best he can through his instinctive recollections. He returns repeatedly to a day buried twenty-nine years in the past—the day when he had not understood that his grandmother's funeral had occurred. At that time, as we gather indirectly from his fragmentary recollections of conversations, his oldest brother Quentin had been nine years old, his sister Caddy had been seven, his brother Jason had been six, and he himself had been four. On that day, Quentin had scolded Caddy for the impropriety of her taking off her dress after she had gotten it wet while playing in the stream on the Compson plantation; as part of his reprimand, Quentin had pushed Caddy so that she had fallen and had gotten the seat of her underpants dirty. During the evening of that same day, Caddy had boldly climbed the tree (only later does it pick up symbolic qualities as a tree of knowledge) while her brothers had enviously watched and had asked her what she saw through the window of the Compson parlor. Ben's rememberings also provide the reader with fragmentary glimpses of Caddy's later growth and sexual development; her first interest in young men; her different forms of sexual play which had finally culminated in her disgrace; and then the wedding which had brought

Quentin home from Harvard in April of his freshman year, to witness his sister's marriage to a man who was not the father of her unborn child. It becomes clear, even in Part One, that Caddy's disappearance after that event, understood by everyone except Ben, had obviously precipitated Ben's unconsolable grieving. His recollections also afford us (but not Ben) hints that, soon after Caddy's wedding, Quentin had committed suicide; that Caddy had not been permitted to return home even after she had been divorced; that she had named her illegitimate daughter after her deceased brother Quentin; and that the girl Quentin had been brought home, during infancy, and had been raised under the harsh rule of Jason, who had become the head of the family immediately after the death of Mr. Compson. Finally, and yet without any hint in Part One as to the significances, Ben's associational blending of past and present is brought full circle by his impressionistic awareness that, while he had been getting ready for bed at the close of his thirty-third birthday, he had seen through the window the seventeen-year-old girl Quentin climbing down the same tree where her mother had sat, years ago, with muddy underpants showing.

Thus Ben's tension of interest becomes our tension of interest throughout Part One. Among the many effects, one cause is quite clear: how it happened that Ben developed his obsessive love for the lost Caddy. From his remembrances we are able to understand that Caddy, during her own childhood, had loved, pitied, and cared for Ben with far greater compassion than had been shown by any other member of the family. Her sensitivity to his needs had brought him whatever moments of happiness and serenity he knew, in his otherwise painful and confused experience. Caddy had discovered ways for satisfying his instinctive and unreasoning hunger for escape from pain through pleasurable moments of touching, tasting, smelling, seeing, and hearing. She had often soothed him by calling his attention to the bright shapes of the dancing flames in the fireplace, and to the attractive colors of red and yellow in a cherished cushion, and to the soft texture of a satin slipper which became his property, and to the fragrance of growing things, and to the music of rain on the roof. Throughout their childhood, Caddy had often lulled Ben to sleep in her arms.

There had been other ways in which they had shared limited forms of response to experience. Within his necessarily primitive world of reality, Ben had made instinctive and unconsciously ritualistic salutes to what might be called the total-value of life-encouraging images: rain, sunlight, the color of blood, and the warmth of the fire. By

33

contrast, he recoiled instinctively from any sensory indications of life-injuring or life-ending forces. Caddy's own childhood empathies had apparently enabled her to participate with Ben in many of these ritualistic experiences. More than that, she had taught him how to double his pleasure in his favorite totem images, by seeing them first in their real forms and then as reflected in mirrors on walls.

The reader is inclined to share Ben's deep affection for his older sister Caddy long before these details of action and imagery begin to pick up poetic and symbolic overtones of meaning. But before we consider any thematic extensions which are derived from Faulkner's ways of building so much initial tension of interest around Caddy, one textual quotation will serve to illustrate Faulkner's power in characterizing Caddy, merely through the dramatic mode of Ben's neutral remembering:

We could hear the roof. I could see the fire in the mirror too. Caddy lifted me again.

"Come on, now." she said. "Then you can come back to the fire. Hush, now."

"Candace." Mother said.

"Hush, Benjy." Caddy said. "Mother wants you a minute. Like a good boy. Then you can come back. Benjy."

Caddy let me down, and I hushed.

"Let him stay here, Mother. When he's through looking at the fire, then you can tell him."

"Candace." Mother said. Caddy stooped and lifted me. We staggered. "Candace." Mother said.

"Hush." Caddy said. "You can still see it. Hush."

"Bring him here." Mother said. "He's too big for you to carry. You must stop trying. You'll injure your back. All of our women have prided themselves on their carriage. Do you want to look like a washer-woman."

"He's not too heavy." Caddy said. "I can carry him."

"Well, I dont want him carried, then." Mother said. "A five year old child. No, no. Not in my lap. Let him stand up."

"If you'll hold him, he'll stop." Caddy said. "Hush." she said. "You can go right back. Here. Here's your cushion. See."

"Dont, Candace." Mother said.

"Let him look at it and he'll be quiet." Caddy said. "Hold up just a minute while I slip it out. There, Benjy. Look."

I looked at it and hushed.

"You humour him too much." Mother said. "You and your father both. You dont realise that I am the one who has to pay for it. . . ."

"You dont need to bother with him." Caddy said. "I like to take care of him. Dont I, Benjy."

"Candace." Mother said. "I told you not to call him that. It was bad enough when your father insisted on calling you by that silly nickname, and I will not have him called by one. Nicknames are vulgar. Only common people use them. Benjamin." she said.

"Look at me." Mother said.

"Benjamin." she said. "Take that cushion away, Candace."

"He'll cry." Caddy said.

"Take that cushion away, like I told you." Mother said. "He must learn to mind."

The cushion went away.

"Hush, Benjy." Caddy said.

"You go over there and sit down." Mother said. "Benjamin." She held my face to hers.

"Stop that." she said. "Stop it."

But I didn't stop and Mother caught me in her arms and began to cry, and I cried. Then the cushion came back and Caddy held it above Mother's head. She drew Mother back in the chair and Mother lay crying against the red and yellow cushion.

"Hush, Mother." Caddy said. "You go upstairs and lay down, so you can be sick. I'll go get Dilsey." She led me to the fire and I looked at the bright, smooth shapes. I could hear the fire and the roof. . . .

You can look at the fire and the mirror and the cushion too, Caddy said.

As there revealed, the apparently careless and lazy inconsistencies in Faulkner's punctuation and spelling have no particular significance. But there is one mechanical feature of that passage which deserves mention. Faulkner employed alternations between roman and italic type faces to indicate changes in tense, throughout Ben's reverie, and elsewhere. At the beginning of Part One, roman type is used to represent Ben's immediate rememberings of certain events which have occurred during the day which is just ending. But when the first psychological association between present and past imagery is represented as causing Ben's consciousness to recall an experience in his past, the only textual indication of that time change or flashback is the type change, from roman to italic. As soon as that change has been indicated by a sentence or two printed in italic, the passage may or may not continue with the same type face; the initial indication of change sometimes seemed to satisfy Faulkner. But occasionally a flashback within a flashback is represented by a change from italic to roman, as in the present case. But sometimes, when that happens, some of the subsequent returns to the immediate birthday rememberings are recorded in italic. This mechanical feature is obviously designed to be helpful, although at times it creates confusions.

In the passage quoted above, the major effect is of course provided by the foil-relationship between Caddy and her mother. Initially Caddy is represented as mothering Ben; but in the close of the scene there is a moment when Caddy is even mothering her self-pitying mother. That scene also reveals Faulkner's capacity for interweaving comical elements with the pathetic, and even with the potentially tragic, throughout the novel. After the reader has witnessed such evidences of Caddy's very tender devotion to Ben, another tension gradually builds up, even as Faulkner arranges to have it build up. The reader of Part One keeps wanting to know how it could have happened that the finely sensitive Caddy came to disgrace herself, in love, to such an extent as to become, eventually, "the shame of the Compsons" along with Ben. As will be shown, Faulkner made several artistic and thematic gains out of postponing answers to that question.

Even in Part One, Ben's unavoidable primitivism enables Faulkner to establish several important motifs. Although Ben has to be completely unaware of moral values, his instinctive responses are represented as permitting him to serve accidentally as a mirror of moral conscience, in which the various members of the family can see their own actions reflected and implicitly evaluated. Only the sensitive and loving Caddy does repeatedly interpret Ben's inarticulate protests and bellowings as, at times, moral judgments. In his reverie, Ben's neutral recollections give us several scenes which reveal different ways in which Caddy's adolescent difficulties created inner moral conflicts which were at least temporarily resolved through Ben's function as a mirror of conscience. For example, he remembers the time when he had escaped from his guardian, one evening, and had gone out on the lawn to find the adolescent Caddy sitting in the lawn swing and playing at love with a young man. Troubled by his appearance, Caddy had left her friend for the apparent purpose of taking Ben back inside the house; but his tears and bellowings had awakened her own sense of guilt:

> Caddy and I ran. We ran up the kitchen steps, onto the porch, and Caddy knelt down in the dark and held me. I could hear her and feel her chest. "I wont." she said. "I wont anymore, ever, Benjy. Benjy." Then she was crying and I cried, and we held each other. "Hush." she said. "Hush. I wont anymore." So I hushed and Caddy got up and we went into the kitchen and turned the light on and Caddy took the kitchen soap and washed her mouth at the sink, hard. Caddy smelled like trees.

Those various actions, in which Caddy tries to wash away her own sense of guilt and shame with water, are implicitly correlated with elements of primitive ritual which are not unrelated to certain limited meanings in the ritual of Christian baptism. In another remembered episode, where a further ritual of incipient washing is combined with another example of Ben's function as a moral mirror for Caddy, the circumstance was brought about by Caddy's self-conscious return from her first complete sexual experience. Ben is represented as having known only that the expression in Caddy's eyes hurt him. Again the meanings are represented through a dramatic action; but the larger context of Part One endows that action with symbolic extensions of meanings which involve moral vision:

> Caddy came to the door and stood there, looking at Father and Mother. Her eyes flew at me, and away. I began to cry. It went loud and I got up. Caddy came in and stood with her back to the wall, looking at me. I went toward her, crying, and she shrank against the wall and I saw her eyes and I cried louder and pulled at her dress. She put her hands out but I pulled at her dress. Her eyes ran. . . . We were in the hall. Caddy was still looking at me. Her hand was against her mouth and I saw her eyes and I cried. We went up the stairs. She stopped again, against the wall, looking at me and I cried and she went on and I came on, crying, and she shrank against the wall, looking at me. She opened the door to her room, but I pulled at her dress and we went to the bathroom and she stood against the door, looking at me. Then she put her arm across her face and I pushed at her, crying.

In that slightly melodramatic passage, the recurrence of such words as "eyes" and "looking" and "seeing" provides an example of how Faulkner lets an action endow an image and its cognates with a gradually increased cluster of poetic meanings. The imagery of eyes is manipulated by Faulkner throughout in ways which establish a counterpoint between moral vision and moral blindness. As will be noticed later, certain contrasting thematic differences between Ben and his older brother Quentin are established through related uses of mirrors and eyes. Quentin is also permitted to remember the final moment when Ben served as a moral mirror for Caddy. The event had occurred during her wedding reception, while most of the Compson family had been trying to wash away guilt with champagne. That ceremony had gone well enough until Ben had climbed on a box, outside, had looked through a window, and had caught a glimpse of Caddy. Then he had broken up the reception with his irrational and bellowing protest, which Caddy could never resist. In Part Two, Quentin impressionistically recalls that he had been watching Caddy's reflection in a mirror when he had heard Ben begin to howl:

37

Only she was running already when I heard it. In the mirror she was running before I knew what it was. That quick, her train caught up over her arm she ran out of the mirror like a cloud, her veil swirling in long glints her heels brittle and fast clutching her dress onto her shoulder with the other hand, running out of the mirror the smells roses roses the voice that breathed o'er Eden. Then she was across the porch I couldn't hear her heels then in the moonlight like a cloud, the floating shadow of her veil running across the grass into the bellowing.

That episode, which marks not only the end of those days when Caddy had helped bring order into Ben's chaotic life but also the end of Ben's instinctive function as moral mirror for Caddy, may serve here as a bridge to the established differences between the moral visions of Ben and his older brother Quentin. Various contrapuntal elements are derived from juxtaposing Quentin's death-day soliloquy against Ben's birthday soliloquy. Each of the two brothers is dependent on Caddy's love. But while that love had given some degree of positive significance to Ben, her disgrace through love and her sham marriage are viewed by Quentin as bringing such disgrace on Quentin as to motivate and justify his plan for suicide. Indeed, his entire death-day monologue, which occurs just before or during his act of suicide, takes the form of a retrospective self-justification. Repeatedly, Quentin is permitted to invert the positive symbolic meanings of images and actions which Ben is permitted to treasure.

Conditioned by his father, the negating Quentin has decided that he is the victim of forces beyond his control, and therefore life is a tale told by an idiot, signifying something worse than nothing. From the moment he awakes in his Harvard dormitory room, on his death-day, to the end of his retrospective soliloquy, Quentin establishes himself repeatedly as an intellectual who has learned to despise all time and all life. One of his first actions, that morning, provides a vividly dramatic self-characterization, with strongly symbolic overtones:

I went to the dresser and took up the watch, with the face still down. I tapped the crystal on the corner of the dresser and caught the fragments of glass in my hand and put them into the ashtray and twisted the hands off and put them in the tray. The watch ticked on. I turned the face up, the blank dial with little wheels clicking and clicking behind it, not knowing any better. Jesus walking on Galilee and Washington not telling lies. . . . There was a red smear on the dial. When I saw it my thumb began to smart. I put the watch down and went into Shreve's room and got the iodine and painted the cut. I cleaned the rest of the glass out of the rim with the towel.

That very tidy ordering of a little chaos can stand as a microcosm of Quentin's death-day. Bothering to paint the cut with iodine, on the day of his suicide, is a nice touch. But the destruction of that time-piece which is a family heirloom can serve as a symbol of self-destruc-tion. Throughout the day, Quentin is annoyed by the Christian notion that time has moral significance. He therefore finds himself made nervous by many conscience-stirring reminders of time, time, time. He keeps hearing bells which strike the hours, and he keeps hearing his own watch, which he carries with him even though he has made it useless. Moreover, his own body becomes a sundial timepiece as the sun casts his shadow before him. After he leaves the dormitory, one of his first remembered observations is this:

> There was a clock, high up in the sun, and I thought about how, when you dont want to do a thing, your body will try to trick you into it, sort of unawares.

What Quentin has intellectually decided he does not want to do is: to live. He has willed himself to death, of his own free choice. Yet his body, motivated like Ben's by the simplest of primitive impulses, instinctively opposes his mind's decision, and therefore seems to be trying to trick Quentin into staying alive. To Quentin's way of think-ing, therefore, his own body has become another enemy which must be outsmarted and tricked. The sun-cast shadow of his body sym-bolizes, for him, the conflict between his death-wish and his life-wish. So whenever he can arrange to perform any ritualistic action which may be viewed by him as an insult to that symbolic shadow, he does it with the proud sense that he has achieved some degree of triumph over both life and time. These little rituals can be represented here by bringing together four scattered symbolic actions:

> Trampling my shadow's bones into the concrete . . .
> I turned my back to it, trampling my shadow into the dust.
> I walked upon my shadow, trampling it into the dappled shade . . .
> . . . my shadow leaning flat upon the water, so easily had I tricked it that it would not quit me.

Quentin never loses an occasion to gloat over what he is realistically and symbolically doing. Early in that day which is the epitome of his life, he walks past a jeweler's window filled with timepieces, all con-tradicting each other and thus creating for Quentin a satisfactory image of what time signifies. Using his broken watch as an excuse, he enters the store and initially asks the jeweler, "Would you mind telling me if any of those watches in the window are right?" Ignoring the answer given, he walks out gloating triumphantly to himself: ". . . each with the same assertive and contradictory assurance that mine had, without any hands at all. Contradicting one another." Like Macbeth in the fifth act, Quentin strikes a posture of self-blinding and self-deafening arrogance as he projects on time and on life his own inner chaos of "assertive and contradictory assurance." But the jeweler's answer to his question had implicitly endowed the entire episode with the quality of a parable: ". . . they haven't been regulated and set yet."

Throughout Part Two of *The Sound and the Fury*, Faulkner's moral preoccupations keep finding reflections in many other actions which are like parables, three of which Quentin is permitted to correlate; but the values he assigns to them always invert the more pertinent meanings. For example, at one moment when Quentin looks down from a bridge over the Charles River, in which he will drown himself that evening, he sees a good-sized trout swimming against the constructive-destructive element in which it has its being. As he recalls the moment, Quentin is permitted to make verbal arrangements which have bearings on the vision-blindness motif:

> I could not see the bottom, but I could see a long way into the motion of the water before the eye gave out, and then I saw a shadow hanging like a fat arrow stemming into the current. . . . The arrow increased without motion, then in a quick swirl the trout lipped a fly beneath the surface. . . . The fading vortex drifted away down stream and then I saw the arrow again, nose into the current, wavering delicately to the motion of the water above which the Mayflies slanted and poised. . . . The trout hung, delicate and motionless among the wavering shadows.

The "poise" of the Mayflies, thus made analogous to the poise of the trout, implicitly establishes a meaning which is extended when Quentin sees and trivially marvels at a sea gull, while he is riding into Boston on a streetcar to buy those flatirons which will assure his drowning:

> I could smell water, and in a break in the wall I saw a glint of water and two masts, and a gull motionless in midair, like on an invisible wire between the masts.

Throughout the rest of the day, that image keeps haunting Quentin. But instead of viewing the gull as instinctively achieving its own kind of "poise" within its own constructive-destructive element in spite of the wind "rushing away under the poised gull and all things rushing," Quentin prefers to invert that poetry:

> Father said a man is the sum of his misfortunes. One day you'd think misfortune would get tired, but then time is your misfortune Father said. A gull on an invisible wire attached through space dragged. You carry the symbol of your frustration into eternity. Then the wings are bigger Father said only who can play a harp.

Thus Quentin inverts the triple imagery to make it fit his concept of predestinating time. With his father's pessimistic help, Quentin can see death as the only element through which he can achieve the poise he wants. In a sense, Quentin's father has arranged to give some truth to Quentin's feeling that he is a victim of forces beyond his control. As the reader becomes better acquainted with all the Compsons, through fragmentary glimpses of injurious family relationships, it would seem that all the Compson children had been poisoned and doomed by parental betrayals. Quentin remembers at one moment in his soliloquy that Caddy had once said, after her fall from grace, "If I'd just had a mother so I could say Mother Mother." Quentin also remembers that he had said to Caddy, "There's a curse on us. It's not our fault. Is it our fault?" But Quentin might have said more pointedly, "If I'd just had a father." Partially correct in passing the blame, Quentin nevertheless finds more consolation in that gesture than Faulkner could tolerate. Here in *The Sound and the Fury*, Faulkner obliquely implies a point which is more strongly conveyed throughout *Absalom, Absalom!* and *Light in August:* he subscribed to the classical notion that tragedy reaches its height when the opposed factors of fate and free will are inextricably operative.

The central irony in Quentin's death-day monologue is provided by the stubborn manner in which he censors all the attempts of his conscience to make him see that he shares with other Compsons the moral responsibility for what happened to Caddy. This fact, which has such an important bearing on theme, is made available in one episode by an ingenious use of free association. It is the episode in which Quentin becomes involved with a little Italian girl whom he keeps calling "sister." He meets her in the bakery shop, befriends her, gives her sugar-cakes and ice cream, even a little money, and then is both flattered and perplexed by her adoring refusal to leave him. He lets her follow him along the river until he has brought her two miles out into the country. There they are overtaken by the girl's older brother who shouts at Quentin, "You steela my seester," and who wants to have Quentin arrested on the charge of criminal intent. But to Quentin the entire affair seems ridiculous. He hasn't stolen her. He hasn't done her any harm. Is he to blame if she followed him? Nevertheless, still protesting, Quentin is dragged before a justice of the peace and found guilty of a misdemeanor. Even after he has paid his fine, Quentin continues to insist that he is the one who has been wronged.

Throughout that episode involving the Italian girl, Faulkner intermittently arranges to let Quentin's psychological associations bring into his consciousness a series of seemingly impertinent memories which have to do with progressive phases in Quentin's relations with his younger sister Caddy, during her adolescence. As these hints accumulate, the reader recalls previously given evidence that Caddy's compassionate love for her younger brother Ben was no greater than her adoration, hero-worship, and imitation of her older brother Quentin. Mrs. Compson is later permitted to sum up Caddy's attitude towards Quentin, in these words: "It was always her and Quentin. When Quentin started to school, we had to let her go, the next year, so she could be with him. She couldn't bear for any of you to do anything she couldn't." In Quentin's fragments of recollection, while he is with the Italian girl, the reader finds dramatizations of how Quentin had played a game of follow-the-leader with Caddy, in matters of adolescent love—a game in which Quentin had enjoyed making his younger sister jealous by teasing her with boasts that he had played some sexual games which she had not yet played. The most revealing of those fragments is a dramatic presentation of a day when Caddy had discovered Quentin playing at love in the Compson barn with a neighbor girl named Natalie:

> *She stood in the door looking at us her hands on her hips*
> *You pushed me it was your fault it hurt me too*
> *We were dancing sitting down I bet Caddy cant dance sitting down*
> *Stop that stop that*
> *I was just brushing the trash off the back of your dress*
> *You keep your nasty old hands off of me it was your fault you pushed*
> *me down I'm mad at you*
> *I dont care she looked at us stay mad she went away*
> *Stay mad. My shirt was getting wet and my hair. Across the roof*
> *hearing the roof loud now I could see Natalie going through the garden*
> *among the rain. Get wet I hope you catch pneumonia go on home Cowface.*
> *I jumped hard as I could into the hogwallow and mud yellowed up to my*
> *waist stinking I kept on plunging until I fell down and rolled over in it*
> *. . . mud was warmer than the rain it smelled awful. She had her back*
> *turned I went around in front of her. You know what I was doing? She*
> *turned her back I went around in front of her the rain creeping into the*

42

mud flatting her bodice through her dress it smelled horrible. I was hugging
her that's what I was doing. She turned her back I went around in front
of her. I was hugging her I tell you.

I dont give a damn what you were doing

You dont you dont I'll make you I'll make you give a damn. She hit my
hands away I smeared mud on her with the other hand I couldn't feel the
wet smacking of her hand I wiped mud from my legs smeared it on her wet
hard turning body hearing her fingers going into my face but I couldn't
feel it even when the rain began to taste sweet on my lips

That remembered scene in the barnyard suggests that Quentin had
smeared mud on Caddy at more than one time and in more than one
sense. Although he sees no analogies between his treatment of the
little Italian girl and his earlier treatment of his own younger sister,
his own recollections are permitted to suggest to the reader that
Quentin had kept teasing Caddy with his follow-the-leader games
until the day she had returned from her first complete sexual experience
and had said to him, as he remembers in Part Two, "You've never
done that, have you?" From Quentin's recollections we also gather
that he himself at first felt so jealous of Caddy that when she became
pregnant he wanted to tell their father that he and Caddy had loved
incestuously, and that Quentin was the father of her unborn child. A
further meaning is implied when the reader recalls that Faulkner had
created a peculiar tension of interest in Part One by letting the
"Quentin he" get mixed up with "Quentin she." Of course Caddy had
named her illegitimate daughter Quentin because of her adoration
for him, even after he had died. In the literal sense, Quentin did not
father her child; but in one figurative sense, he did. These are meanings
which Quentin refuses to see; he prefers to insist that he is the one
who has been wronged.

Regardless of Quentin's gift for blinding himself with self-love, his
death-day conflict is repeatedly dramatized by Faulkner as a struggle
between his conscious will and his subconscious sense of guilt. Late
in the evening of his death-day, after Quentin has gotten mixed up
in another outer conflict which has many past-and-present associations
and analogies, he returns to his dormitory room to tidy himself for
death. As he stands before his mirror, brushing his hair, he is troubled
by the thought that his roommate, Shreve, may return in time to
upset his carefully ordered plans. Or perhaps, he thinks, Shreve may
be coming back into town on a trolley car, just as Quentin is going
out of town on another, to pick up those carefully concealed flatirons.
If so, and if each is looking out of the window, their faces may mo-
mentarily be so close that Shreve may recognize Quentin in passing.

But no, Quentin decides: in the lighted car, Shreve's window will serve him only as a mirror, and Shreve will thus be "seeing on the rushing darkness only his own face." Taken poetically, that phrase fits and summarizes Quentin's own tendencies.

Quentin is represented as being almost as fond of mirrors as is Ben; but here again the counterpoint is obvious. Ben's primitivistic delight is to double his positive or totem values, as Caddy has taught him to do, while Quentin's delight is to double his negative and negating values. If we assume that Faulkner represents Quentin as reviewing the important events of his life during the actual moments when he is committing suicide by drowning, such an adaptation of the old superstition is figuratively appropriate. From the time he begins his carefully ordered descent into chaos by twisting the hands off his watch, he has already willed himself to death. All that remains is to trick the resisting impulses of his body into that ambiguous ritual of death through drowning. The mythic echoes from Eliot's *Waste Land* are pertinent here and elsewhere in *The Sound and the Fury*.

Quentin's entire monologue, if considered by itself, can be viewed as a miniature tragedy which lacks a self-recognition scene. By contrast, Jason's retrospective soliloquy, in Part Three, is handled by Faulkner as bitter comedy and satire, largely established through Faulkner's sustained uses of dramatic irony. The differences are clearly established between the characteristics of the sensitive, brooding, recoiling Quentin and the witty, ruthless, vicious Jason. But the two brothers have one thing in common: each is convinced that Caddy has brought irreparable disgrace on the Compson family. The differences in their reactions to that conviction are enlightening. Caddy has given Quentin his excuse for suicide, while she has given Jason a welcome chance to turn a neat financial profit. During the eighteen years between Quentin's day and Jason's day, Jason has been acquiring a great many of the monthly checks which Caddy has been mailing home for the care and clothing of her daughter Quentin. It has been easy for Jason to deceive his mother into believing that those forged checks which Jason has given her to burn with such a show of self-righteousness are the genuine checks; but Jason has already cashed the genuine ones. Having succeeded in frustrating all of Caddy's attempts to visit her daughter, Jason has almost completed his campaign to drive the seventeen-year-old girl out of the Compson home. Like Quentin, he has no difficulty in convincing himself that he is justified in doing whatever he decides to do. For the reader, however, part of the comedy lies in Faulkner's arrangement to let Jason unintentionally unmask and condemn himself not only in the eyes of the reader but also in the eyes of almost all the characters who deal with him. That effect is clinched by one Negro whom Jason especially despises:

> "You's too smart fer me. Aint a man in dis town kin keep up wid you fer smartness. You fools a man whut so smart he cant even keep up wid hisself," he says, getting in the wagon and unwrapping the reins.
> "Who's that?" I says.
> "Dat's Mr. Jason Compson," he says. "Git up dar, Dan!"

Within the bitterly comic framework of Part Three, there is appropriate irony to be derived from having Jason's day fall on Good Friday. He spends most of his day in a rage because he feels that he is being crucified, repeatedly, by different members of his family, but the reader is more likely to notice that what remains of the family is more nearly crucified by Jason. We want, and are eventually given, a chance to see Jason rewarded with some splendidly ironic form of poetic justice. It occurs when he is "fleeced" by Caddy's daughter Quentin, and the mockeries implicit in Faulkner's indirect uses of the classical Jason myth are not too subtle. There is no need to consider any further relations between art and meaning in Part Three. Jason is gaily handled by Faulkner; but Jason is such a repulsive character that we turn away from him with relief.

The fourth section of *The Sound and the Fury* is cast in the conventional mode of narration. It begins with the Negro servant Dilsey and ends with Ben, those two characters who are most thoroughly despised and rejected by most of the Compsons throughout the narrative. Because Dilsey's day falls on Easter Sunday, there is artistic justification for viewing her as being analogous to "the suffering servant," in the biblical sense. Throughout the story, she is represented as having made her own life a loving sacrifice in her attempts to hold the Compson family together, perhaps largely because of her compassionate pity for Ben. Her own actions make it possible to consider her as another kind of moral mirror, and there is appropriateness in Faulkner's arrangement of the structure so that the negations of Quentin's day and of Jason's day are encompassed and contained symbolically between Ben's day and Dilsey's day. The figurative and mythic significances of those two despised characters is further heightened and correlated through Faulkner's letting Dilsey take Ben to the small Negro church on Easter Sunday. They listen to a homely, even ugly, guest-preacher who so loses himself in his passionate presentation of the crucifixion story that he himself becomes transformed before the eyes of the congregation:

And the congregation seemed to watch with its own eyes while the voice consumed him, until he was nothing and they were nothing and there was not even a voice but instead their hearts were speaking to one another in chanting measures beyond the need for words, so that when he came to rest against the reading desk, his monkey face lifted and his whole attitude that of a serene, tortured crucifix that transcended its shabbiness and insignificance and made it of no moment . . .

✓ Both Ben and Dilsey are represented as instinctively comprehending the point dramatized by the preacher: the transforming power of love.

"Dilsey sat bolt upright, her hand on Ben's knee. Two tears slid down her fallen cheeks, in and out of the myriad coruscations of immolation and abnegation and time. . . . In the midst of the voices and the hands Ben sat, rapt in his sweet blue gaze. Dilsey sat bolt upright beside, crying rigidly and quietly in the annealment and the blood of the remembered Lamb."

In the last scene, Faulkner lets Ben serve once again as a mirror of moral conscience, while Jason plays opposite him. On that Easter Sunday afternoon, the Negro boy Luster hitches the old mare Queenie to the surrey and takes Ben for a ride, intending to visit the cemetery where Quentin and his father are buried. But as they approach the center of Jefferson, and reach the place where the road circles around the monument of the Confederate Soldier, Luster notices that he is being watched by some loitering Negroes. The temptation to "show off" is too great, and he says over his shoulder to Ben, "Les show dem niggers how quality does, Benjy." Turning the mare to the left of the monument, instead of to the right, Luster merely violates a very simple traffic law which is nevertheless calculated to provide one kind of order. Immediately poor stupid Ben begins to howl, merely because he has become conditioned to expect the turn to the right. As it happens, Jason has just returned to Jefferson from his quest for his golden fleece and for that bitch-fleecer Quentin. Appearances are still everything to Jason, and now he finds himself humiliated once again by this public exposure of "the shame of the Compsons," bellowing there in the middle of town. So he runs over to the surrey and with his usual ruthlessness yanks Queenie around, while ordering Luster to "get the hell on home with him." Back they start, and just as soon as that brief chaos gives way to the soothing motion of the surrey, Ben stops crying. Appropriately, *The Sound and the Fury* concludes with this passage:

Queenie moved again, her feet began to clop-clop steadily again, and at once Ben hushed. Luster looked quickly back over his shoulder, then he drove on. The broken flower drooped over Ben's fist and his eyes were empty and blue and serene again as cornice and façade flowed smoothly from left to right; post and tree, window and doorway, and signboard, each in its ordered place.

In that pair of symbolic actions which conclude the tale, the instinctive responses of the idiot Ben to order-giving, in preference to chaos-giving, provide a fitting end to Faulkner's dialectical handling of themes and techniques throughout *The Sound and the Fury*. In the beginning, Ben's monologue seems at first to be a mere verbal chaos; but in retrospect, that monologue is found to be a very carefully ordered chaos wherein Ben, with all his limitations, serves as a mirror of conscience. Now that we can look back at the whole, we can see that the Faulknerian dialectic of thesis, antithesis, and synthesis is largely achieved through protean aspects of counterpoint—that it's all done with mirrors. In the structural pattern, an architectural counterpoint is apparent in the arrangement of the four parts. Ben's birthday is a foil for Quentin's death-day, and Jason's Good Friday is a foil for Dilsey's Easter Sunday. But notice again that in this structural pattern the beginning and end are the positives of Ben's day and of Dilsey's day, so that those positives symbolically bracket and contain the negatives in Quentin's day and Jason's day. Thus the ultimate thematic synthesis is implied by that aspect of form.

As we have seen, another dialectical handling of counterpoint is achieved through the mirror principle of dramatizing the Compson story against the merely hinted and implied backdrop of mythic elements. At first glance, there is an apparent paradox in juxtaposing primitivistic myth against Christian myth against the "mythic" significance of the Macbeth story. Yet the yardstick values of these mythic backdrops can now be summarized: the primitivistic and the Christian frames of this triptych-backdrop implicitly combine to accentuate and honor different ways in which man instinctively affirms faith in the life-encouraging and transforming powers of love. By contrast, the "mythic" framework provided by Macbeth's fifth-act attitude ironically represents a characteristic way in which human beings intellectually deny life and love by projecting the inner chaos caused by self-love. Faulkner's narrative implies that these opposed factors exist in the variables of human response, and that only through creative actions of human beings can these opposed factors achieve meaningful reconciliations.

47

We have also seen that another kind of counterpoint, and of mirroring, is made to work effectively through Faulkner's technical uses of psychological associations between events present, past, and future. (Quentin orders all the events in his day, to make possible one event in the future: death by drowning.) The Christian concept of time here provides the dialectical factor: time was created by God, to implement a divine plan in which human beings may participate, through freely willed and therefore morally responsible actions which imply an understanding that the past, the present, and the future are inseparable parts of a larger whole. Faulkner's poetic handling of time is foreshadowed not only by his using dates as the titles for each part but also by his arranging to have three of those dates fall on the most important days in the Christian calendar.

Attention has also been called to another dialectical factor. As we have seen, a significant act of collaboration between reader and author is made necessary by Faulkner's focus of narration, in which the three Compson brothers provide three different ways of looking at the history of their family. From these opposed and limited aspects of truth, the reader is enabled by Faulkner's techniques to construct a higher and more significant form of truth.

Faulkner's poetic establishment of antitheses between Freudian and Christian concepts throughout *The Sound and the Fury*, implies a further dialectical procedure. One particular character, Ben, is technically endowed with symbolic functions which implicitly combine diametrically opposed Freudian and Christian elements.

There is no need to assume that Faulkner's artistic treatment of the four Compson children consciously applied Freudian notions. Nevertheless, those notions do provide helpful ways of talking about certain thematic meanings which are clearly important to Faulkner. As we have noticed, Ben's instinctive and infantile motivations require the kinds of mothering which are not available to him in any normal fashion, and he transfers his love to his older sister because her compassionate mothering gives order and meaning to his otherwise estranged and chaotic sense of reality. Because Ben's abnormalities are congenital, he particularly needs the forms of love which are blocked off by parental self-love or narcissism. His grievings, after Caddy's disappearance, are best understood as symbolic expressions of his instinctive need and search for love. The scandal he creates when he is "trying to say" love to the Burgess girl is of course misunderstood by Jason, who uses that scandal as justification for having Ben castrated. Taken realistically or figuratively, Ben's instinctive search is for the redeeming power of love.

48

The most appealing character in *The Sound and the Fury* is the child, Caddy, who is permitted to go to the heart of her predicament when she says, "If I'd just had a mother . . ." Nevertheless, she is represented as having an instinctive understanding of love as a two-way process of giving and receiving. Her capacity for love expresses itself just as intensely through her adoration of her older brother Quentin as through her compassion for her younger brother Ben. She is doomed not only by parental failures but also by the misleading actions of Quentin. It is important to notice, however, that Faulkner represents the innocent Caddy as giving herself to Dalton Ames with the same purity of love she has previously given, in different forms, to Ben and Quentin. Thus she stands finally as betrayed by her parents, by Quentin, by Dalton Ames, and by Jason.

When viewed in Freudian terms, the love-predicament of Quentin takes on deeper meanings. Having failed to find in his neurotic mother the basic forms of love, Quentin has transferred his love to his father and has gradually imbibed from his father that form of pessimistic nourishment which eventually enables Quentin to realize his death-wish rather than his love-wish. Warped by two distinct forms of parental failure, Quentin had first made his own experimental quests for love. His incestuous attitude toward Caddy can be taken symbolically as an expression of his peculiar self-love, or narcissism. But on his death-day, Quentin reveals himself as a split personality, figuratively playing father to himself, and viewing his instinctive life-wishes as infantile drives which must be repressed, tricked, conquered, and drowned. By contrast, his brother Jason perverts his instinctive forms of love into the perversions of hatred and narcissism. There would seem to be ironic significance in Faulkner's arranging to let the narrative end by representing Ben as holding in his hand that flower which is indeed symbolically the Compson family flower: a broken-stemmed narcissus. Yet Faulkner's many-sided theme of love combines Freudian and Christian concepts most overtly by permitting three characters to dramatize the positive significances of instinctive responses: Caddy, Ben, and the Negro servant Dilsey. All of Dilsey's actions provide the ultimate synthesis.

If we can say that Faulkner counterbalances the pessimistic psychological determinism of Freud against the optimistic Christian concept of freely willed and therefore morally responsible action, another dialectical aspect of theme is more clearly understood. In a sense, all four of the Compson children are deterministically conditioned by parental failures. No wonder, then, that so many commentators on *The Sound and the Fury* have mistakenly insisted that Faulkner's characters are here caught in a deterministic-naturalistic-fatalistic net. Jean-Paul Sartre, for example, used a brilliant metaphor to indicate what interested Sartre in the predicament of Faulkner's characters. He said they seem to be riding backwards, in a truck-like vehicle which has sides, so that they can not see what is ahead of them, and can not even see what is present, or beside them, until it has passed, or until it has become a part of their past. Fine as that metaphor is, it serves best to represent a very serious and recurrent misunderstanding. Sartre, like others, thus tries to cramp Faulkner's moral vision within a single perspective; but Faulkner has managed to escape from that limitation. As we have seen, he finds different ways of looking at one and the same thing, and he even finds different techniques for making the reader see the same thing from different sides. The tragic elements in *The Sound and the Fury* suggest that Faulkner recognizes and believes in the reality of at least three tragic categories. He believes that human beings are at times deterministically conditioned by factors beyond their control. He believes also that human beings at times commit freely willed actions which, no matter how well-intended, bring on that individual and others a sequence of tragic circumstances for which that individual is morally responsible. But, as we have noticed, the diametrical opposition of those two beliefs affords him sympathy with the classical belief that tragedy reaches its most excruciating form when an individual finds himself in a predicament where the opposed factors of determinism and free will are causally and inextricably operative. In *The Sound and the Fury* alone, the variety of effects which Faulkner derives from those three beliefs is well worth further examination. Up to a certain point, it could be said, the Compson parents as well as the Compson children are victimized. At certain times, however, all of them except Ben assert freely willed actions. So Faulkner can and does play ironically with the different ways in which the Compsons find it convenient to fall back on the notion that they are in no way to blame for their fate. Mr. Compson takes comfort in a very pessimistic form of cosmic determinism and imparts that notion to his children. Mrs. Compson's self-pitying whine is best mocked by Caddy's urging her to "go upstairs and lay down, so you can be sick." Quentin, stubbornly conditioned by and clinging to a ridiculously pathetic Old South code of honor, in regard to sexual matters, at first retreats into those convenient notions of determinism which his father has taught him, and at last asserts his own free will in arranging his own death. That irony is pertinent. Similarly, Jason can pity himself as victimized and crucified, and then can turn around to plan and carry out malicious victimizations of others. Caddy and Ben most completely win our sympathies as characters who are hopelessly victimized; but Faulkner's artistic and symbolic uses of Ben as a mirror of moral conscience further leavens whatever deterministic texture *The Sound and the Fury* may seem to have. It should be obvious that Faulkner has a profound sympathy for the plight of those characters who can not help being what they are. It should also be obvious that his major preoccupations are with those characters who do not see themselves as morally responsible, even when they should. Critics who misunderstand Faulkner's interweaving of three tragic concepts are usually trapped by their inability to cope with the Faulknerian manipulations of dramatic irony.

Perhaps the finest example of dramatic irony in *The Sound and the Fury* is the ambivalent use which Faulkner makes of that title-echo from *Macbeth*, which ultimately serves as a gathering metaphor. We have already noticed various analogies between the attitudes of the Compsons and the attitude of Macbeth, as expressed in that famous fifth-act soliloquy. Most of the Compsons, like Macbeth, try to excuse themselves from predicaments of their own making by projecting their own inner chaos outward upon the ordered universe. With the rantings of the Compsons fresh in our minds, we are now in a good position to appreciate the ironic Faulknerian principle which lets so many Compson negations echo so many of Macbeth's negations:

> Tomorrow, and tomorrow, and tomorrow,
> Creeps in this petty pace from day to day
> To the last syllable of recorded time;
> And all our yesterdays have lighted fools
> The way to dusty death. Out, out, brief candle!
> Life's but a walking shadow, a poor player
> That struts and frets his hour upon the stage
> And then is heard no more. It is a tale
> Told by an idiot, full of sound and fury,
> Signifying nothing.

In his own words, Mr. Compson said much the same thing to his son Quentin, and on his death-day Quentin said much the same thing to himself.

In conclusion, Faulkner's intricate arrangement of counterpoint in *The Sound and the Fury* establishes various thematic counterpoints. The basic antitheses are between chaos and order, erotic love and spiritual love, self-love and self-sacrificial love, deterministic responses and freely willed, moral responses. Faulkner handling of techniques

and themes implies his own conviction that the creative processes of
human action should mirror the divine process of creation by using
chaos as raw materials for human ordering. Love is here represented
as the force which did, and still does, transform and order chaos.
Although human love has its roots in the instinctive sexual drives,
those are the drives which send the branches of love upward and outward. If the negative aspects of those deterministic drives create hindering forms of evil, they also stimulate the will, at times, to assert
morally responsible forms of resistance which are honorable, no matter
how they are limited by human imperfections. Faulkner could have
found other ways of expressing these themes, and other ways of telling
how and why the once distinguished Compson family declined. But
if we now look back at those techniques through those themes, it
becomes apparent that the techniques are inseparable parts of Faulkner's meanings, that the techniques become the meanings.

A Textual Note On *The Sound and the Fury:* The text of *The Sound
and the Fury* has been printed in three different forms: (1) without
any "Appendix," (2) with the "Appendix" printed at the beginning
of the novel, as though it were an introduction, and (3) with the
"Appendix" printed at the end of the novel, where it belongs.

The first edition, published in 1929, appeared without any "Appendix." Approximately twenty-seven years later, Malcolm Cowley
invited Faulkner to straighten out the Compson genealogy for him,
while he was engaged in editing *The Portable Faulkner* (The Viking
Press, 1946). Cowley got more than he bargained for. He published
Faulkner's newly written notes on the Compson genealogy, for the
first time, in *The Portable Faulkner*, with this word of explanation:
"For the earlier history of the Compsons and the fate of the survivors,
see the Compson genealogy printed as an appendix to this volume."

In December, 1946, the first Modern Library edition of *The Sound
and the Fury* contained a reprint of the "Appendix," mistakenly
placed in the front of the volume. Happily that mistake was corrected in 1954, in a volume entitled *The Faulkner Reader:* the full
text of *The Sound and the Fury* there appears on pages 5–237, and the
"Appendix" appears on pages 237–251. Obviously, that "Appendix"
should be read last, and not first.

4

≈§   ABSALOM, ABSALOM!

T HE AVERAGE reader is likely to find that *Absalom, Absalom!* presents so many difficulties in style and plot and structure that the
first discouraging effect may be one of apparent confusion and chaos,
similar to the first effect of starting to read *The Sound and the Fury.*
Yet Faulkner's ways of ordering and controlling his materials and his
meanings in *Absalom, Absalom!* are very strikingly different from the
ways employed in *The Sound and the Fury.* Each of his best novels,
and this is certainly one of them, has its own distinct and original
pattern, which would seem to be determined by what Faulkner wants
to make a particular story emphasize in regard to underlying meanings. If we proceed once again, then, with the assumption that our
understanding and enjoyment of the parts and of the whole may be
increased by a retrospective consideration of a few important technical principles of ordering, a convenient starting place may be found
by noticing that four plots in *Absalom, Absalom!* are interwoven to
make a unified whole. One kind of confusion disappears as soon as a
reader begins to notice which of those plots is made to dominate the
other three.

Of those four plots, a pivotal and yet minor one has a short-story
shape and may be summarized as follows. One day in the autumn of
1909, a neighbor of young Quentin Compson asked a special favor of
him just before he was scheduled to depart from Jefferson for Harvard
College. The neighbor was an elderly lady named Miss Rosa Coldfield,
and she asked Quentin if he would get his father's horse and carriage,
that evening, and drive her to the splendid but decaying Sutpen
mansion on the outskirts of Jefferson. She wanted to make that drive
in order to learn whether a particular son of the late Thomas Sutpen
might be hiding there as a fugitive from justice. Quentin did arrange
to provide the conveyance, and the two of them made that ride to
the Sutpen mansion. They forced their way in, knowing they would
not be welcomed. But as soon as Miss Rosa found the fugitive from
justice, as expected, and found him an invalid, she returned quietly to

Jefferson with Quentin. Some time later, after Quentin had gone to Harvard College, Miss Rosa arranged to have an ambulance drive out to the Sutpen mansion for the purpose of rescuing the invalid from death. But as the ambulance approached, the inmates set the house on fire and two descendants of Thomas Sutpen, including the invalid, willingly perished in the flames. Miss Rosa died, not long afterwards, of natural causes.

Thus summarized, that pivotal plot is very nearly meaningless. But a second plot, more important, may be pieced together from the fragments of information about Thomas Sutpen which Quentin Compson gathered during his talks about Sutpen, at first with Miss Rosa Coldfield and then with his father. That second plot may be summarized briefly, and in a way which also makes it relatively meaningless, as follows. Thomas Sutpen was born a poor white in western Virginia. While still a very young man he conceived an idealistic plan to build a fine mansion on a fine plantation somewhere in the South. Part of his plan was to marry well and to establish a noble line of descent. After many romantic adventures he achieved almost all elements of his plan. He acquired a hundred square miles of land just outside the town of Jefferson, in Yoknapatawpha County, and built a mansion which became a famous showplace. He added further glory to his name by serving as a distinguished officer in the Confederate Army. But he discovered, when he returned from the War, that one event had caused the collapse of his plan to establish a noble line of descent. He never did learn or understand what mistake in his planning might have caused that unforeseen event. His end came unexpectedly when he was murdered by a poor white whose only weapon was a scythe.

That second plot obviously has the makings of a novel in itself; but Faulkner did not choose to handle that plot separately. In fact he interwove it with the third and fourth plots which in turn he interwove with the first and second. The third plot might be described as the story of what happened to Miss Coldfield, in early days, to make her so much interested in the latter days of the Sutpen mansion and the Sutpen descendants. It might be summarized, also somewhat meaninglessly, as follows. Miss Rosa Coldfield had been a child when her older sister Ellen was courted by and married to Thomas Sutpen. She had thus become related by that marriage to the Sutpen family, and she frequently lived for weeks and months in the Sutpen mansion. After the death of her sister Ellen, and after the War, Miss Rosa was courted by Thomas Sutpen. But the courtship was conducted so crudely that his proposal was rejected as an insult, and Miss Rosa never could forgive Sutpen. Yet she could pity Sutpen's children and could worry over them, because they were also the children of her dead sister Ellen. Hence her attempt to rescue one of them from the Sutpen mansion, years later, even though she knew he was a murderer and a fugitive from justice.

Although it might seem that Faulkner could have interwoven those three plots adequately, without any addition, he chose instead to add what might be called a fourth plot, in such a way as to make it determine the entire significance of the other three plots. Instead of merely asserting what that fourth plot is, and of asserting that it achieves a dominant quality of importance, a more convincing way to marshal evidence may be to turn briefly from these considerations of plot to some brief considerations of structure and setting.

There are nine structural units or chapters in *Absalom, Absalom!* and they are built around three meaningful tableaux in three different settings. The first tableau occurs at the beginning of chapter one, where Quentin Compson is sitting in Miss Rosa Coldfield's parlor, listening patiently as he tries to understand her long-winded explanation for wanting to visit the old Sutpen mansion that evening. The second tableau (which is preserved throughout chapters two, three, and four) represents Quentin Compson, again sitting and listening; but this time the setting is the front gallery of his own home, and he is listening to his father's version of the Sutpen story, together with his father's comments on what Miss Rosa had told Quentin. Chapter five is a flashback, and the italics imply a stream-of-consciousness remembering, on Quentin's part, of certain details about the Sutpen story told him by Miss Rosa that afternoon—details which have become more meaningful to him (and to the reader) now that an improved perspective has been provided by new details given in Mr. Compson's version of the story. The third tableau, established at the beginning of chapter eight, represents Quentin Compson sitting and talking with his Harvard roommate Shrevlin McCannon in their Harvard dormitory room—talking across a letter from Mr. Compson announcing the death of Miss Rosa Coldfield. In trying to explain to his roommate why he is so deeply touched by this news, Quentin has to go back over the two stories: what happened to Miss Coldfield, and what happened to Thomas Sutpen. He admits that parts of the story are puzzling and incomplete; so the roommates try to guess, imagine, and create scenes and conversations which would round out the fragmentary versions and would make both stories make sense.

Those controlling aspects of structure and setting, plus those three tableaux, require the reader to realize that Quentin Compson is represented by Faulkner as being more than a center of consciousness through whom the reader "sees" or learns all the details of the other three plots. In a very important sense, Faulkner arranges the focus of the entire narrative to make the reader primarily concerned with what happened to Quentin Compson and what Quentin Compson happened to make out of the other three plots, in terms of *meaning, meaning, meaning*. From start to finish, Quentin is dramatically shown as trying to get at the underlying truth of Miss Coldfield's story and of the Sutpen story; trying to piece the fragments of evidence together; and finally trying to imagine or create fictions which have the quality of truth, in this larger fiction. The climactic action of the entire narrative occurs when Quentin and his Harvard roommate perform an act of collaboration, in order to make the Sutpen story meaningful.

So far, then, some clear advantages should have been gained from noticing the Faulknerian techniques of ordering and controlling his meanings through ingenious and original arrangements of tableaux and structure and setting and plots. Noticing those factors, the reader can be guided and directed by them, until the total story may be seen in a sharper focus. But Faulkner uses these same techniques in ways which further control the reader's attention. Because Quentin is the center of consciousness, through whose restricted vision the reader's own vision is also restricted, a curious effect is achieved. In a sense, the reader is thus forced to dramatize, or to act out, a very important aspect of theme which has to do with the processes by which human beings search for truth through insufficient evidence— the processes by which human beings employ their imaginations creatively to reinterpret knowledge, and thus to endow relatively meaningless facts with significant and useful meanings.

Now we may return to our first observations, and extend them. It would seem that Faulkner had artistic and thematic reasons for confronting the reader, initially, with difficulties in style and plot and structure—with apparent confusion and chaos. As we look more closely at the total structure, and recall the way in which Faulkner made Quentin (and with him the reader) circle back and back over so many of the same details concerning the Sutpen story, it becomes clear that an effect was achieved which was more than mere circling. Each return brought with it some new information, and therefore some improvement in perspective, so that the motion was one of a spiraling ascent. But as we have noticed, all those improvements in perspective bring Quentin (and with him the reader) to the ultimate vantage point only when Quentin and Shreve collaboratively perform their own creative process of imagining fictions within the fiction.

If these insights concerning the relationship between matter and meaning, or techniques and themes, may be extended to include another technical factor of ordering, even the confusing difficulties of style acquire new significance. Much of the narrative is provided through Quentin's stream-of-consciousness rememberings, which dramatize his puzzling search for meanings on the basis of insufficient evidence. The initial motion of Quentin's effort depends on what he is able to make out of Miss Rosa's obscure swirl of rhetoric, warped as it is by the narrowness of her own prejudices. The second motion of Quentin's effort depends on the antithetical, yet still obscure, swirl of Mr. Compson's rhetoric, also warped by the narrowness of his prejudices. Quentin's task is to perform a dialectical process of synthesis by combining Miss Rosa's thesis with Mr. Compson's antithesis. But the reader can go beyond Quentin, in this regard, by noticing that Faulkner arranged to let the rhetoric of each provide a pertinent aspect of characterization for each. For example, Miss Rosa's rhetoric employs a vocabulary which bristles with the terminology of Calvinistic Methodist dogma when she tells Quentin how this demon, this devil named Thomas Sutpen, first saw and courted Miss Rosa's sister Ellen, in church:

> In church, mind you, as though there were a fatality and curse on our family and God Himself were seeing to it that it was performed and discharged to the last drop and dreg. Yes, fatality and curse on the South and on our family as though some ancestor of ours had elected to establish his descent in a land primed for fatality and already cursed with it. . . . I used to wonder what our father or his father could have done before he married our mother that Ellen and I would have to expiate and neither of us alone be sufficient; what crime committed that would leave our family cursed to be instruments not only for that man's destruction, but for our own.

In the counterpoint or antithesis provided by the rhetoric of Mr. Compson, correctives are offered from his very pessimistic and agnostic viewpoint, buttressed with what he understands (or rather misunderstands) of Greek tragedy. Mr. Compson views the long-dead Thomas Sutpen as a modern Agamemnon, doomed by circumstances beyond his control—doomed by a meaningless fate. Readers who have already become acquainted with Mr. Compson's attitude toward life and time and death, as revealed in *The Sound and the Fury*, should enjoy the grim Faulknerian irony of representing him as unchanged here, throughout his entire rant concerning Sutpen as a tragic Agamemnon, unjustly victimized:

> ". . . He [Sutpen] was unaware that his flowering was a forced blooming, and that while he was still playing the scene to the audience, be-

57

hind him fate, destiny, retribution, irony, the stage manager—call him what you will—was already striking the set and dragging on the synthetic and spurious shadows and shapes of the next one."

Even as Quentin makes use of and yet resists the interpretations of Sutpen offered by Miss Rosa and Mr. Compson, so the reader resists. For example, Mr. Compson keeps referring to Sutpen as a modern Agamemnon and guesses that Sutpen mistakenly gave the name of Clytemnestra to one of his daughters by a Negro slave; that he had "intended to name Clytie, Cassandra, prompted by some pure dramatic economy not only to beget but to designate the presiding augur of his own disaster." The reader should use and resist those analogies in ways which have bearing on theme. As yet, however, other factors need to be considered before such bearing becomes sufficiently meaningful. Some of those other factors come into focus nicely if we again make use of and resist an observation digressively made by Mr. Compson:

> "Have you noticed how so often when we try to reconstruct the causes which lead up to the actions of men and women, how with a sort of astonishment we find ourselves now and then reduced to the belief, the only possible belief, that they stemmed from some of the old virtues?"

Which of the old virtues had, and which had not, motivated Sutpen to formulate and carry out his idealistic plan? This question focuses attention on one of the most important parts of Faulkner's thematic concern throughout. One of the old virtues had indeed lain at the heart of Sutpen's plan, as originally conceived. Back in Virginia, during his "poor white" days, he had once been sent by his father to deliver a letter to a plantation owner. Out of ignorance and innocence he had knocked at the front door, which was opened by a Negro butler who told him curtly that the likes of him should knock only at the back door of such a mansion. Hurt by that affront, young Sutpen had vowed that some day he himself would build his own fine home; but that when even the lowliest might come to Sutpen's front door, that person would never suffer the indignity of having that door closed in his face. Apparently motivated by the old virtue of compassion, Sutpen had kept dreaming of his great plan. He grew rich, years later, while serving as a manager of a sugar plantation in Haiti. But he also risked and almost lost his life in saving from a mob of rioting slaves the plantation owner and his family. Then with a properly romantic touch, Sutpen had remained to marry the owner's daughter, after she had nursed him back to health. Not until a son had been born to them did Sutpen learn that his wife had a very slight "taint" of Negro blood. Then, acting as nobly as he knew how, Sutpen had explained his great plan, including his ideal of establishing a noble line of descent. He arranged a thoroughly legal and decent termination of that marriage, including a generous financial settlement. Thus the "old virtues" continued to operate—but now with ironic ambivalence.

As Quentin explained to his Harvard roommate, after Sutpen had built his mansion near Jefferson and after he had married Miss Ellen Coldfield and after he had raised a son named Henry and a daughter named Judith, Henry had brought home from college, as his closest friend, Sutpen's disowned son named Charles Bon. According to Quentin, that must have been the moment when Sutpen felt his plan put to the test. For Shreve's sake, Quentin points up the ironic analogy between those two door-slamming incidents:

> ". . . he stood there at his own door, just as he had imagined, planned, designed, and sure enough and after fifty years the forlorn nameless and homeless lost child came to knock at it and no monkey-dressed nigger anywhere under the sun to come to the door and order the child away; and Father said that even then, even though he knew that Bon and Judith had never laid eyes on one another, he must have felt and heard the design—house, position, posterity and all—come down like it had been built out of smoke . . . And he not calling it retribution, no sins of the fathers come home to roost; not even calling it bad luck, but just a mistake; that mistake which he could not discover himself and which he came to Grandfather, not to excuse but just to review the facts for an impartial . . . mind to examine and find and point to him . . ."

Sutpen had prided himself on his very correct code of moral conduct, and had never been able to see any fault of logic in any phase of his actions. But his own review of the plan, as handed down by Quentin's grandfather, revealed quite clearly which of the "old virtues" he lacked:

> "You see, I had a design in my mind. Whether it was a good or a bad design is beside the point. The question is, where did I make the mistake in it? What did I do or misdo in it? Whom or what injure by it to the extent which this would indicate? I had a design. To accomplish it I should require money, a house, a plantation, slaves, a family —incidentally of course, a wife."

At that same time, Sutpen had told Quentin's grandfather that his first marriage had been annulled, but he had not told him why. Even

Miss Rosa, until the night of her visit to the Sutpen mansion, had known even less than Quentin's grandfather about the background of Charles Bon; hence her previous attempt to add, in her warped way, further evidence as to Sutpen's fiendishness: "I saw Judith's marriage forbidden without rhyme or reason or shadow of excuse." Before Quentin returned from that visit to the Sutpen mansion, his own father had not known about Charles Bon's background. But even after Quentin knew, even after he had told his father, the crux of the mystery in the Sutpen story was a murder. After Sutpen had forbidden the marriage of Judith and Charles Bon, Henry Sutpen had turned against his father and had sided with his half brother without knowing of their blood-relationship. The two young men had served as comrades in arms, throughout the War, and had even ridden as far home together as the gate of the Sutpen plantation. But there at that gate Henry had shot and killed Charles Bon.

Of course, by the time Quentin tried to explain all this to Shreve, at Harvard, they could understand enough to wish to reconstruct the details of that love story, which had involved Henry and Charles and Judith. As Quentin and Shreve try to imagine crucial conversations during crucial moments, Faulkner makes two important editorial intrusions for purposes of commenting on their creative process. The first of those intrusions takes the posture of disparagement:

> It was Shreve speaking, though . . . it might have been either of them and was in a sense both: both thinking as one, the voice which happened to be speaking the thought only the thinking become audible, vocal; the two of them creating between them, out of the rag-tag and bob-ends of old tales and talking, people who perhaps had never existed at all anywhere, who, shadows, were shadows not of flesh and blood which had lived and died but shadows in turn of what were (to one of them at least, to Shreve) shades too, quiet as the visible murmur of their vaporizing breath.

That is one way of looking at the fiction-making game Quentin and Shreve were playing. But it is a way which implicitly belittles the art of fiction. As would be expected, Faulkner very soon counterbalances that passage with another:

> "And now," Shreve said, "we're going to talk about love." But he didn't need to say that either . . . since neither of them had been thinking about anything else; all that had gone before just so much that had to be overpassed and none else present to overpass it but them . . . That was why it did not matter to either of them which one did the talking, since it was not the talking alone which did it, performed and accomplished the overpassing, but some happy mar-

riage of speaking and hearing wherein each before the demand, the
requirement, forgave condoned and forgot the faulting of the other—
faultings both in the creating of this shade whom they discussed
(rather, existed in) and in the hearing and sifting and discarding the
false and conserving what seemed true, or fit the preconceived—in
order to overpass to love, where there might be paradox and inconsistency but nothing fault nor false.

Those two passages concerning these two creators of fictions within
a fiction help to correlate and extend ideas which have been recurrent
and questions hinted earlier concerning not only the limitations of
human knowledge but also the ways in which limited knowledge
searches for truth. The art of fiction, not unlike the art of historiogra-
phy, is an imaginative process of creating possibilities which make the
past, thus interpreted, more meaningful and useful to the present. But
both arts require the collaboration of readers who are willing to arrange a "happy marriage of speaking and hearing," a joint effort of
collaboration "wherein each before the demand, the requirement,
forgave condoned and forgot the faulting of the other."

A more central aspect of a favorite Faulknerian theme is hinted
and foreshadowed when Shreve and Quentin "overpass to love" in
their imaginative creations and interpretations. Part of their imagining
is that Charles Bon, informed by his mother that he has been disinherited by his father, re-enacts the familiar ritual of the orphan seeking
his own identity—the son in search of the father. Quentin should be
particularly interested in this aspect of theme; he himself was already
represented as involved in it, throughout *The Sound and the Fury.*
But now he imagines that when Henry developed an imitative hero-
worship of his older half brother, even after Charles told Henry of
that relationship, Charles might have thought:

> ". . . what cannot I do with this willing flesh and bone if I wish; this
> flesh and bone and spirit which stemmed from the same source that
> mine did . . . what could I not mold of this malleable and eager
> clay which that father himself could not—to what shape of what good
> there might, must, be in that blood and none handy to take and mold
> that portion of it in me until too late."

They imagine that Charles does finally arrange to make Henry do
precisely what Charles wants him to do. But before they reach that
stage in their creative process they imagine that when Charles Bon
first knew he was to be taken home as a guest at Christmas time, by
Henry, Bon must have hoped for some kind of recognition-scene between his father and himself:

61

. . . there would be that flash, that instant of indisputable recognition between them and he would know for sure and forever—thinking maybe *That's all I want. He need not even acknowledge me; I will let him understand just as quickly that he need not do that, that I do not expect that, will not be hurt by that, just as he will let me know that quickly that I am his* son . . .

Quentin and Shreve imagine that perhaps Henry's deep love for Charles, after he learned of their half-brother relationship, was so powerful that during the War he gradually overcame his repugnance to the unavoidably incestuous element in the possible marriage of Bon to Judith; they imagine that only after the War, when Sutpen still refused to show Bon any indication of their kinship, and yet privately revealed to Henry that Bon had the very slightest "taint" of Negro blood, then and only then Henry may have found himself faced with what Henry might consider to be a tragic choice. Or perhaps Bon had precipitated the final crisis from motives of revenge and retaliation, bitterly and desperately planned, not against Henry but against the father who had refused to be a father. Maybe, Quentin and Shreve agree, Bon had decided to deprive Sutpen of two sons by making the gesture of insisting that he would marry Judith unless Henry stopped him. Quentin imagines this possible conversation between the brothers:

—*So it's the miscegenation, not the incest, which you cant bear.*
Henry doesn't answer.
—*And he sent me no word? . . . He didn't need to tell you I am a nigger to stop me. He could have stopped me without that, Henry . . .*
—*You said, could have stopped you. What do you mean by that? . . . You mean you——*
—*Yes. What else can I do now? I gave him the choice. I have been giving him the choice for four years.*
—*Think of her. Not of me: of her.*
—*I have. For four years. Of you and her. Now I am thinking of myself.*

That imagined conversation suggests the ironic possibility that the two sons of Thomas Sutpen, each finding his own way to force the crisis into a tragic conclusion, thus brought the Sutpen saga full circle by figuratively re-enacting precisely the same kind of self-centered and ruthless logic which their father had employed when he unconsciously established the matrix for this tragedy. That possibility is strengthened by a refrain which Quentin establishes and repeats, while considering the love stories of the Sutpens: "But it's not love," Quentin said. "That's still not love."

Throughout the narrative, Faulkner has arranged to concentrate more and more attention on those two sides of his thematic coin, love and not-love; but once again he has arranged to define the positive largely in terms of the negative. Because love was not one of the "old virtues" possessed by Thomas Sutpen, all the other virtues came to naught. And the last two love stories involving Thomas Sutpen put the clinching evidence on that thematic point. The lesser of those love stories involves the crude way in which Thomas Sutpen had courted Miss Rosa Coldfield, after the death of her sister Ellen, and after the war. Having lost both his sons, he became obsessively anxious to re-establish a noble male line of descent, to perpetuate his name, at any cost. ("You see, all I wanted was a son.") If he married again and if a new wife produced for him only daughters, he would fail again. The cold logic of his need was so clear that he proposed to Miss Rosa Coldfield that "they breed together for test and sample and if it was a boy they would marry." That was the end of that love story. The final love story brought the end of Sutpen. Wash Jones was the poor white who worshiped Sutpen as he wanted to be worshiped. So when the desperate Sutpen transferred his biological attentions from the disgusted Miss Rosa to the passive and submissive granddaughter of Wash Jones, no complaint was possible: "And I know that whatever your hands tech, whether hit's a regiment of men or a ignorant gal or just a hound dog, that you will make hit right." For Wash Jones, the terrible moment of disillusionment came only when he stood outside his own shack on the morning Milly gave birth to a girl, and heard Sutpen say to her as he stood beside the bed holding mother and child, "Well, Milly; too bad you're not a mare too. Then I could give you a decent stall in the stable." Having uttered those casual not-love words, Sutpen left the shack to find Wash Jones waiting for him with the nearest weapon handy. It happened to be a rusty old scythe. Like Father Time, or like Fate, the furious man effectively used that symbolic weapon and mowed old Sutpen down. As one character in *The Unvanquished* phrased it, "Sutpen's dream was only Sutpen."

By way of conclusion, we are now in a position to notice how Faulkner has arranged to reinforce and corroborate his thematic meanings, throughout, by manipulating mythic analogies. One of these is Hellenic in its source and the other Hebraic: the Oresteia trilogy of Aeschylus, in which the violation of sacred family ties brings retribution and tragedy, and the Old Testament story of David and Absalom, again involving the violation of sacred family ties and again bringing retribution and tragedy. Quite obviously, Faulkner gives his first hint of the primary mythic analogy by drawing his title for this novel from David's celebrated lament. But he reinforces that first hint by invoking and implying repeated analogies. Also quite obviously, Faulkner permits Mr. Compson's comparisons of Sutpen with Agamemnon to hint at the secondary mythic analogy. The less important of the two will be treated, here, first.

Any correlation which is made between what might be called the Sutpen myth and the pertinent Hellenic myth must be held loosely and must be taken poetically. But remember that in the Oresteia trilogy the curse on the house of Atreus was heightened by that violation of sacred family ties which occurred when Agamemnon sacrificed one of his children, for reasons he considered idealistic and noble. As a result, he brought on himself the vengeful fury and retribution of Clytemnestra, and the sins of the parents were at least figuratively "inherited" by the children, in a succession of tragic consequences. That may press the analogies far enough. But it should be clear that when Faulkner arranges to endow the Sutpen story with elements of a Greek tragedy he did not accept Mr. Compson's reading of Greek tragedy. As was noted in the previous chapter, Faulkner variously revealed his awareness that in Greece the concept of tragedy evolved through various stages; that originally the fall of a man of high degree, through a meaningless and inexplicable act of Fate, was considered an adequate concept of tragedy; and that Aeschylus modified that concept in his plays and also in one celebrated remark: "I hold my own mind and think apart from other men. Not prosperity but human faults and failures bring misery." But Faulkner's fondness for dialectical procedures may have made him enjoy the reconciliation of those two opposed concepts. As we have noticed, he was willing to admit that human beings were indeed victimized, at times, by inexplicable and meaningless forces beyond their control. He was also willing to admit that human faults and failures bring tragedy. But in novel after novel he demonstrated his preference for that concept of tragedy which represented an inextricable relationship between determinism and freely willed actions. So here, is the tragedy of Thomas Sutpen; a tragedy without a self-recognition scene.

Perhaps the mythic analogy drawn from the Old Testament has less to do with illuminating the Faulknerian concept of tragedy and more to do with corroborating the reader's awareness of what was lacking in Thomas Sutpen. But first notice how many analogies between the story of David and the story of Thomas Sutpen are arranged by Faulkner, before any of those analogies pay off significantly, in terms of Faulknerian themes. It will be remembered that Sutpen, like David, was sent by his father on an errand which changed the entire course of his life. David was told that whoever should kill the giant Goliath would receive as wife the daughter of the king. But after David had killed Goliath he was tricked by Saul, who promised him one daughter and gave him another. As a result, David felt morally justified in leaving that wife and in fleeing from that country. Much later, after he had established himself as a king, David used questionable means to obtain another wife, Bathsheba, even as Sutpen used questionable means in obtaining Ellen Coldfield. For that theft of Bathsheba, David was reprimanded by the prophet Nathan: "Thus saith the Lord, Behold, I will raise up evil against thee out of thine own house . . . the child also that is born unto thee shall surely die." That prophecy fits Thomas Sutpen's predicament. But consider further analogies. David had his own family problems involving incest. There came a time when David's son Amnon forced incestuous relations with his half sister Tamar, and was killed by his brother Absalom, who rebelled against his father and thus ruined the house of David. Even so, when David received the news of the death of Absalom, he uttered his grief-stricken lament:

> "O my son Absalom, my son, my son Absalom! would God I had died for thee O Absalom, my son, my son!"

Thus David took on himself or at least shared part of the responsibilities for the estrangements between father and son which caused the ultimate death of two sons. More than that, David achieved the tragic height of anguished dignity and nobility, through self-reproach and repentance. How do the analogies operate here? Did Thomas Sutpen make any such lament? He did not. It is thus at the very point where the mythic analogy breaks down, or becomes inverted, that the most important values of all those analogizings illuminate the crucial point in the Sutpen story. The ultimate tragedy here is that Sutpen's dream was indeed only Sutpen.

5

✑ LIGHT IN AUGUST

A MONG THE many peculiarities of form which make *Light in August* distinct from any of Faulkner's other works, two aspects are particularly worth noticing. The more obvious one is the structural antithesis established between two interwoven stories. What happens to Lena Grove serves as foil for what happens to Joe Christmas. Less obvious is the Faulknerian counterpoint between two tragic predicaments: that of Reverend Gail Hightower and that of Joe Christmas.

One way to begin demonstrating the difference between the mere raw materials of narrative and the effects made meaningful in particular ways by Faulkner's artistic orderings is to ignore the art entirely and simply reduce the narrative to a cause-and-effect summary of the most important events. That initial approach, which will be used here, requires that the account of what happened to Lena Grove shall be disentangled from the account of what happened to Joe Christmas.

Lena Grove, a simple and naïve country girl, gives herself in love to a ne'er-do-well named Lucas Burch, who leaves her after she becomes pregnant. Innocently trusting in the kindness of people, Lena undertakes a long pilgrimage on foot from her home in Alabama, and follows the trail of Lucas Burch until she arrives in Jefferson, Mississippi, on the very day Burch is thrown in jail. He is suspected of having caused, or at least of having taken part in, the murder of a spinster lady named Miss Joanna Burden, and then of having tried to conceal the murder by setting fire to her house. Lena is befriended in Jefferson by a stranger named Byron Bunch, who finds a temporary home for her in a former Negro cabin on the estate of the late Joanna Burden. Until arrested, Lucas Burch had been living in that same cabin. There Lena gives birth to her child; there Lucas Burch is brought from jail, by the law, unaware of the planned confrontation. Escaping from Lena and from his captors, through a window, Burch disappears. Lena is also befriended, while in the cabin, by a defrocked Presbyterian minister named Gail Hightower, to whom Byron Bunch has appealed for assistance. After Lucas runs away, Byron Bunch returns to continue his timid courtship of Lena, and the novel ends with the departure of Bunch from Jefferson, with Lena and her child.

Joe Christmas is the man who murdered Joanna Burden, and the story of his life helps to explain how he became that murderer. Born an illegitimate child, he was kidnaped by his grandfather, old Doc Hines, who could not bear the disgrace of having an illegitimate child in his house. Hines insisted, in spite of his daughter's denial, that the Mexican father's dark skin was proof of Negro blood. He disposed of the baby by leaving it anonymously on the doorstep of an orphanage on Christmas Eve; hence the choice of surname, for the child, by the orphanage. Concealing his relationship to the child, Hines became a janitor in the orphanage and remained there for years, partly for the obsessive purpose of encouraging the other orphans to call Joe a "nigger" and to teach Joe what it meant to be cursed with Negro blood. When old enough to work, the white-skinned Joe Christmas was adopted by a God-fearing farmer named McEachern, whose rigorous discipline of Joe took the form of sadistic brutalities. When Joe became involved in a clandestine love affair, he brought down the wrath of McEachern, lost the girl, and ran away from his foster parents. Thereafter, for years, he tried unsuccessfully to subdue those inner conflicts motivated by his assumption that he must be cursed with black blood. Having circled as far north as Chicago and Detroit, Joe returned compulsively to Jefferson. He thought of himself as an outcast, although anyone who did not know his story accepted him as a white man. After he and Lucas Burch had worked together at the planing mill, they went into partnership selling bootleg whisky. While they lived together in the abandoned Negro cabin on the Burden plantation, Joe told Burch about the Negro blood. Miss Burden took a particular interest in him, after he had also told her the same story. She was descended from Yankee abolitionists and had been taught that she must love the Negroes. When Joe took cynical advantage of her conditioning, she found twisted sexual pleasure in her relations with him. Eventually they quarreled over religious matters, and when she tried to kill him, after he had refused to pray, he killed her. He escaped from Jefferson and remained in hiding for some time; but then he chose to return, knowing that he would be captured. After he had been taken into custody, he again escaped and sought refuge in the home of the Reverend Gail Hightower, where he was overtaken by his pursuers, mortally wounded by Percy Grimm, and then castrated.

So much for the very raw materials of subject matter in *Light in August*. Any three novelists, working with those same materials from their own separate points of view, would obviously endow those materials with different meanings. But the form which Faulkner employs is the factor which enables him to endow that double story with meanings congenial to his own particular point of view. Now we are in a position to consider certain elements of that controlling form.

Take first an artistic procedure which can be described easier than it can be named. In the first few chapters, the rapid and disjointed shifts in time can be explained retrospectively as providing Faulkner with a chance to introduce Lena Grove, Byron Bunch, Joe Christmas, Lucas Burch, Gail Hightower, and Doc Hines, each as an isolated character, not merely alone but also lonely. At the start, most of them do not know much about each other; most of them do not know much about themselves. But that initial fragmentation of narrative, involving abrupt changes in time and setting, provides Faulkner with his method of establishing a cluster of motifs involving loneliness and not-knowing; motifs which are later to be developed thematically.

Take next a more elaborate formalizing element which, once again, can be described easier than it can be named. The life and death of Joe Christmas can be viewed as influenced primarily by his relationships with five characters, distinctly different from each other and yet artistically made analogous because of their peculiar obsessions: Doc Hines, McEachern, Miss Burden, Gail Hightower, and Percy Grimm. These five are permitted to represent a cross section of that social group which helped mold their assumptions, even as their own assumptions help mold Joe Christmas into the tragic figure he becomes. One of the most ironic assumptions which Faulkner arranges to let each of these five characters dramatize, and thus reinforce thematically, is that any action may be justified or excused if it can be seen as inspired by the will of God. Another irony is the social assumption that God has willed white men to find that Negro blood is cursed and cursing. The recurrent tone of anguished brooding, in so many of Faulkner's novels, suggests the persistence with which he probes the riddle as to how and why his own beloved South has become an arena for peculiar kinds of violence and brutality. But in *Light in August*, his way of surrounding Joe Christmas with these five analogously motivated characters enables him to suggest that various warped and vicious religious assumptions have strongly contributed to the predicament of the South.

To improve our understanding of how Joe Christmas becomes a microcosm of his immediate social-religious macrocosm, and a symbolic battleground wherein certain misconceptions clash, we may profitably juxtapose Faulkner's handling of these five characters.

Doc Hines is first introduced merely as a janitor in the orphanage, and the reader is not immediately aware that, even in that first description of him, many of the images, there used, foreshadow his peculiarities. As we have already noticed, Faulkner likes to start with effects, in ways which heighten our curiosity as to causes; he likes to postpone the revelations as to causes until moments when those revelations can have the strongest impact on tensions carefully established. After describing Doc Hines as just sitting in a hard splint chair, reading through steel-rimmed spectacles the Bible which lies open on his knees, Faulkner as narrator establishes the first tension concerning him by pretending that Faulkner himself does not know why Doc Hines is there:

> He was not an old man. In his present occupation he was an incongruity. He was a hard man, in his prime; a man who should have been living a hard and active life, and whom time, circumstance, something, had betrayed, sweeping the hale body and thinking of a man of forty-five into a backwater suitable for a man of sixty or sixty-five. . . . His eyes were quite clear, quite gray, quite cold. They were quite mad too.

The tension thus created, concerning the possible causes and motives behind this exterior, is heightened as soon as Doc Hines begins talking with the orphanage dietitian. Quite clearly, he likes to think of himself as an instrument of God, even as he likes to think of Satan and the prophets of the Old Testament as instruments of God, so that there is no inconsistency for him in his playing both roles. The dietitian, trying to enlist the help of Doc Hines in getting the now five-year-old Joe Christmas out of the orphanage, finds that Doc is at once for and against her. He agrees that the "little nigger bastard" should not be in this white orphanage; but he insists that Joe, as a symbol of sin, is being used by God as an accuser of the sinfulness of the dietitian. Just a sampling of his rant sets the tone:

> "Ah," the janitor said. "I knowed he would be there to catch you when God's time came. I knowed. I know who set him there, a sign and a damnation for bitchery. . . . I know evil. Aint I made evil to get up and walk God's world? A walking pollution in God's own face I made it. Out of the mouths of little children He never concealed it. You have heard them. I never told them to say it, to call him in his rightful nature, by the name of his damnation. I never told them. They knowed. They was told, but it wasn't by me. I just waited, on His own good time, when He would see fitten to reveal it to His living world. And it's come now. This is the sign, wrote again in woman-sinning and bitchery."

Much later in the story, Faulkner permits Doc Hines to reveal the same distorted religious obsession when Hines explains to Hightower how he had known that his daughter Milly's Mexican lover had Negro blood: ". . . telling old Doc Hines, that knowed better, that he was Mexican. When old Doc Hines could see in his face the black curse of God Almighty." Byron Bunch, listening to that explanation, with Hightower, explains who the Mexican was and adds that Hines "knew somehow" that the Mexican was part Negro: "He never said how he found out, like that never made any difference. And I reckon it didn't." Bunch is correct, and the irony is obvious. What made the difference was that Hines found it convenient to know, even as the dietitian found it convenient to call Joe a "little nigger bastard." But Hines also explains to Hightower how he had taught Joe about the curse:

> "Because he didn't play with the other children no more now. He stayed by himself, standing still, and then old Doc Hines knew that he was listening to the hidden warning of God's doom, and old Doc Hines said to him, 'Why don't you play with them other children like you used to?' and he didn't say nothing and old Doc Hines said, 'Do you think you are a nigger because God has marked your face?' and he said, 'Is God a nigger too?' and old Doc Hines said, 'He is the Lord God of wrathful hosts, His will be done. Not yours, not mine, because you and me are both a part of His purpose and His vengeance.'"

That is enough to represent Doc Hines, and his share in conditioning his grandson. During the next phase of his development, Joe's analogous conditioning at the hands of the farmer McEachern took only a slightly different form. Like Hines, McEachern prided himself on being guided at all times by the voice or word of God. So when he found that Joe was unable to learn certain lines from the Presbyterian Catechism, as ordered, during Joe's first Sunday in his new home, McEachern whipped the boy until he fainted. That evening, the austere man appeared in the boy's room and commanded him to kneel beside the bed:

> The boy knelt; the two of them knelt in the close, twilit room: the small figure in cutdown underwear, the ruthless man who had never known either pity or doubt. McEachern began to pray. He prayed for a long time, his voice droning, soporific, monotonous. He asked that he be forgiven for trespass against the Sabbath and for lifting his hand against a child, an orphan, who was dear to God. He asked that the child's stubborn heart be softened and that the sin of disobedience be forgiven him also, through the advocacy of the man whom he had flouted and disobeyed, requesting that Almighty be as magnanimous as himself, and by and through and because of conscious grace.

On that passage, Faulkner makes no comment. He trusts his ironic art, even as he also trusts that the reader will have no difficulty in noticing how certain meanings are controlled through the establishment of analogies between McEachern and Hines, in their self-justifying sense of self-righteousness. Consider further analogies between them. Hines described his errant daughter Milly in biblical terms as a Jezebel and a whore of Babylon; he also spoke in the manner of an Old Testament prophet when he hurled the same epithets at the orphanage dietitian. As though echoing Hines, McEachern invaded the schoolhouse dance to save Joe from womansinning and bitchery, and Faulkner's narrative style helps point up the ironies:

> Perhaps, if he were thinking at all, he believed that he had been guided and were now being propelled by some militant Michael Himself as he entered the room. Apparently his eyes were not even momentarily at fault with sudden light and the motion as he thrust among bodies with turned heads as, followed by a wake of astonishment and incipient pandemonium, he ran toward the youth whom he had adopted of his own free will and whom he had tried to raise as he was convinced was right. . . . "Away, Jezebel!" he said. His voice thundered, into the shocked silence, the shocked surrounding faces beneath the kerosene lamps, into the ceased music, into the peaceful moonlit night of young summer. "Away, harlot!"

That is enough to represent the conditioning of Joe Christmas, at the hands of McEachern. The analogies between Miss Joanna Burden and Hines and McEachern are implicitly established as she tells Joe about her heritage, and about how her abolitionist forebears had stemmed from a New Hampshire runaway whose first name was, appropriately, Calvin. He had wandered westward to California, had married a Spanish girl, and had learned to read Spanish. His way of rearing his children was in part like McEachern's:

> "I'll learn you to hate two things, or I'll frail the tar out of you," Calvin Burden told them. "And those two things are hell and slaveholders. Do you hear me? . . . Let them all go to their own benighted hell. But I'll beat the loving God into the four of you as long as I can raise my arm." . . . interspersing the fine, sonorous flowing of mysticism in a foreign tongue with harsh, extemporized dissertations composed half of the bleak and bloodless logic which he remembered from his father on interminable New England Sundays, and half of immediate hellfire and tangible brimstone of which any country Methodist circuit rider would have been proud.

Joanna Burden, warped and twisted by the abolitionist version as to what was meant by "the curse of the black race," grew up to assert a self-sacrificial missionary zeal in trying to love the Negroes, even though she feared them. Her confused and obsessive need to expiate some vaguely believed curse on herself is represented by Faulkner as reaching ironic extremes in the clash between her pleasure in sexual orgies with Joe Christmas and her guilty conviction that such love was a sin against God:

> "I'm not ready to pray yet," she said aloud, quietly, rigid, soundless, her eyes wide open, while the moon poured and poured into the window filling the room with something cold and irrevocable and wild with regret. "Don't make me have to pray yet. Dear God, let me be damned a little longer, a little while."

Other analogies bring Hightower into this "wheel of faces" ultimately surrounding Joe Christmas. Starting again with effects, Faulkner makes the reader wait until the very climax of the action before completing Hightower's portrait. Eventually we discover that, since childhood, his greatest obsession had taken the form of romantic hero worship of his fabulous grandfather, who had made a daring and successful raid, with his Confederate raiders, on Union supplies in Jefferson, only to be killed, ignominiously, in a henhouse while stealing a chicken a few hours later. Although he had not been born in Jefferson, Hightower had nevertheless formed a passionate conviction that some day he must live on the very street along which his heroic grandfather had entered and left that town. Under the conveniently deceptive and self-deceiving disguise of a "religious calling," he gratified his desires. While still a student of divinity, he married a girl whose father could and did eventually help him to secure a pastorate in Jefferson. His wife, estranged by his introversions, and finding love elsewhere, was driven by her own shame to commit suicide. After that scandal had caused Hightower's congregation in Jefferson to repudiate him, he had been content to claim that he had thus bought immunity from the present, and was free to devote more time to the worship of his grandfather's glorious days. But his peculiar sanctuary was invaded, first by Byron Bunch's appeal for aid to Lena Grove, then by old Doc Hines and wife, and finally by Joe Christmas. Faulkner's ambiguous handling of Hightower fluctuates between compassionate pity and sarcastic indignation, the latter best illustrated by acid editorial intrusions on the account of Hightower's attempt to recapture his lost religiosity:

> "Yes," he thinks. "I should never have let myself get out of the habit of prayer." He turns from the window. One wall of the study is lined with books. He pauses before them seeking, until he finds the one

which he wants. It is Tennyson. It is dogeared. He has had it ever since the seminary. He sits beneath the lamp and opens it. It does not take long. Soon the fine galloping language, the gutless swooning full of sapless trees and dehydrated lusts begins to swim smooth and swift and peaceful. It is better than praying without having to bother to think aloud. It is like listening in a cathedral to a eunuch chanting in a language which he does not even need to understand.

Although the artistic faults of those intrusions are obvious, and sharply at odds with Faulkner's predilection for achieving at least the illusion of detachment, they throw an interesting light on Faulkner's point of view concerning Tennyson, and prayer. Another kind of artistic fault occurs when Faulkner brings Hightower to a sequence of self-recognition scenes, in which Hightower is permitted to serve as a too obvious mask, or persona, through whom Faulkner too pointedly communicates his own distaste for professional Christians:

> It seems to him that he has seen it all the while: that that which is destroying the Church is not the outward groping of those within it nor the inward groping of those without, but the professionals who control it and who have removed the bells from its steeples. He seems to see them, endless, without order, empty, symbolical, bleak, sky-pointed not with ecstasy or passion but in adjuration, threat, and doom. He seems to see the churches of the world like a rampart, like one of those barricades of the middleages planted with dead and sharpened stakes, against truth and against that peace in which to sin and be forgiven is the life of man.

The same Faulknerian fury and indignation may be found obtruding throughout most of Hightower's utterances of self-recognition. Turning now to consider analogies which bring Percy Grimm into this "wheel of faces," we find that Grimm is also ironically represented as claiming God's guidance as the justification for his final action in castrating and killing Joe Christmas. During his boyhood, Grimm blamed his parents because he was not born early enough to become a soldier in World War I. When he is old enough, he makes compensations by joining the National Guard, and becomes a Captain by the time he is twenty-five. With continuing irony, Faulkner describes Grimm as motivated by "a sublime and implicit faith in physical courage and blind obedience, and a belief that the white race is superior to any and all other races and that the American uniform is superior to all men, and that all that would ever be required of him in payment for this belief, this privilege, would be his own life." Of course, he joined the American Legion. When Joe Christmas made his last masochistic bid for torture, and Grimm appointed himself the officer in charge of the pursuers, Faulkner's irony blends with sarcasm in pretended praise for the heroic bravery of this young man who dared chase, with only an automatic pistol, that dangerous murderer and rapist whose hands happened to be manacled:

> . . . in this too he seemed to be served by certitude, the blind and un-troubled faith in the rightness and infallibility of his actions. . . . He was moving again almost before he had stopped, with that lean, swift blind obedience to whatever Player moved him on the Board. . . . He seemed indefatigable, not flesh and blood, as if the Player who moved him for pawn likewise found him breath.

Joe Christmas, viewed as encircled by this "wheel of faces," might seem to be a character completely conditioned and determined and victimized by his heritage and his environment. Many critics have used that character as evidence that Faulkner's own viewpoint, throughout *Light in August* and elsewhere, is strongly deterministic and naturalistic. That mistake can be avoided if the reader notices that the tragic interaction of determinism and free will, operative in *Light in August*, is analogous to those interactions found in *The Sound and the Fury* and in *Absalom, Absalom!* Consider first, Faulkner's way of treating the predicament in which Joe Christmas finds himself. The motives for most of his actions are beautifully complicated by the fact that neither he nor the reader ever knows whether he does or does not have any Negro blood; but Christmas has become convinced by his grandfather that he probably does have it. As a result, he is represented as being torn between consciously trying to act as a white man, because he looks like a white man, and consciously trying to act as a Negro, even though his Southern conditioning makes him detest that possibility. What he craves most is some kind of reconciliation or armistice which will end his inner warfare and give him a sense of peace, of belonging—a sense of home and of roots. By the time he has wandered as far north as Chicago and Detroit, he is confronted with the possibility that a great many people will accept him on any terms, regardless of whatever mixture of blood he may have in his veins. At that point, Joe Christmas is confronted with a choice which will determine the rest of his life: the possibility of escape from his conditioning long enough to make a freely willed choice. (It is very doubtful if Faulkner himself would have wanted to decide on that point.) But at least Joe thinks he chooses to circle back to the region which has helped make him what he is. And whether he acts compulsively or of his own free will, he devotes his life to a sadistic-masochistic pattern of action which constitutes a form of retaliation, if not vengeance. The reader first sees him on the day he reappears in Jefferson, and Faulkner introduces him (even as he introduced Doc Hines) as though he were an enigma:

> He did not look like a professional hobo in his professional rags, but there was something definitely rootless about him, as though no town or city was his, no street, no walls, no square of earth his home. And that he carried his knowledge with him always as though it were a banner, with a quality ruthless, lonely and almost proud. . . . with his dark, insufferable face and his whole air of cold and quiet contempt.

After this introduction, Faulkner gives the reader a foundationless description of the events immediately leading up to the murder of Joanna Burden. Then after the long flashback which helps the reader understand the initially offered effects in terms of causes, one of the most revealing exchanges occurs between Christmas and Joanna Burden when he tells her that he is "part nigger," and she challenges him:

> She was still looking at him; her voice told him that. It was quiet, impersonal, interested without being curious. "How do you know that?"
> He didn't answer for some time. Then he said, "I don't know it." Again his voice ceased; by its sound she knew that he was looking away, toward the door. His face was sullen, quite still. Then he spoke again, moving; his voice now had an overtone, unmirthful yet quizzical, at once humorless and sardonic: "If I'm not, damned if I haven't wasted a lot of time."

That passage should be correlated with another which occurs when Joanna Burden suggests to Christmas that he and she get married:

> "Why not?" she said. And then something in him flashed *Why not? It would mean ease, security, for the rest of your life. You would never have to move again. And you might as well be married to her as this* thinking, "No. If I give in now, I will deny all the thirty years that I have lived to make me what I chose to be."

Faulkner thus continues to worry the reader with conflicting evidences as to whether Joe's determining circumstances would seem to have given him any chance to make a genuine choice. The reader is also reminded by Faulkner that Christmas, having been conditioned by his grandfather and by McEachern to know and hate the Calvinistic form of determinism called predestination, has also learned to fall back on the posture of appealing to predestination whenever he finds it convenient. That irony becomes crystallized when Christmas decides that he will be forced to kill Joanna Burden:

He believed with calm paradox that he was the volitionless servant of the fatality in which he believed that he did not believe. He was saying to himself, "I had to do it," already in the past tense. "I had to do it. I had to do it."

The questions thus thematically raised in the reader's mind concerning Faulkner's variable attitudes toward free will and predestination are further heightened by Christmas's final choices. After the murder and after the escape, he chooses to circle back, within the larger circle of his runnings, to avail himself of that ultimate and masochistic luxury of death at the hands of his enemies—the death he expects and wants. At this point in the narrative, Faulkner's attitude toward Christmas seems to vary again, as he explicitly assigns the following values:

He is like a man who knows where he is and where he wants to go and how much time to the exact minute he has to get there in. It is as though he desires to see his native earth in all its phases for the first or the last time. He has grown to manhood in the country where like the unswimming sailor his physical shape and his thought had been molded by its compulsions without his learning anything about its actual shape and feel. For a week now he has lurked and crept among its secret places, yet he remained a foreigner to the very immutable laws which earth must obey.

Faulkner's protean attitude there reveals more than a hint, in that reference to the "immutable laws which earth must obey." The point to remember is that while Faulkner can and does pity some of his characters enough to excuse them, the concept of moral responsibility (implying choices freely willed) keeps cropping up. It appears most articulately, in *Light in August*, in the episode where Byron Bunch appeals to Hightower, and asks him to talk with the grandmother of Joe Christmas, after he has finally been captured. Hightower, still hiding behind his claim that he has bought immunity from the present, thus precipitates this exchange with Bunch, who begins:

"But you are a man of God. You cant dodge that."
"I am not a man of God. And not through my own desire. Remember that. Not of my own choice that I am no longer a man of God. . . ."
"I know that. Because a man aint given that many choices. You made your choice before that." Hightower looks at him. "You were given your choice before I was born, and you took it before I or her or him either was born. That was your choice. And I reckon them that are good must suffer for it the same as them that are bad."

Bunch is thoroughly "in character" when he makes that indignant

76

retort; but so is Faulkner, in letting Bunch say it. As one might therefore expect, when Hightower reaches his own self-recognizing and self-
condemning scene, he accepts and applies to himself the criticism
which Byron Bunch made. That penitence comes immediately after
he condemns himself implicitly by condemning Christian profession-
alism:

> "I acquiesced. Nay, I did worse: I served it. I served it by using it
> to forward my own desire. I came here where faces full of bafflement
> and hunger and eagerness waited for me, waiting to believe; I did not
> see them. Where hands were raised for what they believed that I would
> bring them; I did not see them. I brought with me one trust, perhaps
> the first trust of man, which I had accepted of my own will before God;
> I considered that promise and trust of so little worth that I did not
> know that I had even accepted it. And if that was all I did for her,
> what could I have expected? what could I have expected save disgrace
> and despair and the face of God turned away in very shame? Perhaps
> in the moment when I revealed to her not only the depth of my hunger
> but the fact that never and never would she have any part in the
> assuaging of it; perhaps at that moment I became her seducer and her
> murderer, author and instrument of her shame and death. After all,
> there must be some things for which God cannot be accused by man
> and held responsible. There must be.

The speaker, there, is obviously Hightower; but once again the voice
that sounds through the stage-mask of that persona is unmistakably
the voice of Faulkner. So at last, one central theme, which has been
picking up cumulative illumination throughout Faulkner's manipulation of the "wheel of faces" around Joe Christmas, comes into sharp
focus. *Light in August* provides an intensely ironic representation of
those analogous characters who find it convenient to lay their burdens
on the Lord and thus excuse themselves from any moral responsibility
which is inconvenient.

That ironic theme, or that thematic irony, reaches a point of excruciating intensity when Faulkner presses it one step further by
implying one particular analogy between Joe Christmas and Jesus
Christ. Although many critics and interpreters have raised troubled
questions as to the significance of the various parallels which Faulkner
establishes between events in the lives of these two characters who
are so unlike each other, most of those critics seem to miss the deeper
significances which artistically and thematically justify this particular
mythic analogy. There is only one truly significant sense in which
Joe Christmas is "Christ-like," and it is, with obvious irony, this:
he is misused as a scapegoat by those elements of his society who have

first made him in their own image and have then dodged their own moral responsibilities by attempting to heap their own sins on him, as they crucify him, so that they may obtain the illusion of having thus achieved some form of purification and redemption. All the other analogies merely foreshadow this ultimate reversal of conventional meanings in the Christian myth. Faulkner uses Hightower once again to extend this scapegoat theme. On Sunday evening, less than a day before the lynching (the inverted crucifixion), Hightower is represented as sitting in his home listening to the church music:

The organ strains come rich and resonant through the summer night, blended, sonorous, with that quality of abjectness and sublimation, as if the freed voices themselves were assuming the shapes and attitudes of crucifixion, ecstatic, solemn, and profound in gathering volume. Yet even then the music has still a quality stern and implacable, deliberate and without passion so much as immolation, pleading, asking, for not love, not life, forbidding it to others, demanding in sonorous tones death as though death were the boon, like all Protestant music. It was as though they who accepted it and raised voices to praise it within praise, having been made what they were by that which the music praised and symbolised, they took revenge upon that which made them so by means of the praise itself. Listening, he seems to hear within it the apotheosis of his own history, his own land, his own environed blood: that people from which he sprang and among whom he lives who can never take either pleasure or catastrophe or escape from either, without brawling over it. Pleasure, ecstasy, they cannot seem to bear: their escape from it is in violence, in drinking and fighting and praying; catastrophe too, the violence identical and apparently inescapable *And so why should not their religion drive them to crucifixion of themselves and one another?* he thinks. It seems to him that he can hear within the music the declaration and dedication of that which they know that on the morrow they will have to do. It seems to him that the past week has rushed like a torrent and that the week to come, which will begin tomorrow, is the abyss, and that now on the brink of cataract the stream has raised a single blended and sonorous and austere cry, not for justification but as a dying salute before its own plunge, and not to any god but to the doomed man in the barred cell within hearing of them and of the two other churches, and in whose crucifixion they too will raise a cross. 'And they will do it gladly,' he says, in the dark window. He feels his mouth and jaw muscles tauten with something premonitory, something more terrible than laughing even. 'Since to pity him would be to admit selfdoubt and to hope for and need pity themselves. They will do it gladly, gladly. That's why it is so terrible, terrible, terrible.'

Of course the crucifixion is beautifully conducted for them by Percy

Grimm, and Faulkner's use of irony lapses into sarcasm once again as he describes how the people who approve what Grimm has done gather round to stare at the bleeding body; then he describes how they will take pleasure in remembering that image of their own presumed self-redemption, actually their own self-crucifixion.

Another use of irony occurs when Faulkner establishes a brief analogy between the responses of the most ignorant elements of society and the best educated. First we are permitted to overhear one of the countrypeople talking about how Joe Christmas was captured. "He dont look any more like a nigger than I do. . . . He went into a white barbershop like a white man, and because he looked like a white man they never suspected him." Against that nice passage Faulkner plays off the post-mortem opinions of Gavin Stevens, "the District Attorney, a Harvard graduate, a Phi Beta Kappa." He "explains" all of Joe's final actions, in words and thoughts which are just as compulsively blinded by his environment as are the words of the ignorant country-people. Here is one illustration: ". . . Because the black blood drove him first to the Negro cabin. And then the white blood drove him out of there, as it was the black blood which snatched up the pistol and the white blood which would not let him fire it." Faulkner trusts to his dramatic irony, there, and it becomes clear if we apply the same kind of reasoning to the actions of Percy Grimm. Was it Grimm's white blood which would not let him shoot the manacled Joe Christmas through the table? Was it also the white blood which would not let him use the knife to castrate Joe after Percy had angrily snatched it up? Ah, but he used both. Then, according to the reasoning of Gavin Stevens, there must have been more black blood than white in Percy Grimm.

One element of form has been saved for a final consideration. It is the structural antithesis or counterpoint established between the story of what happened to Joe Christmas and the story of what happened to Lena Grove. One aspect of theme acquires implicit illumination from Faulkner's arrangement of those two narratives in such a way that the action starts and ends with Lena Grove. Here, as in *The Sound and the Fury*, the structural arrangement lets the positives bracket and contain the negatives. Lena Grove is another of Faulkner's primitive and pagan characters; a social outcast who has made herself vulnerable to social criticism because she has violated certain moral conventions. At first glance, her innocent attitudes toward love and hate appear to be merely naïve. Yet from the start Lena Grove is represented as having a peculiar power to evoke from others various reflections of her own gentleness, kindliness, and compassion. Implicitly, Faulkner establishes an important counterpoint between Lena Grove's capacity for placing herself in accord with "the old earth of and with and by which she lives," and Joe Christmas' placing himself at odds with "the very immutable laws which earth must obey." If interpreted within the framework of Faulkner's moral vision, those "laws" have to do with the "verities of the heart." They include an awareness of the practical necessity implicit in positive expressions of courage, endurance, compassion, aspiration, sacrifice, pride, and love. Faulkner begins by establishing her pagan kinship with Mother Earth and with the fruitful light of August: "swollen, slow, deliberate, unhurried and tireless as augmenting afternoon itself . . . with that providential caution of the old earth of and with and by which she lives." The analogies implied between her inner light and the outer light of August becomes reinforced when Hightower says of her, after her child has been born on the morning of the day Joe Christmas is to die, "That will be her life, her destiny. The good stock people, in tranquil obedience to it, the good earth; from these hearty loins without hurry or haste descending mother and daughter." Those passages suggest why Faulkner chose to bracket, structurally, the negations and hatreds of the Joe Christmas story within the affirmations of the Lena Grove story.

In conclusion, any statement of Faulkner's major thematic concerns in *Light in August* should point out that in none of his other novels does Faulkner unburden himself quite so furiously as to what he believes to be certain aberrations in Christian practice. He might even be giving conscious support to Nietzsche's claim that Christianity has found ways for poisoning human strength and dignity through preaching excessive self-contempt and self-immolation. A careful reading of *Light in August* should clarify the fact that the basic antithesis or counterpoint or polarity, here, is derived from Faulkner's rebellious insistence on contrasting certain pagan attitudes with certain Christian attitudes for purposes of honoring the pagan. Whatever concepts Faulkner here salvages from his own Christian heritage he reinterprets, as a means of separating them from those meanings in Christian dogma. If he chose largely to define the positive elements of his themes in terms of negatives, he may have done so because once again he wanted to shock, hurt, and upset Christian complacencies.

6

⋙ GO DOWN, MOSES

THE SEVEN short stories in *Go Down, Moses* are so successfully integrated and unified by elements of subject matter and theme that they may be viewed as constituting a good experimental novel. Yet if the claim were made that these qualities alone give distinction to *Go Down, Moses*, the counterclaim could easily be made that the successful use of the same processes in *The Unvanquished* places the two works on an equal footing when evaluatively considered. It almost does. But *Go Down Moses* is here preferred, not only because those integrated stories activate more profound themes but also because one of those profound themes does so much to unify and correlate the significance of the stories which dramatize that theme. It is built around different concepts of "freedom" and "bondage" (or "enslavement"). In a typical Faulknerian fashion, the stories develop variations of meaning out of those counterpoint concepts—variations which begin with the first story, "Was," and swell to an impressive climactic crescendo of meanings, in the last episode of "The Bear." The significances of that theme, and of the variations, may be followed easily throughout most parts of the narratives by anyone who pays careful attention to possibilities. Therefore, interpretive analysis of each story, here, would be an act of supererogation. But Faulkner's final resolution of his theme and variations, occurring as it does in the commissary episode of "The Bear," has often caused trouble for many readers and has often been misunderstood and misinterpreted. So an attempt will be made to clarify at least the central difficulties in *Go Down, Moses*.

The important point to notice, in Faulkner's handling of themes built around "freedom" and "bondage," is that after he has arranged to make various narratives dramatize and implicitly explore different ways in which human beings construe and misconstrue meanings implicit in those terms, he finally implies which of those possibilities he considers most pertinently illuminated, by these narratives. Once again, the counterpoint principle provides Faulkner with a new chance to develop a dialectical thesis, antithesis, and synthesis.

Viewed abstractly, and quite apart from *Go Down, Moses*, the terms "bondage" and "freedom" may be seen as lending themselves to para-doxical extensions of meanings. The term "bondage" may apply not only to a condition of serf-like enslavement but also to any condition in which an individual or group may be subjected to some particular force or compulsion either good or bad. One "good" of bondage and enslavement was marveled at, by the enslaved Prince Ferdinand, in Shakespeare's *Tempest*, when he explained to Miranda that the bond-age of his love for her made his physical enslavement by Prospero bearable, and even pleasant. The same paradoxical viability may be found in the term "freedom." Its possible meanings may be arranged in a descending order, from the most highly honored forms of liberty (personal, social, political, religious), downward to various forms of license, and still further downward to jungle law. Freedom, thus con-sidered, is a term which may suggest a state or quality of liberation which can operate in a constructive way or in a destructive way, or perhaps (under certain circumstances) in both ways simultaneously.

These considerations of possible meanings for those terms would be impertinent, here, if Faulkner did not implicitly invite the reader of *Go Down, Moses* to notice how and when and why they all are given thematic manipulations throughout. But here, as always, in Faulk-ner's works, Faulkner's double vision gave him apparent pleasure in giving ambivalent and ironic enrichments to his handlings of his thematic counterpoint. With these observations in mind, we need next to consider some broad glimpse of subject matter in *Go Down, Moses*, before we are in position to appreciate the ordering and controlling significances of the themes built around "freedom versus bondage."

Once again, the subject matter has to do with the history of one family—this time, the McCaslin family. Implied as background for the immediate stories, and fragmentarily sketched in, is the saga of the growth and the flourishing (this time, not the decline and fall) of several generations of the McCaslin family tree, in several branches. The central setting, from which all the actions fan out, is the pros-perous McCaslin plantation, situated some seventeen miles northeast of Jefferson, in Yoknapatawpha County. A rearrangement of the scrambled fragments of background information, and a chronological presentation of the sort which Faulkner never gives us, would reach back to pioneer days, when Carothers McCaslin, the "Abraham" of this clan, came from Carolina with his wife, their twin sons, their daughter, and slaves, to start life anew by purchasing land from the Indians, and by beginning to develop a plantation.

Faulkner selects and presents the seven stories in such a way as to give us a representative pattern of conflicts between blood relatives in three genealogical branches of descent from Carothers McCaslin: the brief male line of descent, from one of the twin sons; the distaff line, descended from the one daughter; and the Negro line of descent, from one of Carothers McCaslin's slave girls. Interminglings of love and hate are most vividly dramatized in relationships between four generations on the distaff side, and four parallel generations on the Negro side. A central aspect of the saga is finally brought full circle in the story entitled "Delta Autumn," where we learn that a fourth-generation distaff-side descendant named Carothers Edmonds loves and breeds with, and then abandons, a part-Negro girl who also happens to be a fourth-generation descendant from the original Carothers McCaslin. That brief glimpse of subject matter suggests some interesting possibilities for the functioning of the central and unifying "freedom-bondage" theme.

Genealogical facts are used by Faulkner as a tantalizing means of focusing attention on theme. He forces the reader to worry over, struggle with, and piece together, various clues as to family relationships, in order to understand even the surface significance of the actions. In most cases, however, the stress thus placed on family relationships would seem calculated to heighten the reader's awareness of underlying meanings. For example, the first story or chapter is entitled "Was," and it begins exasperatingly, thus:

> Isaac McCaslin, 'Uncle Ike,' past seventy and nearer eighty than he ever corroborated any more, a widower now and uncle to half a county and father to no one
> this was not something participated in or even seen by himself, but by his elder cousin, McCaslin Edmonds, grandson of Isaac's father's sister and so descended by the distaff, yet notwithstanding the inheritor, and in his time the bequestor, of that which some had thought then and some still thought should have been Isaac's, since his was the name in which the title to the land had first been granted from the Indian patent . . .

Troublesome as that opening gambit may be, during a first reading, it does more than to start the reader worrying about McCaslin family relationships, genealogically considered. Anyone who returns to that opening passage, after reading all the way through *Go Down, Moses*, may then realize how many important tensions were thus initially foreshadowed. Although the passage does not inform us that Isaac

McCaslin was the grandson and last male descendant of old Mc-
Caslin to bear his name, it significantly represents him as remembering in old age a family legend told to him earlier by his cousin,
McCaslin Edmonds. Gradually we find that all the stories in *Go Down,
Moses* are Isaac's old-age recollections, and that he is thus made the
center of consciousness and (in a faulty but well-intended sense) the
center of conscience, as he reviews these pertinent events in the history
of the McCaslin family. But even in that first paragraph of the first
story, the hint is given that Isaac's life has somehow been a disap-
pointment to him, at least in the sense that he is "uncle to half a
county and father to no one." It also hints that he is troubled by the
memory that his cousin became the inheritor, and that he himself,
during his own lifetime, had been the bequeather of that plantation
"which some had thought then and some still thought should have
been Isaac's." Relatively meaningless at first glance, these hints of
tensions in the retrospective consciousness of Isaac McCaslin are later
developed in ways which are of major importance to subject matter
and theme.

On first reading, it is also easy for anyone to overlook the ironic
operation of the freedom-bondage theme in "Was." This particular
family legend or anecdote deals with an amusing family crisis which
had occurred in "the good old days" of slavery, before Isaac was born,
but after the McCaslin slaves had been set free by the twin sons of old
Carothers McCaslin: Amodeus and Theophilus, better known as Uncle
Buddy and Uncle Buck. Idealists, both of them, and troubled by the
evils and injustices of slavery, they had done more than liberate their
own slaves. With a quaint and well-intended largess, they had hired
their slaves as well-paid laborers, and then had provided a communal
home for them, by turning over to them the McCaslin plantation
house, after the twins had moved their necessary belongings into a
very modest two-room log cabin. Although this background information is gradually acquired by the reader of *Go Down, Moses*, the central
action in "Was" has to do with the odd courtship which had taken
place between the future parents of Isaac McCaslin. The protagonist
in that courtship had been Miss Sophonsiba Beauchamp, a neighbor
who had conducted her approaches to the reluctant Theophilus with
shrewdness and with ultimate success. But during the particular phase
of the courtship described in this narrative, she had been defeated.

But even the courtship is not mentioned at the beginning of "Was."
Instead, the yarn starts with a swirl of action, as Theophilus conducts
a chase for a runaway Negro worker, and pursues him with all the
excitement, gaiety, and spirit of a fox hunt. The worker is Tomey's

Turl, who has skipped away from work to court a slave girl on the Beauchamp plantation. So when Theophilus arrives there, in pursuit, he has to cope with the latest stratagems of Miss Sophonsiba, and is rescued this time only through the card-playing skills of his twin brother. The entire story is handled comically, on the surface. In fact, if the reader does not take the trouble to work out the genealogical hints, no serious overtones or undertones touching on the "freedom-bondage" theme may be noticed. But the runaway worker, Tomey's Turl, so gaily pursued in the spirit of a fox hunt and so centrally involved in the entire story, as chattel, is half brother to the man who playfully treats him as half-animal.

The ramifications and extensions of the freedom-bondage theme acquire cumulative importance without taking any particular direction, during the next two stories: "The Fire and the Hearth" and "Pantaloon in Black." But the direction begins to become more pointed when the stories concentrate on the early life of Isaac McCaslin himself. In the first of these, entitled "The Old People," it becomes apparent that Isaac, born in 1867 and soon orphaned, had been adopted informally by his older cousin, McCaslin Edmonds, and that Edmonds in turn had agreed to manage the family plantation until Isaac should come of age to accept his birthright responsibilities of ownership. In the meantime, the boy's outdoor education was handled by a part-Indian, part-Negro retainer known as old Sam Fathers. Under his guidance, Isaac acquired expert training as a hunter of squirrels and rabbits. But Sam Fathers, continuing to suffer indignities from whites and Negroes alike because of his mixed blood, finally asked permission to leave the McCaslin plantation and go down into the wilderness, alone, to live as year-round guardian of a camp where the best huntsmen in Jefferson gathered at least once a year, in search of big game. Isaac interceded for Sam Fathers, and asked his foster-father-cousin to let Sam do as he wished. They are both troubled by an expression in the eyes of Sam Fathers:

. . . and the boy's cousin McCaslin told him what that was: not the heritage of Ham, not the mark of servitude but of bondage; the knowledge that for a while that part of his blood had been the blood of slaves. "Like an old lion or a bear in a cage," McCaslin said. "He was born in the cage and has been in it all his life; he knows nothing else. Then he smells something. It might be anything, any breeze blowing past anything and then into his nostrils. . . . But that's not what he smells then. It was the cage he smelled. . . . That's what makes his eyes look like that."

"Then let him go!" the boy cried. "Let him go!"

That passage, foreshadowing much in "The Bear," would also seem to end with echoes and overtones of the celebrated Negro spiritual from which Faulkner borrowed his title for this volume. This time, the biblical echo does far more than invoke mythic analogies which may serve ambivalently as backdrop for the entire saga of the McCaslin clan. Initially it serves as a subtle reminder of the freedom-bondage theme; but ultimately the freedom-bondage theme endows the title itself with greatly enriched meanings. In the biblical myth, the voice of God had spoken to Moses from out of the burning bush and had indeed said to him, at least in effect,

> "Go down, Moses, way down in Egypt's land;
> Tell old Pharoah to let my people go."

But Faulkner's titular reminder of mythic analogies should keep troubling the reader with unanswered questions. Within this narrative, who are God's chosen people? Within this narrative, which kinds of freedom are constructive and which kinds are destructive? Within this narrative, which kinds of bondage are constructive? As the focus keeps closing on these questions, the stories provide answers which are angled from Faulkner's own viewpoint. But we are not yet ready to consider them.

In a sense, old Sam Fathers helps to set young Isaac McCaslin free from several different kinds of bondage. After the former slave was granted permission to live permanently in the wilderness hunting camp, he helped initiate Isaac into the mysteries of the big woods. For Isaac that camp became a training ground in primitive rituals. The scene which occurs at the beginning of "The Old People" describes how Sam Fathers actually baptized Isaac with blood and consecrated him, just after the ten-year-old boy shot and killed his first deer:

> The boy did that—drew the head back and the throat taut and drew Sam Fathers' knife across the throat and Sam stopped and dipped his hands in the hot smoking blood and wiped them back and forth across the boy's face . . . the white boy, marked forever, and the old dark man sired on both sides by savage kings, who had marked him, whose bloody hands had merely formally consecrated him to that which, under the man's tutelage, he had already accepted, humbly and joyfully, with abnegation and with pride too; the hands, the touch, the first worthy blood which he had been found at last worthy to draw, joining him and the man forever . . .

Sam Fathers had thus already begun to teach young Isaac an attitude toward the "verities" of life which made the boy an incipient

alien among his own kin. But as Isaac looks back at that day from the
vantage point of old age, he is represented as recalling the crucial
moments in it as tableaux—urn-like, bas-relief tableaux of beauty and
truth. He remembers particularly how he had felt as he had left that
camp with the hunting party, and with his deer, only a few hours after
that ritualistic baptism:

> . . . There could have been (and were) other trophies in the wagon.
> But for him they did not exist, just as for all practical purposes he and
> Sam Fathers were still alone together as they had been that morning.
> The wagon wound and jolted between the slow and shifting yet con-
> stant walls from behind and above which the wilderness watched them
> pass, less than inimical now and never to be inimical again since the
> buck still and forever leaped, the shaking gun-barrels coming instantly
> and forever steady at last, crashing, and still out of his instant of im-
> mortality the buck sprang, forever immortal; —the wagon jolting and
> bouncing on, the moment of the buck, the shot, Sam Fathers and
> himself and the blood with which Sam had marked him forever one
> with the wilderness which had accepted him since Sam said that he
> had done all right, when suddenly Sam reined back and stopped the
> wagon and they all heard the unmistakable and forgettable sound of
> a deer breaking cover.

During the hunt for that particular deer, the crucial moment for
Isaac had occurred as he had stood watching in amazement while
Sam Fathers refrained from shooting the huge buck passing their
station—refrained, and then saluted the old-timer of the wilderness,
as a living totem image. That night, when Isaac had told the story of
that salute to his older cousin, back at the plantation, McCaslin
Edmonds had refused to believe that there had been any flesh-and-
blood deer for Sam Fathers to refrain from shooting. He dismisses the
incident as merely a buck-fever hallucination on Isaac's part. But the
reader, given no previous or subsequent hints which cast doubt on the
actuality of that salute, is inclined to feel that Cass is thus represented
as becoming more and more blinded by and enslaved to practical
matters, even while Isaac is becoming liberated from the merely practical, by Sam Fathers. These first minor clashes of viewpoint between
the boy and his older cousin foreshadow their more complicated conflicts, as dramatized in "The Bear." But again, the theme picks up
new meanings.

Old Isaac's recollections of his boyhood participation in the hunt
for Old Ben the bear begins with another tableau of beauty and
"verities":

> He was sixteen. For six years now he had been a man's hunter. For

six years now he had heard the best of all talking. It was of the wilderness, the big woods, bigger and older than any recorded document . . . It was of the men, not white nor black nor red but men, hunters, with the will and hardihood to endure and the humility and skill to survive, and the dogs and the bear and deer *juxtaposed and reliefed* [italics added] against it, ordered and compelled by and within the wilderness in the ancient and unremitting contest according to the ancient and immitigable rules which voided all regrets and brooked no quarter . . .

Even the surface or literal level of meaning, in this entire hunting story which constitutes the next phase of young Isaac's education, is handled by Faulkner with such lyric power and sympathy that the style itself approaches a mode of incantation, particularly as it describes the lore of camp life in the wilderness, remembered through the innocent and wondering eyes of the boy. Here again, however, the literal and the figurative levels of meaning are blended by Faulkner as Isaac explores more complicated realms of freedom and bondage, all new to him. The huge and seemingly immortal bear had become endowed with contradictory sets of values, even for Isaac, during those years when he had been too young to take part in the annual hunt for Old Ben. All the reported evidence of the bear's marauding forays had indicated that he was a destructive menace; yet the very boldness of the creature's courses had provided the boy with new ways of looking at certain aspects of freedom, liberty, license, and jungle law. Two passages may be juxtaposed, here, to represent the bear's ambiguous significance. The first merely collects a few signs of his dangerous destructiveness:

. . . the long legend of corn-cribs broken down and rifled, of shoats and grown pigs and even calves carried bodily into the woods and devoured and traps and deadfalls overthrown and dogs mangled and slain and shotgun and even rifle shots delivered at point-blank range yet with no more effect than so many peas blown through a tube by a child—a corridor of wreckage and destruction beginning back before the boy was born . . . an anachronism indomitable and invincible out of an old dead time, a phantom, epitome and apotheosis of the old wild life . . .

Old Ben, we are told, was "not malevolent," at least when measured by the laws of the wilderness, and yet his kind of freedom had become obsolete. At the same time, Isaac and Sam Fathers could not help but admire the bear as a totem image of freedom in a different sense:

. . . fierce and ruthless not just to stay alive but ruthless with the fierce pride of liberty and freedom, jealous and proud enough of liberty and freedom to see it threatened not with fear nor even alarm but almost with joy, seeming deliberately to put it into jeopardy in order to savor it and keep his old strong bones and flesh supple and quick to defend and preserve it . . .

Understanding the bear in that double sense, as destroyer and totem, Sam Fathers and Isaac could not help but hunt him with mixed motives. Their annual attempts to seek and destroy such a fine old ruler of the wilderness had to take on the quality of pageant rites because, for the mentor and the boy, there was always an element of reverence and worship in their particular kinds of pursuit. One of Isaac's strongest desires was to find and confront the bear, alone—not from a desire to kill but, partly out of sheer curiosity and partly out of a deep respect for such primitive power, to observe. If that was what the boy wanted, Sam Fathers told him, he would have to leave the gun behind. He did, and kept searching. At last, after relinquishing his watch and compass because they were also metallic and odorous, Isaac did achieve one brief moment when he and the bear stood looking at each other, in another tableau of beauty and truth which would remain vivid for Isaac as long as he lived. Thereafter, he and Sam Fathers were even more willing to postpone the denouement as long as possible.

More than once, each of them had the chance to shoot Old Ben, and each refrained. A particularly dramatic moment in their ritualistic hunting took the form of another meaningful tableau, in Isaac's memory and education. He had brought his fyce, his little mongrel dog, down into the wilderness from the plantation, to use in tracking the bear. Even before the dog was needed, and even while he was still being carried in Isaac's arms, the boy and Sam Fathers came unexpectedly on Old Ben. Without thinking, Isaac set the dog free, and saw him start to close in. The bear was ready for him:

> It turned at bay against the trunk of a big cypress, on its hind feet; it seemed to the boy that it would never stop rising, taller and taller, and even the two hounds seemed to have taken a kind of desperate and despairing courage from the fyce. Then he realized that the fyce was actually not going to stop. He flung the gun down and ran. When he overtook and grasped the shrill, frantically pinwheeling little dog, it seemed to him that he was directly under the bear. He could smell it, strong and hot and rank. Sprawling, he looked up where it loomed and towered over him like a thunderclap. It was quite familiar, until he remembered: this was the way he had used to dream about it.

That time, the dog had done the teaching: he had inspired the boy to act out the same kind of courage and loyalty which the dog itself had displayed. After the boy returned home from that particular hunt, his cousin Cass asked him why he had not used his gun when his fyce charged the bear. Isaac had no ready answer, and so his cousin did a strange thing, as it seemed to the boy. He took from the bookcase a volume of poems and read aloud Keats' "Ode on a Grecian Urn," an urn containing a bas-relief frieze of tableau scenes. Concluding, Cass read the second stanza again, ending,

> She cannot fade, though thou hast not thy bliss,
> For ever wilt thou love, and she be fair.

Unschooled in the ways of formal poetry, and seeing no connection, Isaac protested, "He's talking about a girl." So Cass had been forced to explain the underlying meaning, as he saw it:

"He had to talk about something. . . . He was talking about truth. Truth is one. It doesn't change. It covers all things which touch the heart . . . Courage and honor and pride, and pity and love of justice and of liberty. They all touch the heart, and what the heart holds to becomes truth, as far as we know truth. Do you see now?"

Isaac had not been sure. Perhaps the reader is not sure, at least on the point as to whether Cass is in character when he reaches for Keats's "Ode on a Grecian Urn." But his remarks throw light on, and actually express, Faulkner's definition as to "the verities of the human heart." Those remarks also illuminate the recurrent significance of tableaux, throughout "The Bear." Furthermore, the "liberty" reference is more than a reminder of the theme.

The end of the hunt for Old Ben approached only after Sam Fathers trapped and subdued and trained the wild dog he named Lion. Convinced that he had at last found a beast which could bring Ben to bay and hold him there, Sam was willing to admit that the end was in sight, perhaps for himself as well as for the bear. Having identified his sympathies first with the freedom of the wilderness, then with the freedom of the bear, and finally with the freedom of the wild dog he himself had enslaved, Sam seemed to find something fitting in the possibility that they should all go together. In a sense they were all obsolete, anachronistic. Isaac thought he understood that well enough to see, at least in retrospect, why Sam had wanted Lion to help him effect that end:

And he was glad, he told himself. *He was old. He had no children, no people, none of his blood anywhere above earth that he would ever meet again. And even if he were to, he could not have touched it, spoken to it, because for seventy years now he had had to be a negro. It was almost over now and he was glad.*

In the epic close of the hunt, on the last day, Lion and Old Ben met in combat as two opposed totem images, and the end became simultaneously a death-struggle and an embrace: "the bear, on its hind feet, its back against a tree while the bellowing hounds swirled around it and once more Lion drove in, leaping clear of the ground. This time the bear didn't strike him down. It caught the dog in both arms, almost loverlike, and they both went down." Because Isaac could find no chance for a shot, the half-breed Indian, Boon Hoggan-beck, who could never use a gun adequately, found his instinctive moment for displaying a courage which gave him his moment of heroic dignity. As though intent only on going to the rescue of his beloved Lion, Boon completed the ritual in the traditionally primitive manner by killing the bear with a knife: "For an instant they almost resembled a piece of statuary: the clinging dog, the bear, the man astride its back, working and probing the buried blade."

Immediately after the kill, while Boon was tending to the mortally injured Lion, with no regard for his own serious wounds, someone found Sam Fathers lying on his face in the mud, unhurt and yet apparently dying, or at least ready to die. Isaac pleaded with his cousin for permission to stay with Boon to care for Sam Fathers, and might have been refused if old General Compson had not defended his right to stay, by talking obliquely about various forms of freedom and enslavement:

"All right," General Compson said. "You can stay. If missing an extra week of school is going to throw you so far behind you'll have to sweat to find out what some hired pedagogue put behind the covers of a book, you better quit altogether. —And you shut up, Cass," he said, though McCaslin had not spoken. "You've got one foot straddled into a farm and the other foot straddled into a bank; you aint even got a good hand-hold where this boy was already an old man long before you damned Sartorises and Edmondses invented farms and banks to keep yourself from having to find out what this boy was born knowing and fearing too maybe without being afraid . . . maybe by God that's the why and the wherefore of farms and banks. —I reckon you still aint going to tell what it is?"

Isaac stayed, and with the death of Sam Fathers came the end of this section of the story—the end of the boy's education. Just what he has learned from Sam Fathers, or rather just what effect Sam Fathers has in shaping his future action, becomes clear in the next

91

section of the story, where Isaac says to his cousin McCaslin Edmonds, "Sam Fathers set me free."

Prior to any consideration of that next section, which has for its symbolic setting the commissary store on the McCaslin plantation, a textual note is in order, for purposes of making an important point about the freedom-bondage theme. When "The Bear" was first published, in *The Saturday Evening Post* (on May 9, 1942, just two days before the publication of *Go Down, Moses*), that *Post* version of the story did not contain the commissary episode. When Faulkner subsequently supervised the reprinting of "The Bear" as a short story in *Big Woods* (1955), that version again omitted the commissary episode. It would seem clear, then, that the commissary episode was designed to make "The Bear" thematically integrated with the other parts of *Go Down, Moses*. It does more than that. The commissary episode constitutes the thematic center of the entire volume, by enriching, extending, and complicating Faulkner's previous and subsequent dramatizations of the ways in which human beings use and abuse and construe and misconstrue freedom and bondage. Specifically, the commissary episode represents Isaac McCaslin as misusing and misconstruing his own freedom, but with the best of intentions.

In the commissary, on his twenty-first birthday, Isaac McCaslin confronts his cousin and foster father, McCaslin Edmonds, and sells his birthright. That is, he repudiates his claim to the ownership of the McCaslin plantation. His motives are clear. He thus intends to set himself free from all the evils and injustices and bondages which, he feels, have cursed and continue to curse his legal inheritance. But in retrospect, Isaac himself admits that his noble and idealistic gesture of repudiation had been a tragic error. In various ways it had ruined his life to such an extent that he might almost say with Cordelia, "We are not the first who, with best meaning, have incurred the worst." The irony, the tragedy, of that free choice has been foreshadowed repeatedly, in the earlier pages of *Go Down, Moses*, starting with one passage in the very first paragraph of the first story: ". . . that which some had thought then and some still thought should have been Isaac's, since his was the name in which the title to the land had first been granted . . ." Two very closely related evaluations of that freely chosen act of repudiation occur in the second story entitled, "The Fire and the Hearth." The first of these is provided by Lucas Beauchamp, a Negro relative of Isaac, who is represented as thinking, years after the event, that he himself is "almost as old as old Isaac who in a sense, say what a man would, had turned apostate to his name and lineage by weakly relinquishing the land which was right-

KING GUSTAVUS VI AWARDING WILLIAM FAULKNER THE NOBEL PRIZE, 1950

fully his to live in town on . . . charity . . ." The reference to "charity" indicates the allowance of fifty dollars a month, given to Isaac after the relinquishment, for living expenses, according to the terms of the contract he made with his cousin, McCaslin Edmonds. The second evaluation is made by Isaac himself, on the day when Lucas Beauchamp had reached the age of twenty-one and had come to claim the disinheritance money, the birthwrong money which had been left to him through his father by old Carothers McCaslin, and which was disbursed by Isaac. Wishing that he could help Lucas more, by giving him some of his own money, and yet having none to give, Isaac upbraided himself by thinking, as he stood facing Lucas Beauchamp, "Fifty dollars a month. He knows that's all. That I reneged, cried calf-rope, sold my birthright, betrayed my blood, for what he too calls not peace but obliteration and a little food." Those two passages in "The Fire and the Hearth" forewarn the reader that Isaac's idealistic gesture, dramatized in the commissary episode of "The Bear," can and should be viewed as being at least in part a tragic mistake. A further contextual sidelight is thrown on the same action in the later story entitled "Delta Autumn." When the niece of Lucas Beauchamp stands before Isaac and holds in her arms the disinherited child she had borne to the grandson of McCaslin Edmonds, she reproaches the old man whom she impulsively calls "Uncle Isaac," in this exchange:

"You spoiled him. You, and Uncle Lucas and Aunt Molly. But mostly you."
"Me?" he said. "Me?"
"Yes, when you gave to his grandfather that land which didn't belong to him, not even half of it by will or even law."
"And never mind that too," he said. "Never mind that, too."

With these contextual controls of meaning in mind, the reader is better able to recognize the dramatic ironies and ambiguities with which Faulkner endows the counterpoint of argument on the subject of freedom between Isaac and his cousin in the commissary. Furthermore, certain elements in the first three episodes of "The Bear" take on ironic colorings when viewed in the light of the commissary episode. For example, old Sam Fathers had initiated young Isaac into certain Indian beliefs concerning the communal ownership of land. The boy had accepted the notion that the wilderness had been and should remain a realm free from even the possibility of any one man's ownership—a realm bigger than "white man fatuous enough to believe he had bought any fragment of it, of Indian ruthless enough to pretend that any fragment of it had been his to convey." By the time

Isaac had reached manhood, he had apparently applied this idealistic attitude toward the wilderness to his larger fund of reasons why he himself should not accept ownership of the McCaslin plantation. Faulkner handles all of Isaac's beliefs ambiguously, as though to imply that even the reader should be able to preserve sympathies for both sides of the argument between the two cousins.

The commissary episode is prefaced with another tableau, artistically counterbalanced against the wilderness tableau which occurs in the first episode of "The Bear." This time, Isaac is represented as recalling, retrospectively, that day of decision which had been made possible to him only when he had finally come of age: ". . . himself and his cousin juxtaposed not against the wilderness but against the tamed land which was to have been his heritage . . . not in pursuit and lust but in relinquishment, and in the commissary as it should have been." The figurative and poetic overtones of that phrase, "as it should have been," are worth noticing. Literally, the word commissary refers to the plantation store; but the same word is also used to represent a person to whom is committed some charge or office, by a superior power, and Isaac is about to preach a sermon on the Christian doctrine of stewardship, to his decidedly anti-Christian cousin. He begins, not by appealing to beliefs he has learned from Sam Fathers but rather to beliefs acquired from his Christian heritage:

> . . . He told in the Book how He created the earth, made it and looked at it and said it was all right, and then He made man . . . to be His overseer on the earth and to hold suzerainty over the earth and the animals on it in His name, not to hold for himself and his descendants inviolable title forever, generation after generation, to the oblongs and squares of the earth, but to hold the earth mutual and intact in the communal anonymity of brotherhood . . .

That idealistic notion of stewardship is too impractical for Cass Edmonds, who is not at all impressed with scriptural evidence, and who scornfully refers to the Bible as that "tedious and shabby chronicle of His chosen sprung from Abraham." He continues his retort by asking Isaac what God could have been doing throughout the various historical cycles of time in which various men had possessed both property and people as "chattel and revokeless thrall":

> ". . . while He—this Arbiter, this Architect, this Umpire—condoned —or did He? looked down and saw—or did He? Or at least did nothing: saw, and could not, or did not see; saw, and would not, or perhaps He would not see—perverse, impotent, or blind: which?"

Isaac's answer is that God was permissively dispossessed by man's misuse of his own freedom, his own free will, divinely given. He further suggests to his cousin that perhaps it had been a part of the divine purpose to let white man fashion a curse and bring it on himself by introducing the institution of slavery, which had certainly brought retribution on the South in the form of the War Between the States. When Cass quotes Scripture to remind Isaac of the biblical justification for slavery, Isaac protests,

> "There are some things He said in the Book, and some things reported of Him that He did not say. And I know what you will say now: That if truth is one thing to me and another thing to you, how will we choose which is truth? You dont need to choose. The heart already knows. . . . Because the men who wrote his Book for Him were writing about truth and there is only one truth and it covers all things that touch the heart."

Later in this episode, Isaac is to remember how his cousin had explained the "Ode on a Grecian Urn" by saying that Keats had been writing about truth, which is one, which does not change, and which covers all things that touch the heart. Just now, in this argument across the counter of the commissary story, Cass prefers appeals based on reason, and he employs sarcasm as he ridicules Isaac by saying that perhaps everything is for the best, after all, "if, as you say, the heart knows truth, the infallible and unerring heart." For Cass, there is something simultaneously comic and tragic in Isaac's claim that perhaps it was even a part of God's plan to choose old Carothers McCaslin as one of God's stewards, and that perhaps God had found "already in Grandfather the seed progenitive of the three generations He saw it would take to set at least some of His lowly people free." (Again the echo.)

More than once, during their discussion, Isaac and his cousin glance toward the ledgers on the shelf of that commissary store—the ledgers which have provided Isaac with evidences as to "the injustice and a little at least of its amelioration and restitution" on the plantation. He remembers finding, in those ledgers, hints that the slave girl Eunice, having borne a daughter, Tomasina, to old Carothers McCaslin, had lived long enough to see that daughter grow up and bear her own father a son, Terrell, later known as Tomey's Turl. He also remembers finding hints that Eunice had drowned herself on Christmas Day of 1832, after learning that Tomasina was pregnant, and that Tomasina had died soon after the birth and disinheritance of her son. (The reader is thus reminded of the first episode in *Go*

Down, Moses, and of that comic chase after that same Tomey's Turl, conducted in the spirit of a fox hunt.) Isaac tries to explain to his cousin that those repeated porings over the ledgers in that commissary have played a large part in driving him to this act of repudiation, even to the act of defending the Negroes:

> . . . those upon whom freedom and equality had been dumped over-night and without warning or preparation or any training in how to employ it or even just endure it and who misused it not as children would nor yet because they had been so long in bondage and then so suddenly freed, but misused it as human beings always misuse freedom, so that he thought *Apparently there is a wisdom beyond even that learned through suffering necessary for a man to distinguish between liberty and license* . . .

Precisely there, in that passage, Faulkner permits Isaac to make explicit an important part of the freedom-bondage theme which operates metaphorically as a drawstring throughout all the stories in *Go Down, Moses.* The reader should notice, however, that Faulkner keeps that passage balanced, artistically, through the dramatic irony of Isaac's being completely unaware of having thus characterized his own misuse of freedom. His cousin is permitted to turn the tables on Isaac, finally, by implying that this repudiation of what Isaac almost refers to as the original sin and innate depravities, which are part of his own heritage, provides a strikingly tragic example of how human beings can and do misuse freedom. The peripeteia occurs just after Isaac summarizes his own version of the divine plan for Negroes and whites alike by saying that all will come out for the best in the end. Sarcastically, his cousin adds, "And anyway, you will be free." Then he contradicts Isaac's claim that his repudiation has liberated him once and for all from the evils and injustices of his heritage: "No, not now nor ever, we from them nor they from us."

Implicitly, that remark touches the most profound factors in Faulkner's theme, and those factors may be summarized as follows: Man should live under the permanent awareness of his moral obligation to accept and honor that blood-bondage which binds all men together within the human family; but man validly accepts and shares in the responsibilities of imputed guilt, only by taking repeated steps of positive action in trying to correct and make restitution for that imputed guilt. Isaac's motives are represented by Faulkner as being idealistic, spiritual, and noble. But as we have seen, Faulkner also represents Isaac as discovering, too late, the many ways in which his repudiation denied him the chance to exercise, adequately and constructively, his own sense of moral responsibility. Remember that Isaac arrives at one moment of self-recognition and self-condemnation when he faces Lucas Beauchamp, on that blood-relative's twenty-first birthday, and regrets that he can not offer Lucas more financial aid. The most bitter parts of Isaac McCaslin's tragedy is that after he has thus hamstrung himself with good intentions, on his own twenty-first birthday, he goes on living "past seventy and nearer eighty than he ever corroborated any more, a widower now and uncle to half a country and father to no one." Within the Faulknerian premises, the essential irony of his tragedy is that he has abrogated the very same doctrine of stewardship which he expounded so eloquently to his decidedly anti-Christian cousin.

There is no need to consider further textual evidence that Faulkner achieves extraordinary success in manipulating so many different strands of his freedom-bondage theme, in tying together the separate parts of the McCaslin saga. If any single point deserves reiteration, it might be that Faulkner chose a brilliant metaphor when he borrowed as title for *Go Down, Moses* that fragment from the recurrent refrain in the familiar Negro spiritual. The head of the pin, on which Faulkner heaps so much, is the additional phrase of refrain thus activated: "Let my people go." The unfolding of the various episodes in the history of the McCaslin family forces the reader to find repeated and even paradoxical meanings in that phrase. But the ultimate extension of Faulkner's theme would seem to be this: If "my people," as thus used, encompasses all mankind, then the ultimate freedom is derived from individual and social acceptance of moral bondage, within the family of man.

 ❧ SANCTUARY

FAULKNER's best-known story, *Sanctuary*, is also the most criticized and reviled of his novels, perhaps because the relationship between manner and matter therein is easily misunderstood. Unfortunately, *Sanctuary* is too often the first and sometimes the only Faulkner novel which many people have read. But anyone who reads *Sanctuary* for the first time, after having read *The Sound and the Fury*, *Absalom, Absalom!*, *Light in August*, and *Go Down, Moses*, should be able to recognize the peculiar technical quality and tone which gives *Sanctuary* an honorable place among Faulkner's works. Nowhere else does he interweave such comic, ironic, satiric, sarcastic, and tragic bitterness. More than that, the mockery throughout is double-barreled: one load is fired at certain vulnerable foibles in human nature at large, and the other load is fired simultaneously at the low tastes of the vulgarly common reader.

Many critics of *Sanctuary* have glanced so casually through Faulkner's mordant "Introduction" to the Modern Library edition that they have seemed to take the first two sentences only at face value without noticing the subsequent contextual modifications: "This book was written three years ago. To me it is a cheap idea, because it was deliberately conceived to make money." The modifications which follow those first two sentences constitute a typically self-conscious and self-deprecatory Faulknerian smoke screen of explanations, which combine fact and fiction, about how it happened that he wrote *Sanctuary*. He explains that he had not made money from his first two novels, *Soldiers' Pay* and *Mosquitoes*. He also admits that publishers had "consistently refused for two years" to accept for publication the manuscript of *Sartoris* (the matrix of the Yoknapatawpha saga), presumably on the grounds that it would not sell any better than his first two novels. Faulkner does not say that his pride was thus wounded. He merely says that he continued to write merely for his own enjoyment: "Meanwhile . . . I had just written my guts into *The Sound and the Fury* though I was not aware until the book was published that I had done so, because I had done it for pleasure. I believed then that I would never be published again. I had stopped thinking of myself in publishing terms." Not quite, apparently, for he goes on to admit that he offered the manuscript of *The Sound and the Fury* to a publisher who refused it. Now he had two unpublished manuscripts, and it is safe to assume that his pride was thus doubly wounded.

Then a change came in his fortunes, along with an accompanying change in his attitudes. The manuscript of *Sartoris* was accepted by one publisher, and the manuscript of *The Sound and the Fury* was accepted by another publisher who, according to Faulkner, "warned me at the time that it would not sell." It was at that stage, he admits, that he began to ask himself (and, it may be presumed, with bitterness) what kind of a story would sell. He knew the answer, and he had even stated it obliquely in *Sartoris*, where he had caustically described the impatience with which one of his characters, a very respectable Southern lady, waited each day for the arrival of a Memphis tabloid newspaper so that she could indulge her sentimental passion for luxuriating in bloody and horrific accounts of rape, murder, and the gang warfares of rumrunners. Of course such a reader would not be interested in even the best of the four novels Faulkner had already written and published. But his desire to make money at the expense of such a common reader seems to have been coupled with his desire to avenge himself sarcastically and satirically on the common reader. He does not say so, in his "Introduction" to the reprint of *Sanctuary*, but he does say this:

> . . . I began to think of books in terms of possible money. I decided I might just as well make some of it myself. I took a little time out, and speculated what a person in Mississippi would believe to be current trends, chose what I thought was the right answer and invented the most horrific tale I could imagine and wrote it in about three weeks and sent it to Smith, who had done *The Sound and the Fury* and who wrote me immediately. "Good God, I can't publish this. We'd both be in jail."

For the moment, then, Faulkner's very sardonic plan for money-making, and possibly for retaliation and revenge, seemed to have failed. But the act of writing that satirical shocker had apparently enabled Faulkner to vent so much spleen that he began writing again to please himself; he tossed off *As I Lay Dying* in six weeks, and sent it to his publisher "without changing a word." It was accepted. Then came the surprise of receiving from his publisher, without warning, the galley proof of *Sanctuary*. Faulkner explains, in the reprint "Introduction," that when he reread his little satirical shocker in that form he himself found it "so terrible" that he refused to let it be published: ". . . there were but two things to do: tear it up or rewrite it." He chose to make heavy revisions, even though he knew that he would have to pay for the privilege, at the standard cost for making too many galley-proof corrections. On that note he concludes his "Introduction," dryly:

> I had to pay for the privilege of rewriting it, trying to make out of it something which would not shame *The Sound and the Fury* and *As I Lay Dying* too much and I made a fair job and I hope you will buy it and tell your friends and I hope they will buy it too.

The tart snap of that conclusion echoes a little of the sarcastic bitterness which must have gone into the first draft of *Sanctuary*. Some of that same bitterness remains in the revised and published draft. But by the time Faulkner was invited to write that "Introduction" for the reprint of *Sanctuary* he had already received grimly satisfactory proof that the tabloid-reading public had solemnly swallowed the satirical bait. One may imagine his mixed emotions as he watched those readers "buy" *Sanctuary* well up into the best-seller list—as he also watched Hollywood solemnly pay him plenty of money for the privilege of transforming *Sanctuary* into a soap-opera film entitled "The Story of Temple Drake."

The following interpretation of *Sanctuary* is based on the assumption that the stylistic virtuosity which Faulkner had previously demonstrated in writing novels as different as *The Sound and the Fury* and *Sartoris* made it quite possible for him to endow a conventional narrative style with a tone of detachment and indifference, as though he were merely a tabloid reporter turned novelist. But in the process he achieved a considerable degree of subtlety; otherwise the sardonic-sarcastic-satiric-burlesque flavor and tone of *Sanctuary* would have been described by Faulkner's critics long ago. Part of that flavor and tone was achieved through Faulkner's strategy of making no comment on the actions of his characters in *Sanctuary*. Once again, however, that posture of seeming detachment merely meant that he counted on his various formal and technical procedures to convey his thematic meanings indirectly and figuratively. Once again, also, he made heavy use of dramatic irony, by permitting one character after another to establish unintentional and unselfconscious discrepancies between things said and things done.

Faulkner employed another familiar convention of the comic mode in *Sanctuary*. He did not permit any character to change, by arriving at any significant self-recognition scene. Such a change would have deprived Faulkner of the opportunity to keep using such characters, from beginning to end, as targets for satirical unmasking. Although Faulkner's goal in *Sanctuary* would seem to have been to ridicule certain forms of human stupidity and folly and vice, he simultaneously invoked yet another convention of the comic mode. He arranged to define his positive thematic concerns in terms of their opposites. More than that, he took the risk of interweaving various elements of tragedy throughout this primarily satirical and comic narrative.

The sentimental type of reader was quite easily seduced by Faulkner into serving as unwitting target for ridicule, through such a blend of narrative detachment, irony, and satire. For example, if any reader chooses to extend sentimental sympathies to Temple Drake (who is ironically permitted to protest that she is more sinned against than sinning, even while her actions belie the protest) that reader gets weighed in Faulkner's satirical balance, and found wanting, along with Temple Drake. In the conclusion of this chapter, two splendid illustrations will be given of how some other kinds of readers choose their own peculiar ways of walking glibly into Faulkner's not too subtly baited satire-trap.

In the chapter devoted to *Light in August,* an attempt was made to establish contrasts between the minimal and almost meaningless values implicit in the raw materials of that narrative, and the meanings implicitly assigned to those raw materials through Faulkner's formal and technical ordering. The same procedure will be employed in this chapter because it is particularly effective when applied to *Sanctuary*. By way of beginning, then, the following paragraph is devoted to a deliberately flat, neutral, and almost meaningless recapitulation of the mere story or plot in *Sanctuary*.

A lawyer named Horace Benbow, plagued by marital difficulties, escapes from the insults of his twice-married wife, and her daughter. His excuse for escape is his distaste for the smelly task of carrying home from the railroad station, once a week, a package of shrimps. After he has run away from home, he hopes to find refuge with his widowed sister, Narcissa Benbow Sartoris, who lives in the nearby town of Jefferson. En route, Horace leaves the road to drink at a spring near the Old Frenchman place, and thus accidentally meets a small-time bootlegger-gangster called Popeye. Horace is told by Popeye that if he can wait until after dark he will be given a ride to Jefferson in one of Popeye's rumrunning trucks. So the lawyer goes with Popeye into the Old Frenchman place, meets the moonshine-maker, Lee Goodwin, talks with Goodwin's common-law wife, Ruby Lamarr, and shares their supper with them. Afterwards, he rides into Jefferson as planned. Then he goes to the old Sartoris home, where his sister is living with her young son and with a Sartoris relative, Aunt Jenny. Horace there meets a young man named Gowan Stevens who has just returned from the University of Virginia for the spring vacation. Although Gowan seems to be courting the young widow, Narcissa, he apparently becomes discouraged by her coldness and moves on to the State University in the neighboring town of Oxford. He seeks out and finds, there, a redheaded girl named Temple Drake, whom he takes to a local dance. After Gowan has brought Temple back to her dormitory, he spends the rest of the night carousing. As a result, he is in poor physical condition to take Temple to an out-of-town baseball game in his mother's car, the next day, as planned. But they meet at a designated rural station, where Temple makes her spectacular arrival by using the emergency signal to stop the excursion train, and then by jumping off before anyone can stop her. Gowan explains that their first call must be made at the Old Frenchman place because Gowan needs more liquor. At the entrance to Popeye's hide-out, Gowan wrecks the car against a fallen tree. So the young people are stranded at the Old Frenchman place during the remainder of a wild day of drinking, and through an even wilder night. In the morning, as Gowan sets out to find another car, he becomes so ashamed of remaining drunk that he decides not to return for Temple. Later that same morning, as the impotent Popeye is courting Temple, a feeble-minded innocent named Tommy gets in the way, and Popeye casually kills him. Then he rapes Temple with a corncob. That afternoon, Popeye drives Temple to a Memphis whorehouse, where she is to be kept indefinitely against the day when she may be needed as an alibi or false witness, in case Popeye is accused of killing Tommy. Temple falls in love with one of Popeye's gangsters, a handyman nicknamed Red, and so she does not try to escape from the brothel. Meanwhile, back at the Old Frenchman place, Lee Goodwin had immediately reported to the police the murder of Tommy. Suspected of the crime, and jailed, Goodwin refused to name Popeye as the murderer because he fears retaliation. In Jefferson, Horace Benbow hears of Goodwin's arrest, suspects injustice, and offers his own legal services to Goodwin, free of charge. After Horace discovers that Gowan Stevens and Temple Drake were somehow involved, he buys from Senator Clarence Snopes the information that Popeye is keeping Temple in a Memphis whorehouse. Then he visits her and arranges to have her testify in defense of Goodwin, at the trial. But Senator Snopes has already sold the same information to the District Attorney, who is further assisted by hints from Horace's sister Narcissa. During the trial, Temple testifies for the prosecution and identifies Goodwin as the man whom she saw kill Tommy. She also implies that Goodwin was the man who raped her with the corncob. That evening, after Goodwin has been convicted of both murder and rape, he is taken from the jail by a mob and lynched. Benbow returns to his wife. Temple goes with her father, Judge Drake, to Europe. Popeye, caught in another miscarriage of justice, some time later, is executed in Alabama on the charge of having killed a man in one town, at precisely the hour when he was actually in another town, killing someone else.

That bald summary raises the immediate question as to how even a satiric variety of literary treatment can effect any salvage. Again it may be worth remembering that two different authors, given that summary of raw materials, could so order it as to endow it with diametrically opposed meanings. Because we are already familiar with Faulkner's themes, however, it should not be surprising to notice that one of his major formalizing strategies in *Sanctuary* is to handle the whole sardonically as a montage of love stories, arranged in a counterpoint pattern. Of course there are several different kinds of love involved. Temple Drake is the mock-heroine, and her Gothic romance is ironically projected against a rich background of contrasting love interests. The hollow marital love of Horace Benbow and his wife Belle provides one element in that background; the pathetic but genuine and self-sacrificial love of Ruby Lamarr for her common-law husband Lee Goodwin provides another; all of the love interests represented by Miss Reba's sporting house in Memphis provide others; then finally we are given the love story which explains Popeye's heritage. Thus *love-love-love* serves ambiguously as the center of subject matter. It also serves ambiguously as one of Faulkner's themes.

Another broad category of technical factors which helps to focus attention on a somewhat separate and yet related theme is first hinted by the title word, *Sanctuary*. A cumulative sequence of actions dramatize meanings for that title, and thus gradually endow the word with enrichments of meaning until the title becomes metaphorical. Taken out of context, the word "sanctuary" might suggest, initially, only its etymological root, *sanctus:* something consecrated or sacred. It might further suggest, if still considered out of context, any sacred place of refuge, protection, shelter, where a fugitive might feel secure. If misused, such a sanctuary could provide even a fugitive from the law with a temporary hiding place. In Faulkner's context, that latter meaning is particularly pertinent. The total action of *Sanctuary*, viewed in retrospect, can be seen as being not only a montage of love stories but also a cluster of symbolic actions made analogous: various characters dodging, running, ducking, hiding, always for purposes of seeking false sanctuaries, and frequently finding sanctuary behind nothing more sacred than *words-words-words*.

Chief among those artful dodgers, of course, is the mock-heroine Temple Drake. Her Christian name is implicitly related to the title of the novel in a way which can scarcely be called subtle. The very strong associations of that name may be derived, in a Christian frame of reference, from a familiar biblical passage in the third chapter of Paul's first letter to the Corinthians: "Know ye not that ye are the temple of God, and that the Spirit of God dwelleth in you? If any man defile the temple of God, him shall God destroy; for the temple of God is holy, which temple ye are. Let no man deceive himself." The Pauline austerity of that passage is not greatly different from what we have already seen of the Faulknerian austerity. Temple Drake, in all her sanctuary-seekings, ignores the figurative significance of her Christian name. But she repeatedly makes appeal to the social weight attached to her family name. Whenever she reiterates, "My father's a judge," particularly when she stumbles into the utterance of that phrase while trying to say the Lord's Prayer, the poetic overtones suggest that Temple Drake is not entirely free from twinges of conscience.

Among Temple's most futile and ironic gestures are her self-deceptive attempts to find sanctuaries in illusions, so that she more than once becomes the victim of circumstances beyond her control. Quite early in the story, all of her subsequent attempts in this regard are foreshadowed by thoughts which cross her mind as she sees that Gowan Stevens' car is about to crash into the tree at the entrance to the Old Frenchman place: ". . . it seemed to her the logical and disastrous end to the train of circumstances in which she had become involved." The reader recognizes the ambiguous possibilities in that thought. But Temple would be out of character if she saw herself as a causal agent, in any way responsible for her predicament. As detached and seemingly indifferent narrator, Faulkner makes no comment here; he merely lets Temple's later actions continue to unmask her capacity for gagging and blinding her conscience.

Technically and thematically considered, the sharpest foil for Temple Drake is Ruby Lamarr, whose love for Goodwin gets her into trouble with the more prudent citizens of Jefferson. Faulkner makes it ironically clear that Ruby is maligned and insulted by the townspeople, not because she had been living in sin but because she has been caught at it. As her name implies, she had red-blooded qualities which give more dignity to her total action than is achieved by any other character. No sacrifice is too great for her to make for the man she loves, even though that man may not be worth her sacrifices. She has tried before to rescue him from predicaments of his own making, and she has failed. She tries one last time, and continues trying until Goodwin is lynched for a crime he did not commit. Ruby Lamarr is another Faulknerian primitive, related symbolically to Lena Grove, Dilsey, and Nancy Mannigoe. Playing opposite the red-haired Temple Drake, Ruby is the actual and tragic heroine of *Sanctuary*, while her husband is a weaker tragic victim. At times, Ruby is permitted to serve quite inartistically as a persona for Faulkner, particularly in that early scene where she upbraids Temple:

> "Oh, I know your sort," the woman said. "Honest women. Too good to have anything to do with common people. You'll slip out at night with the kids . . . and burn their gasoline and eat their food, but just let a man so much as look at you and you faint away because your father the judge and your four brothers might not like it. . . . But you good women. Cheap sports. Giving nothing . . . You poor little gutless fool," the woman said in her cold undertone. "Playing at it . . . do you think you've got the only one in the world? . . . Nobody asked you to come here. Nobody cares whether you are afraid or not. Afraid? You haven't the guts to be really afraid, any more than you have to be in love."

If Ruby speaks too pointedly for Faulkner, there, she at least speaks accurately. Appearances provide Temple with sanctuaries, and therefore a mirror is one of her favorite yardsticks. The story ends, appropriately, with Temple's gazing at herself in a mirror. Near the beginning, during her drive to Memphis with Popeye, Faulkner makes another ironic dramatization of Temple's character as he permits Popeye to silence her sobbing with a mirror:

> "Shut it," he said, "shut it;" gripping her silent. "Look at yourself. Here." With the other hand he swung the mirror on the windshield around and she looked at her image, at the uptilted hat and her matted hair and her round mouth. She began to fumble at her coat pockets, looking at her reflection. He released her and she produced the compact and opened it and peered into the mirror, whimpering a little. She powdered her face and rouged her mouth and straightened her hat, whimpering into the tiny mirror on her lap while Popeye watched her. He lit a cigarette. "Aint you ashamed of yourself?" he said.

Temple is far too much ashamed of her appearance to worry very long about anything else. As Popeye stops his car at a gasoline station in Jefferson, leaves his car, and thus inadvertently gives Temple a chance to escape, she gets out to see a young man whom she knows. Immediately her one concern is to avoid having the young man see her, and this time she seeks sanctuary behind a trash barrel, where Popeye finds her. Temple explains: "He nearly saw me! He was almost looking right at me!"

Faulkner's ruthless unmasking of Temple increases as he describes her response to the sanctuary provided by Miss Reba's house in Memphis—particularly after Red has taught Temple to love his kind of love, even while the impotent Popeye leans over the end of the bed watching them and whinnying like a gelding. So long as Temple can get Red's love she does not care where or how she is kept. Apparently she said as much, and more, in those letters to Red which reappear in *Requiem for a Nun*.

The ultimate self-degradation of Temple Drake occurs in the trial scene, where her complete indifference permits her to help send an innocent man to his death without even the slightest twinge of conscience. Faulkner's handling of those implicitly sarcastic ironies reaches its height when he lets the District Attorney laud Temple as a most sacred epitome of Southern Womanhood.

Irony again provides a means of unmasking, throughout Faulkner's representation of Horace Benbow as a professional upholder of the law. Horace is an idealist, a gentleman, a preserver of the traditions of the Old South, and a sensitive exponent of justice in all its forms. But readers who have previously met him in *Sartoris* will remember that he did not show up very well there. The same is true here. At the start of *Sanctuary*, when he is first represented as playing opposite Popeye at the spring near the Old Frenchman place, the moral advantage would seem to be entirely in favor of Horace: he is the one who consciously and even formally places himself in accord with nature, as he kneels beside the spring to drink, while Popeye suggestively squats on the other side and spits into the water. But Horace says, at the Old Frenchman place, a short time later, "You see, I lack courage. That was left out of me. The machinery is all here, but it wont run." Ruby Lamarr is one listener and watcher who sees through Horace and says, "The fool. The poor fool." Later, when Horace is prompted by the best of intentions, and asserts his belief in the noble dignity of man by going into court as lawyer for the unjustly accused Goodwin, Faulkner merely hints that Horace has found in the predicament of Goodwin and Ruby a new form of sanctuary from his own marital troubles. As represented, his well-meaning and yet cowardly efforts in behalf of Goodwin actually work against justice. By confiding indiscreetly to his equally cowardly and gossiping sister, Horace provides the whole town of Jefferson with all the information needed to incite the persecution of Ruby and the lynching of Goodwin. During the trial, which provides the crisis in the total action of *Sanctuary*, Horace lets the District Attorney get away with the bribery and theft of Benbow's own star witness, Temple Drake. He obstructs justice by keeping out of the trial the fact that Popeye was the actual murderer and rapist. He has evidence enough to break the case wide-open, and he never tries to use it. He does not even appeal the case. Why?

Faulkner gives no direct answer. Having cast himself in the role of a seemingly indifferent narrator, he would violate the rules of his own artistic game if he did. Instead, he lets Horace provide answers, indirectly, through what he does do and does say. Eventually Horace seeks that familiar sanctuary of insisting that he is in no way to blame for what happens, because the forces of evil are so highly organized and powerful that they have reduced the forces of good to impotence. After he has finished hearing Temple's grotesque story from her own lips, long before the trial, Horace pessimistically sees only one solution. He wishes all these people involved, including himself, might enter a lethal gas chamber where they could get life over with, quickly and painlessly. Faulkner thus reminds us of all the other Horaces in the world who perennially fashion different kinds of death chambers out of the same self-excusing rationalizations. Horace's best death-wish compresses that same world into a little ball and throws it away thus:

> Perhaps it is upon the instant that we realize, admit, that there is a logical pattern to evil, that we die.

No comment from Faulkner on that; no need for comment, in a context where the satire is so austere and biting. But Faulkner's view would seem to be that just as soon as any individual comes to realize there is a logical pattern to evil, that individual discovers his duty to assert his own moral responsibility to others and to himself by going into action against that logical pattern, regardless of the possible consequences of such a struggle. By contrast, Faulkner implies, the individual who submits to Horace's sense of impotence might just as well be dead. He is already worse than dead because he unintentionally collaborates with evil. In the trial scene, Horace's passivity baffles even the judge. A few excerpts will illustrate, starting with the District Attorney's hypocritical and sentimental play to the jury and the audience, in his cross-examination of his bribed star-witness, Temple Drake:

"Speak out. No one will hurt you. Let these good men, these fathers and husbands, hear what you have to say and right your wrong for you."

The Court glanced at Horace, his eyebrows raised. But Horace made no move. He sat with his head bent a little, his hands clutched in his lap.

". . . Speak a little louder. These men will not hurt you. They are here to right the wrong you have suffered. . . . You are your father's only daughter?"

Again the Court looked at Horace; again he made no move.

". . . You were hiding, then, because something had happened to you and you dared not—"

"I object!" Horace said. "The question is lead—"

"Sustained," the Court said. "I have been on the point of warning you for some time, Mr. Attorney, but defendant would not take exception, for some reason."

. . . The District Attorney turned away. "Your honor and gentlemen, you have listened to this horrible, this unbelievable, story which this young girl has told; you have seen the evidence and heard the doctor's testimony: I shall no longer subject this ruined, defenseless child to the agony of—" he ceased; the heads turned as one and watched a man come stalking up the aisle toward the Bench. . . .

"Your Honor," the old man said, "is the Court done with this witness?"

"Yes, sir, Judge," the Court said: "yes sir. Defendant, do you waive—"

Of course Horace does waive, and in so doing he makes his most crucial waiver of both his legal and his moral duties. Through that default, Goodwin is convicted, and as a result he is lynched. Pertinently, brief notice may be given here to a comment made by another District Attorney, later in *Sanctuary*, when another travesty on law and justice leads to the conviction of Popeye. Assuming that the decision will be appealed, and that Popeye's gangster world will help him escape from hanging, this District Attorney observes with an Horatian wail, "It's them thugs like that that have made justice a laughing-stock, until even when we get a conviction, everybody knows it won't hold." The dramatic ironies, there, suggest that to make justice a laughing-stock, a thug needs a skillfully crooked lawyer, and adequately weak opposition. Horace's weak opposition leads him into collusion with a crooked District Attorney, and even into collusion with an assenting society, to make justice unjust.

Faulkner never lets the reader forget that Horace happens to be in Jefferson, acting like a shrimp, because he has dodged his own problems of shrimphood at home. Goodwin had said to Horace, quite early, "Look here, you go home." Ruby Lamarr had said much the same thing. Aunt Jenny had meant even more in what she said when Horace gave her the opening:

> "If you know of any way in which I can get him out of that jail by tomorrow . . ."
> "You know what that way is," Miss Jenny said. "If you aint got any backbone."
> "I'll know whether or not I have any backbone when you tell me what the other way is."
> "Go back to Belle," Miss Jenny said. "Go back home."

Miss Jenny would seem to represent, there, much the same austere attitude toward seeking sanctuaries from moral difficulties which Faulkner permitted Miss Rosa Coldfield to express in *Absalom, Absalom!:* ". . . before it became fashionable to repair your mistakes by turning your back on them and running." But Faulkner saves the crowning irony for Horace until after he has failed to appeal the Goodwin case—until even after he has failed to talk with his client at the conclusion of the trial. Horace merely sneaks out of the courtroom, climbs into his sister's car, and drives back with her toward the Sartoris home. On the way, he again notices that logical pattern of nature which has repeatedly made some impression on him throughout the story. Those references to spring, and to nature, have accumulated typically Faulknerian symbolism until they provide a fairly overt metaphysical backdrop of order, against which all these chaotic human actions are being performed. Now Horace opines, "It does last. Spring does. You'd almost think there was some purpose in it." Horace eventually goes home to Belle; but without any indication that he has achieved any self-recognition. It is more appropriate to the satiric mode of *Sanctuary* to conclude that Faulkner leaves Horace unchanged: having initially escaped from lesser shrimphood, at home, and having acted like a shrimp in Jefferson, he then returns supinely to his lesser shrimphood.

Faulkner achieves one kind of counterpoint by playing off Horace's emotional-mental-spiritual impotence against Popeye's physical impotence until that particular antithesis helps to illuminate and extend certain thematic values. Technically, the strategy of establishing that antithesis requires that the cause of Popeye's impotence, as it might be figuratively and symbolically considered, must be explained late in the action. He is introduced as a mysterious figure. Apparently he is the villain of the piece; he might seem to be a personification of evil. Out of tune with nature, at odds with life, he is unnatural. The sign for Popeye is black, and his black suit becomes correlated not only with evil but also with death, particularly when the literate Horace thinks, "He smells black; he smells like that black stuff that ran out of Bovary's mouth and down on her bridal veil, when they raised her head." By contrast, Horace would like to think that his own sign-value is white, symbolizing his lofty and pure idealism. From Horace's viewpoint, of course, Popeye is the motive-force behind the immediate logical pattern of evil and injustice. So when Horace explains to Miss Jenny that he himself "cannot stand idly by, and see injustice done," he reacts to Miss Jenny's correction by saying, "Well, call it that irony which lurks in events, then." The major irony which lurks in all the events concerning Popeye is that when the reader finally is given the story of Popeye's background, the moral responsibility for his actions can no longer be assigned to Popeye.

Popeye did of course kill Tommy. He did unnaturally rape Temple Drake. He also murdered Temple's lover, Red. Those facts are not changed, but the significance of those facts does change when Faulkner eventually makes it clear that Popeye, congenitally ill, can not be held morally responsible for what he did; that, instead, society can be held morally responsible for letting Popeye out of confinement. A brief review of the information thus deliberately withheld may suggest how the ironies accumulate to provide a savagely strong reinforcement of meaning.

Popeye was a love-child, we are told. The ironic love story, involving his parents, builds quickly to the nice detail that he was born, illegitimately, on the birthday of the supreme exponent of the gospel of love. The child was gifted, congenitally gifted, with certain effects of a love-disease or a social disease: syphilis. His abnormalities expressed themselves in picturesque ways even during his childhood. (In describing those ways, Faulkner again reveals an almost insolent attitude toward those tabloid-readers for whom he initially wrote *Sanctuary*. He tauntingly hammers them with overt symbolism, as though to say, "Get it? Get it?") We are told that when Popeye practiced vivisection, during childhood, by cutting up two little birds with a pair of scissors, they were not just any old birds; they were lovebirds. Next, he practiced vivisection on a couple of kittens. But even after he had repeatedly demonstrated his incapacity for assuming responsibility for his own actions, this unnatural victim of a love-disease or a social disease should clearly have become the permanent responsibility of society, and of charity. Instead, on the day when Popeye was pronounced fit to go free, society thus turned loose on itself, or thus brought on itself, an incipient retribution. In that sense, Popeye is figuratively akin to Joe Christmas. With these facts of Popeye's background in mind, the reader would seem invited by Faulkner to reconsider at least some aspects of the question as to who is the villain of this grotesque and Gothic romance. Ostensibly, Popeye; actually, those attitudes, those individuals, and that society which created Popeye, and then turned him loose.

One technical factor in *Sanctuary*, not yet considered, further reinforces Faulkner's thematic preoccupation with ducking and dodging moral responsibilities through seeking sanctuary in appearances. Temple's tendencies, in this regard, have been illustrated. But Faulkner arranges a recurrence of analogous actions which involve many other characters. A few quotations will illustrate these analogous actions and the bearing they have on theme. When Horace's own sister (significantly named Narcissa) asks Horace to drop the Goodwin case, because his association with Ruby Lamarr has already caused gossip, this dialogue occurs:

> "I don't care where else you go, nor what you do. I don't care how many women you have, nor who they are. But I can not have my brother mixed up with a woman people are talking about."
> "Oh. So you think that, do you?"
> "I don't think anything about it; I don't care. That's what people in town think. So it doesn't matter whether it's true or not. . . . Go away from here, Horace."

Thematically, that passage takes care of Narcissa, if she has not previously been disposed of. A similar concern for appearances is revealed when the hotel keeper in Jefferson explains to Horace why Ruby Lamarr had to leave the hotel:

> "It's these church ladies," he said. He lowered his voice, his toothpick in his fingers. "I got a certain position to keep up, myself," he said, "and I know some more folks around here that better do the same thing. No miles off, neither."
> "Where is she now?" Benbow said. "Or did they drive her out of town?"
> "That aint my affair, where folks go, after they check out. I reckon somebody took her in, though."
> "Yeah," Horace said. "Christians, Christians."

The appearances of religious respectability provide even Miss Reba Rivers with a sense of sanctuary, as Temple has a chance to notice (and of course does not) just after Temple and Miss Reba are introduced to each other by Popeye:

> "Anybody in Memphis can tell you who Reba Rivers is. Ask any man on the street, cop or not. I've had some of the biggest men in Memphis right here in this house, bankers, lawyers, doctors—all of them. . . ."
> Almost as soon as they entered the house she began to tell Temple about her asthma, toiling up the stairs in front of them, planting her feet heavily in worsted bedroom slippers, a wooden rosary in one hand and the tankard in the other. She had just returned from church . . .

Even the Snopes boys are concerned with appearances. After they have mistakenly found lodging in Miss Reba's "hotel" they sneak out to find a Negro brothel, and then apologize to Miss Reba on their return by saying that they are just returning from a prayer meeting. An even nicer concern for appearances occurs when two of Miss Reba's quondam fellow workers, Miss Myrtle and Miss Lorraine, visit her with the little boy called Uncle Bud, accidental son of Miss Myrtle. ("Children are such a comfort to a body.") The trouble with Uncle Bud is that he embarrasses Miss Myrtle by stealthily sipping too many drinks:

> "You, Uncle Bud," she said. "Didn't I tell you to come out from behind there, and play? Would you believe it? The other afternoon when we left here I was so mortified I didn't know what to do. I was ashamed to be seen on the street with a drunk boy like you."

Throughout that entire passage, Faulkner's handling of satire descends to burlesque—a familiar failing of satire. Faulkner generally avoids that descent. But his sardonic handling of the wake and funeral elaborately conducted for the gangster Red, in the night club, offer too many possibilities for burlesque, and Faulkner does not even try to resist them. One sampling, which further unmasks human concerns for appearances, will suffice:

> From the dance hall came a strain of music. The people entered and found seats. On the platform was the orchestra from a downtown hotel, in dinner coats. The proprietor and a second man were conferring with the leader.
> "Let them play jazz," the second man said. "Never nobody liked dancing no better than Red."

"No, no," the proprietor said. "Time Gene gets them all ginned up on free whiskey, they'll start dancing. It'll look bad."

"How about the Blue Danube?" the leader said.

"No, no; don't play no blues, I tell you," the proprietor said. "There's a dead man in that bier."

"That's not blues," the leader said.

"What is it?" the second man said.

"A Waltz. Strauss."

"A wop?" the second man said. "Like hell. Red was an American. You may not be, but he was. Don't you know anything American? Play I Cant Give you Anything but Love. He always liked that."

. . . The orchestra played Nearer, My God, to Thee. The audience grew quiet. A woman in a red dress came in the door unsteadily. "Whoopee," she said, "so long, Red. He'll be in hell before I could even reach Little Rock."

Such entertaining lapses into burlesque do obviously constitute artistic faults; but they at least heighten the reader's awareness that Faulkner is consistently employing variants on the comic and satiric mode, as a means of keeping his moral indignation under artistic control. That same function is also served by many other technical procedures which further illuminate meanings. The general reader might be unconvinced by any assertion that Faulkner once again invokes various references to time, even to the seasons, for purposes of achieving poetic reminders of the Christian myth that time is the factor which enables man to collaborate with God, in a divinely planned order, if man so chooses. But there is one particular passage which might convince. Temple, lying on her bed in Miss Reba's house, languidly stares at a clock, in the dusk:

> She watched the final light condense into the clock face, and the dial change from a round orifice in the darkness to a disc, suspended in nothingness, the original chaos, and change in turn to a crystal ball holding in its still and cryptic depths the ordered chaos of the intricate and shadowy world upon whose scarred flank the old wounds whirl onward at dizzy speed into darkness lurking with new disasters.

Temple Drake has to be forced quite out of character before she can perceive those poetic and theological metamorphoses. But when the dial of that timepiece changes into a "disc, suspended in nothingness, the original chaos," it figuratively serves as a microcosm of the entire earth. The consequent mutations suggest ways in which that symbol of divinely purposed order becomes perverted into a symbol of man-made and man-ordered chaos.

The interaction of so many poetic controls endows Faulkner's thematic meanings with a moral earnestness which is quite sternly and austerely puritanical. Beneath the dead pan of his apparently indifferent narrative posture, even beneath the grim laughter of the satiric implications, Faulkner's attitude gradually reveals a savage indignation not unlike that of certain Old Testament prophets. Because Faulkner himself was so thoroughly familiar with biblical texts, and because he so frequently chose to establish biblical analogies, one can not help but guess that he himself was aware of one striking parallel between what he arranged to have happen to Temple Drake, and what Ezekiel prophesied, in equally poetic and symbolic terms. In the King James version, the seventh chapter of Ezekiel bears the running head, "Enemies defile the sanctuary," and the sixteenth chapter contains the following condemnations:

> Is this of thy whoredoms a small matter, that thou hast slain my children . . . ? [Slain, that is, through acts of contracepting or perverting the life-source.] . . . Thou . . . hast made thy beauty to be abhorred, and hast opened thy feet to every one that passed by . . . Behold, therefore I have stretched out my hand over thee, and have diminished thine ordinary food, and delivered thee unto the will of them that hate thee . . . And I will judge thee . . . and I will give thee blood in fury and jealousy. And I will also give thee into their hand, and they shall . . . bring up a company against thee, and they shall . . . thrust thee through with their swords. . . . Because thou hast not remembered the days of thy youth, but hast fretted me in all these things; behold, therefore I also will recompense thy way upon thine head . . .

Like Ezekiel, Faulkner is "fretted" by the actions of Temple Drake and her kind. The essence of his themes, in this tragicomic satire can be summarized in terms of cause and effect. That which seems to trouble Faulkner most, in representing the logical pattern of evil, is the motivation reflected in various human acts of dodging moral responsibility until the consequent chain reaction brings its own retribution, not only on the individual but also on any units of society which tolerate that dodging and dismiss it as unimportant. That which motivates the kinds of actions which do not dodge and duck is the kind of self-sacrificial love which Ruby Lamarr showed for Lee Goodwin.

In conclusion, just two examples may be offered to illustrate the unfairness with which Faulkner's critics have so often misrepresented and misinterpreted *Sanctuary*. The first is one of the most unfortunate and yet one of the most widely accepted misinterpretations, perpetrated by George Marion O'Donnell in 1939. With facetious joy, O'Donnell insisted that Faulkner had intended *Sanctuary* as an allegory, the meanings of which O'Donnell thus paraphrased:

> In simple terms the pattern of the allegory is something like this: Southern Womanhood Corrupted but Undefiled (Temple Drake), in company of Corrupted Tradition (Gowan Stevens, a professional Virginian), falls into the clutches of Amoral Modernism (Popeye), which is itself impotent, but which with the aid of its strong ally Natural Lust ("Red") rapes Southern Womanhood unnaturally and then seduces her so satisfactorily that her corruption is total, and she becomes the tacit ally of Modernism. Meanwhile Pore White Trash (Goodwin) has been accused of the crime which he, with the aid of the Naif Faithful (Tawmmy), actually tried to prevent. The Formalized Tradition (Horace Benbow), perceiving the true state of affairs, tries vainly to defend Pore White Trash. However, Southern Womanhood is so hopelessly corrupted that she wilfully sees Pore White Trash convicted and lynched; she is then carried off by Wealth (Judge Drake) to meaningless escape in European luxury. Modernism, carrying in it from birth its own impotence and doom, submits with masochistic pleasure to its own destruction . . . In this sense, the book is a "cheap idea" —as Mr. Faulkner himself calls it in his preface to the Modern Library. Its defects are those of allegory in general . . .

Criticism could scarcely be more irresponsible than that. As Popeye says, "There ought to be a law." Yet O'Donnell's fashioning of an allegorical mold, into which he tries to pour *Sanctuary*, has made its appeal to the thoughtless reader and has been widely praised, widely paraphrased. As late as 1957, Richard Chase could do no better than quote that same passage and add, "This interpretation, with all of its ridiculous personifications, strikes me as essentially correct. It illustrates the fact that Faulkner's mind, like Hawthorne's, is less discriminating than many Faulkner devotees want to admit—at least in the sense that it entertains the lowest of lowbrow fantasies." One way to correct such misinterpretations is to demonstrate, in some such way as has been attempted throughout this chapter, that the mode of *Sanctuary* is insolently satirical, and that Faulkner fired this double-barreled satire at some persistently lowbrow and highbrow "fantasies."

8

~~≈§~~ REQUIEM FOR A NUN

F AULKNER repeatedly urged that, because of his own human and artistic limitations, he would like to have each of his literary works evaluated twice: first, in the light of the artistic risks dared, therein, and finally in the light of "the splendor of the failure." As we have already noticed, the variety of his experimental innovations is proof enough that he liked to take artistic and thematic risks in all his major works. But the risks he took in writing *Requiem for a Nun* set that work apart from anything else he wrote. The boldness of that particular effort made failure inevitable. Nevertheless, the splendor of that failure deserves our attention.

There are two other important reasons why a consideration of *Requiem* deserves a place among these introductory essays. Any reader who is troubled by the degradation which Faulkner arranged for Temple Drake in *Sanctuary* can scarcely fail to be interested in *Requiem* as a sequel in which Faulkner tries to arrange at least the possibility of Temple Drake's redemption. More than that, *Requiem* gives overt artistic illumination to some major themes which operate covertly and centrally throughout Faulkner's entire work. Any reader who has resisted the interpretive hints I have given, in previous chapters, concerning that aspect of Faulkner's moral vision which indicates his metaphysical preoccupations, should find evidence in *Requiem* that those preoccupations are truly Faulkner's, that they are validly deduced from his themes, and that they are not merely superimposed, here, through arbitrary mistakes of critical interpretation.

When Faulkner took the artistic risk of transforming this sequel to *Sanctuary* into a blend of dramatic and narrative modes, he did more than create three separate acts of drama, each with its own prologue. Taken literally, not figuratively, each prologue may be said to constitute a preliminary "stage direction" for the act of drama which follows it. The one image which provides the title for each prologue denotes the dominant setting for each act. For example, the setting for the first scene of Act One is the Courthouse of Yoknapatawpha

County, in the city of Jefferson, and the prologue to Act One is entitled, "The Courthouse (A Name for the City)." Similarly, the setting for Act Two is the Statehouse in Jackson, Mississippi, and the
prologue to Act Two is entitled, "The Golden Dome (Beginning Was
the Word)." Finally, the setting for Act Three is the County Jail in
Jefferson, and the prologue to Act Three is entitled, "The Jail (Nor
Even Yet Quite Relinquish)." Courthouse, Statehouse, and Jail are
each endowed, gradually, with symbolic meanings which are pertinent to the dramatic action. But each prologue endows each title-
image with even broader symbolism, and each prologue surrounds
the immediate title-image and the immediate narrative with a mythic
pattern of metaphysical action involving all time and all space. The
artistic risks thus taken were indeed so bold that the artistic failure
was almost inevitable.

At the beginning of the first prologue, nothing in the story suggests
the kind of theme which Faulkner will gradually derive from it. We
are given an early chapter in the mythic history of Jefferson, and the
yarn is an amusing account of how it happened that the pioneers
and frontiersmen in that corner of Mississippi happened to build a
courthouse and happened to name their town Jefferson. Humorously,
laconically, ironically, and with a typically mysterious ordering of
effects prior to causes, Faulkner builds the continuities of the yarn
around the image of a huge padlock:

> . . . the iron monster weighing almost fifteen pounds, with a key al-
> most as long as a bayonet, not just the only lock in that part of the
> country, but the oldest lock in that cranny of the United States,
> brought there by one of the three men who were what was to be Yokna-
> patawpha County's coeval pioneers and settlers . . .

We further learn that the lock was not particularly useful until
someone thought of putting it on the bimonthly mail-pouch in the
combined store and postoffice of the little settlement, "and that was
the second phase of the monster Carolina lock's transubstantiation
into the Yoknapatawpha County courthouse." The narrative goes
on to reveal that the third phase of that metamorphosis occurred
when the lock was borrowed for temporary use on the door of the
local jail, just after three bandits were incarcerated there for one
night. In the morning the bandits had disappeared, with the lock,
and the problem of paying the original donor, Holston, for the loss
of his lock produced several suggestions which were not exactly
ethical. In protest, the wilderness mail-carrying rider named Thomas
Jefferson Pettigrew pointed out that whoever put Holston's lock on

the mail bag had made a gift of it to Uncle Sam and so the community now had a responsibility to make some kind of compensation for that loss to the United States. The lofty moral idealism of Pettigrew's remarks so touched and impressed one of the three original settlers that he said they should pay back their debt to the United States by building a courthouse. Out of curiosity, someone asked Pettigrew how he came by his name. "My ma named me for him," he answered, "so I would have some of his luck. . . . She didn't mean luck. She never had any schooling. She didn't know the word she wanted to say." Thus doubly inspired, they built a temporary courthouse, named the town Jefferson, and began to draw up plans which expressed their visions of things to be:

> . . . a Square, the courthouse in its grove the center, quadrangular around it, the stores . . . school and church and tavern and bank and jail each in its ordered place. . . . But above all, the courthouse: the center, the focus, the hub; sitting musing, brooding symbolic and ponderable . . . protector of the weak, judiciate and curb of the passions and lusts, repository and guardian of the aspirations and the hopes . . .

The recurrence of that phrase, "each in its ordered place," previously noticed as the concluding phrase in *The Sound and the Fury*, suggests that Faulkner assigned a special burden of meaning to it. Additional meanings will be acquired by it, and will be noted later. Immediately, as the vision is translated into actuality, and as the orderly procedure for building the Courthouse gets under way, that final phase in the metamorphosis or transubstantiation of the huge lock is represented as a symbolic action:

> . . . working . . . black and white, free and unfree, shoulder to shoulder in the same tireless lift and rhythm as if they had the same aim and hope . . . as one because it was theirs, bigger than any because it was the sum of all and, being the sum of all, it must raise all of their hopes and aspirations level with its own aspirant and soaring cupola, so that, sweating and tireless and unflagging, they would look about at one another a little shyly, a little amazed, with something like humility too, as if they were realizing, or were for the moment at least capable of believing, that men, all men, including themselves, were a little better, purer maybe even, than they had thought, expected, or even needed to be.

In a sense, all of those early citizens were helping to realize certain truths which had been held self-evident by the namesake of their town. The poetry of that passage invites further extension, to suggest even a metaphysical vision of a plan or purpose or design or order, binding all men and all things and all time. Faulkner helps to convey that overtone of meaning by representing the storekeeper, Ratcliffe, as troubled by the way the problem of the lock had been solved. Ratcliffe feared that if the President, up in Washington, and those in power with him, should hear about these doings, they might misunderstand. Ratcliffe's own summary of the possible attitude of those in power is given an arrangement, by Faulkner, in words which pick up figurative and metaphysical overtones:

> It's like Old Moster and the rest of them up there that run the luck, would look down at us and say, Well well, looks like them durn pecker-woods down there dont want them fifteen dollars we was going to give them free-gratis-for-nothing. So maybe they dont want nothing from us. So maybe we better do like they seem to want, and let them sweat and swivet and scrabble through the best they can by themselves.

Although a reader may be inclined to minimize the metaphysical overtones of meaning in that passage, the second prologue strengthens and reinforces those overtones. Even the title of the second prologue uses a biblical phrase which hints at pertinent metaphysical extensions: "The Golden Dome (Beginning Was the Word)." While the first prologue merely hints at mythic continuities in the early history of Jefferson, the second prologue poetically invokes the Christian concept of continuities by reaching backwards through time to the beginning of beginnings, where and when the divine act of ordering the universe foreshadowed the incipient development of historical and cosmological events to realize a divine "Idea." Faulkner's backward-reaching through time had been nicely prepared, at the conclusion of the first prologue, where sparrows and pigeons in the cupola of the Courthouse were so continuously startled by each striking of the clock, there, that they always burst "in one swirling explosion out of the belfry, as though the hour instead of merely adding one puny infinitesimal more to the long weary increment since Genesis, had shattered the virgin pristine air with the first loud dingdong of time and doom." As implied above, the motto of the second prologue also makes an implicit invocation of certain ideas in the familiar opening passage of the Gospel according to John:

> In the beginning was the Word, and the Word was with God, and the Word was God. The same was in the beginning with God. All things were made by him; and without him was not any thing made that was made. In him was life; and the life was the light of men. And the light shineth in darkness; and the darkness comprehended it not.

That passage operates with familiar meanings within the context of Christian doctrine; reinterpreted within the rebellious and yet theistic context of Faulkner's moral vision, it operates with related and yet separable meanings, as will be explained in the concluding chapter. The highly poetic verbiage of the major passage in the second prologue of *Requiem* not only establishes the symbolic significance of "The Golden Dome" atop the Statehouse but also reviews the symbolic significance of all time and of all evolutionary developments which paved the way for the creation of that man-made center of whatever is for the common good in that Commonwealth. Through literal and figurative uses of evolutionary, geological, geographical, and historical images, Faulkner spins out a prodigious lyric rhapsody of growth and change in that continuity which is viewed as reaching all the way from God's original concern for man's common wealth to man's creation of that symbolic microcosm, the Capitol dome. The passage builds to this concluding image:

> . . . the golden dome, the knob, the gleamy crumb, the gilded pustule longer than the miasma and the gigantic ephemeral saurians, more durable than the ice and the pre-night cold, soaring, hanging as one blinding spheroid above the center of the Commonwealth, incapable of being either looked full or evaded, peremptory, irrefragable, and reassuring . . .

A further mirroring of continuities is provided, in the prologue to the third act, by the Jefferson Jail. It is made to reflect, poetically, the strengths and the weaknesses of human beings who (like the saurians) served their functions in the divine plan before becoming obsolete and dispossessed by better and worse, on the world-stage. Like the Court and the Capitol, the Jail is implicitly associated with the phases of universal history, even down to the contemporary re-enactments of age-old conflicts between human beings bent on corrupting life back into chaos, against the wishes of the more enlightened who still remember the dream, the truth, the "Idea" which is man's heritage and birthright:

> . . . one universe, one cosmos: contained in one America: one towering frantic edifice poised like a card-house over the abyss of the mortgaged generations . . . until the vast hollow sphere of his air, the vast and terrible burden beneath which he tries to stand erect and lift his battered and indomitable head—the very substance in which he lives and, lacking which, he would vanish in a matter of seconds—is murmurous with his fears and terrors and disclaimers and repudiations and his aspirations and dreams and baseless hopes . . .

Faulkner's art sags quite deplorably in such passages where he will not trust his narrative to convey his meanings. Yet the very pressure of those meanings on his art indicates the importance of physical-metaphysical continuities to Faulkner. One particular passage in the third prologue further accentuates his theme of continuity, in a way which fuses the three tenses thus:

> So only the old citizens knew the jail any more, not old people but old citizens; men and women old not in years but in the constancy of the town, or against that constancy, concordant (not coeval of course, the town's date was a century and a quarter ago now, but in accord against that continuation) with that thin durable continuity born a hundred and twenty-five years ago out of a handful of bandits captured by a drunken militia squad, and a bitter ironical incorruptible wilderness mail-rider, and a monster wrought-iron padlock—that steadfast and durable and unhurryable continuity against or across which the vain and glittering ephemerae of progress and alternation washed in substanceless repetitive evanescent scarless waves . . .

Within that framework of continuities, and against that backdrop of meanings, Faulkner presents the sequel to the earlier story of Temple Drake. As might be anticipated even from the first prologue, the primary stress of the central dramatic action is placed on moral continuities. The new action takes place some eight years after the events of *Sanctuary*, some eight years after Gowan Stevens had acted the part of a Southern gentleman by marrying Temple Drake not because he loved her but because he felt he should make amends for abandoning her at the Old Frenchman place. Thus outwardly and socially re-established, Gowan and Temple are represented as having settled down to rear a family—the older child a boy, the younger child a girl, six months old. In the drama, the crucial action hinges on the fact that Temple Drake's daughter had recently been strangled in her crib by a Negro maid named Nancy Mannigoe. Starting from effects, the first act begins in the courtroom, with the pronouncing of the death sentence on Nancy. Thereafter, the action is arranged to probe beneath the facts for causes, motives, and consequences. All of the symbolism implicitly established throughout the first prologue is now correlated by Faulkner in his first stage direction:

> The curtain rises, symbolising the rising of the prisoner in the dock, and revealing a section of the courtroom. It does not occupy the whole stage, but only the upper left half, leaving the other half and the bottom of the stage in darkness, so that the visible scene is not only spotlighted but elevated slightly too, a further symbolism which will be

clearer when Act II opens—the symbolism of the elevated tribunal of justice of which this, a county court, is only the intermediate, not the highest stage.

It is only implicitly suggested, in that stage direction, that the highest tribunal of justice is the mercy seat of God. But the stage direction for Act Two, Scene One, in describing the symbolic significance of the governor's office, clarifies and reinforces that implicit suggestion:

> The whole bottom of the stage is in darkness, as in Scene I, Act One, so that the visible scene has the effect of being held in the beam of a spotlight. Suspended, too, since it is upper left and even higher above the shadow of the stage proper than the same in Scene I, Act One, carrying still further the symbolism of the still higher, the last, the ultimate seat of judgment . . . The Governor stands in front of the high chair. . . . He is symbolic too: no known person, neither old nor young; he might be someone's idea not of God but of Gabriel perhaps, the Gabriel not before the Crucifixion but after it.

Even without those stage directions, the extremely brief dialogue and action of Act One, Scene One has related overtones of symbolic meaning. The Judge summarizes the findings of the Court, that Nancy Mannigoe did "wilfully and with malice aforethought kill and murder the infant child of Mr. and Mrs. Gowan Stevens." She is therefore sentenced "to be hanged by the neck until you are dead." Then the formal conclusion: "And may God have mercy on your soul." Immediately Nancy creates a minor chaos in the courtroom by answering, "Yes, Lord." As the shocked spectators react protestingly, the Bailiff shouts, "Order! Order in the court! Order!" On those words, the curtain descends, thus reinforcing the order-chaos theme, established in the prologue. The later action makes it implicitly clear that Nancy has her own reasons for feeling that she had made her peace with God, before the murder, and that while an earthly court of justice has condemned her to death for her action, such death is now unimportant to her, or rather important only because it will translate her to the realms of eternal life, mercy, and salvation. Although Nancy is not sufficiently articulate to express her own intuitions adequately, it later becomes clear that before she resorted to murder she had done her fumbling best to resist and overcome an evil which threatened to destroy Temple Drake Stevens and both her children; that only as a last resort, after she had failed in those other attempts, she had deliberately chosen to sacrifice her own life, together with the life of the infant, in her attempt to save the other child, and Temple, and a precarious marriage.

Scene Two of Act One dramatizes the reactions of both Temple and Gowan, after the trial, as they return to their own home accompanied by Gavin Stevens, who is the lawyer for the defense and the uncle of Gowan Stevens. In that second scene, Temple's words and actions imply her suspicion that the lawyer has not tried to employ all his skills to save Nancy Mannigoe from the death-sentence, and that he may have had from Nancy certain information which he did not choose to present in the trial. Temple's first bit of stage business, after her entrance, is a significant symbolic action. While Gowan goes to get refreshments, Temple lights the fire in the fireplace by applying a flame from a mechanical cigarette lighter to the mechanically controlled flow of gas around fake logs. All her motions are at first mechanical, and without genuine feeling. The reader may recall the antithetical symbolism of "The Fire and the Hearth" in *Go Down, Moses*.

While her husband is out of the room, in Scene Two of Act One, Temple tries to penetrate the lawyer's mystery. The quickness with which she changes the subject when Gowan returns implies that she is not on completely intimate terms even with her husband, and that in some way she has deceived him. It later becomes clear that she has withheld from him, and from the District Attorney, certain information pertinent to the murder. Now she is forced to lie to the lawyer for the defense when he asks (while Gowan is again offstage) if a man was in the Stevens home on the night of the murder: "There was no man there. You see? I told you, warned you, that you would get nothing from me." So she leaves the two men alone, and Gowan unburdens himself of self-pitying sentimentalism toward all that has happened to him:

"Six years on the wagon—and this is what I get for it: my child murdered by a dope-fiend nigger whore that wouldn't even run so that a cop or somebody could have shot her down like the mad-dog—You see? Six years without the drink, and so I got whatever it was I was buying by not drinking, and now I've got whatever it was I was paying for and it's paid for and so I can drink again. And now I dont want the drink. You see? Like whatever it was I was buying I not only didn't want, but what I was paying for it wasn't worth anything, wasn't even any loss. So I have a laugh coming. That's triumph. Because I got a bargain even in what I didn't want. I got a cut rate. I had two children. I had to pay only one of them to find out it wasn't really costing me anything—Half price: a child, and a dope-fiend nigger whore on a public gallows: that's all I had to pay for immunity."

In trying to awaken the consciences of both Gowan and Temple, the lawyer-uncle answers with Faulknerian austerity, in the next exchange, concerning immunity within time.

> Stevens: "There's no such thing."
> Gowan: "From the past. From my folly. My drunkenness. My cowardice, if you like."
> Stevens: "There's no such thing as past either."

Further meanings of the lawyer's reprimand, there, are made clear by the larger context. He is trying to help Gowan and Temple face up to a concept of moral responsibility which gives to all three tenses of time a particular kind of continuity. Misunderstanding him completely, Gowan jeers at the notion that there is no such thing as "past," and immediately begins to review the circumstances which caused him to make amends to Temple, after she had been "kidnapped into a Memphis whorehouse—and loved it." His uncle immediately presses in:

> "Is that what you can never forgive her for?—not for having been the instrument creating that moment in your life which you can never recall nor forget nor explain nor condone nor even stop thinking about, but because she herself didn't even suffer, but on the contrary, even liked it—that month or whatever it was like the episode in the old movie of the white girl held prisoner in the cave by the Bedouin prince?—That you had to lose not only your bachelor freedom, but your man's self-respect in the chastity of his wife and your child too, to pay for something your wife hasn't even lost, didn't even regret, didn't even miss? Is that why this poor lost doomed crazy Negro woman must die?"

The lawyer is there permitted to imply, among other things, that both Gowan and Temple are again trying to seek sanctuary in the act of heaping their own sins on a scapegoat, and that Nancy, by contrast, is willing to die for them. His remarks so nearly awaken Gowan's conscience that the young man ineffectually orders his uncle out of the house. Ignoring the command, the lawyer relentlessly continues his cross-examination of Gowan, and concludes:

> "What else happened during that month, that time while that madman held her prisoner there in that Memphis house, that nobody but you and she knew about, maybe not even you know about?"

That insinuation is too much for Gowan, who restrains himself from violence by shouting profanely, "So help me, Christ . . . So help me, Christ." In this context, Faulkner can even get thematic overtones out of profanity thus phrased. At the end of Scene Two, then, the psychological tensions are compactly established and brought into the open by truths which the lawyer either knows or suspects—truths which may not save Nancy Mannigoe but which may keep her sacrifice from being wasted.

The third scene of Act One occurs several months later, after Temple and her husband have sought another kind of immunity by running away to California, and after they have returned, unexpectedly, two days before Nancy Mannigoe is to be hanged. Apparently the lawyer has succeeded in doing something to Temple's conscience. She now admits that she has returned in the hope of saving Nancy from hanging. But the lawyer is not trying to save Nancy. Instead, he employs the psychiatric (or rather the religious) process of helping Temple confess, and acknowledge for the first time, that her own past actions have precipitated a sequence of events in which she stands ultimately to blame for the death of her own child and for the imminent hanging of Nancy. The lawyer knows he is dealing with a stubborn and hardened kind of spiritual and emotional blindness. Temple thinks she can adequately salve her conscience by saving Nancy with lies: "All we need is an affidavit. That she is crazy. Has been for years." If so, Stevens asks, how can Temple explain her own previous motives in court? For Temple, falsehoods even as to motives will do. But when Stevens insists that "Temple Drake will have to save" Nancy, Temple corrects him: "Mrs. Gowan Stevens will. . . . Cant you get it through your head that I will do anything, *any*thing?" Then comes this thematically pertinent exchange:

> Stevens: "Except one. Which is all. We're not concerned with death. That's nothing: any handful of petty facts and sworn documents can cope with that. That's all finished now; we can forget it. What we are trying to deal with now is injustice. Only truth can cope with that. Or love."
> Temple (harshly): "Love, Oh, God. Love."
> Stevens: "Call it pity then. Or courage. Or simple honor, honesty, or a simple desire for the right to sleep at night."

After further pressures, Temple quite scornfully and contemptuously asks, "Why blink your own rhetoric? Why dont you go and tell me it's for the good of my soul—if I have one?" Stevens answers, "I did. I said, so you can sleep at night." He goes on to insist that the issue is one to be settled by Temple Drake, not by Mrs. Gowan Stevens. When Temple says, "Temple Drake is dead," Stevens answers with his persistent moral reiteration, "The past is never dead. It's not even past." He has admitted that if Temple will tell her entire story to the Governor, it is possible that the Governor may save Nancy with a reprieve. But when Temple yields far enough to ask, "How much will I have to tell?" and Stevens replies, "Everything," Temple refuses. She sends Stevens away, only to phone his home immediately: She will go.

In the first scene of Act Two, as Temple and Stevens confront the Governor, by arrangement, in his office late at night, Temple starts talking about Nancy Mannigoe (". . . I—have come to ask to save her") and soon finds herself confessing more and more about Temple Drake. Now she is willing to admit that of her own free will she chose the pattern of action which involved her with Gowan and Popeye and Red:

> ". . . because Temple Drake liked evil. . . . So I saw the murder, or anyway the shadow of it, and the man took me to Memphis, and I know that too, I had two legs and I could see, and I could have simply screamed up the main street of any of the little towns we passed . . . [in Memphis] I could have climbed down the rainspout at any time, the only difference being that I didn't."

(Faulkner is never more puritanical, never more Calvinistic, than in his treatment of sexual matters. When he makes Temple play that reiterative emphasis on could, could, could, it almost sounds like John Calvin's unintentional jingle concerning Adam: "He could have stood if he would.") Temple obliquely acknowledges that there was still a lie, a dodging, a seeking of false sanctuary, in her choosing to marry Gowan Stevens, without love. Stevens points out to the Governor (without any protests from Temple) that the marriage did not trouble her greatly because "she still had the legs and the eyes; she could walk, escape, from it any moment she wished. . . ." It is still Stevens who explains to the Governor how Temple must have felt trapped by her first pregnancy. Again the stern tone is Faulknerian:

> "Now she couldn't escape; she had waited too long. But it was worse than that. It was as though she realized for the first time that you—anyone—must, or anyway may have to pay for your past; that past is something like a promissory note with a trick clause in it which, as long as nothing goes wrong, can be manumitted in an orderly manner, but which fate or luck or chance, can foreclose on you without warning."

Between them, Temple and Stevens explain to the Governor that the initial foreclosure occurred in the form of blackmail, when Red's brother Pete had demanded money for the obscene love letters which

Temple had written to Red; that instead of paying the money and
getting the letters, Temple had tried to use Pete as a means of escape
back into her old ways, and had even promised Pete the money if
he would take her and her baby daughter with him; that the Negro
servant Nancy had tried various words and actions to block this incipient elopement by making Temple see and feel her moral responsibility to herself, her husband, and, most of all, to her children.
When Stevens has nearly completed putting together such pieces of
the puzzle, for the Governor, as a means of correcting Temple's
mechanical half truths, he requires Temple to put in place the key
piece: the image of what actually had happened on the night of the
murder. Faulkner, instead of permitting Temple merely to recall
that night, recreates the essentials of it, dramatically, in the second
scene of Act Two. The final crisis between Temple and Nancy, while
Pete waits outside the Stevens home, takes this form:

> Temple: "I'm sorry. Why do you force me to this—hitting and
> screaming at you, when you have always been so good to my children
> and me—my husband too—all of us—trying to hold us together in a
> household, a family, that anybody should have known all the time
> couldn't possibly hold together? even in decency, let alone happiness?"
> Nancy: "I reckon I'm ignorant. I dont know that yet. Besides, I
> aint talking about any household or happiness neither—I'm talking
> about two little children."
> Temple: "I said, hush."
> Nancy: "I cant hush. I'm going to ask you one more time. Are you
> going to do it?"
> Temple: "Yes!"
> Nancy: "Maybe I am ignorant. You got to say it out in words your-
> self, so I can hear them. Say, I'm going to do it."

After Temple has coldly put her plan into words, and has ordered
Nancy out of her way, Nancy makes one speech which seems addressed more to God than to Temple, by way of explanation and
apology for the as yet uncommitted murder: "I tried everything I
knowed. You can see that." At the beginning of the third scene in
Act Two, Temple is still talking: "And that's all. The police came,
and the murderess still sitting in a chair in the kitchen in the dark
saying, 'Yes, Lord, I done it,' and then in the cell at the jail, still
saying it." Temple does not know that at some moment during her
dramatized confession, the Governor has left the room and Temple's
husband has taken the place of the Governor, behind the desk, so
that this part of her confession is symbolically addressed to her husband. At this phase of the action she does not care who has heard her.

She now seems only concerned to know why the Governor had refused to save the life of Nancy, even before they had come. When the lawyer begins to explain by mentioning the Governor's talk about Temple's son, she interrupts with furiously sustained sarcasm:

"That's right. Make it good: the same little boy to hold whose normal and natural home together, the murderess, the nigger, the dopefiend whore, didn't hesitate to cast the last gambit—and maybe that's the wrong word too, isn't it?—she knew and had: her own debased and worthless life. Oh yes, I know that answer too; that was brought out here tonight too: that a little child shall not suffer in order to come unto Me. So good can come out of evil."

Stevens replies, "It not only can, it must." So far, Temple does not even care whether it can or must. The experience through which she has passed seems to her to represent suffering just for the sake of suffering, even though she has progressed far enough to admit the continuity between her story and that of the self-sacrificial and in that sense the Jesus-imitating Nancy, who will die on Friday:

"Friday. The black day. The day you never start on a journey. Except that Nancy's journey didn't start at daylight or sunup or whenever it is polite and tactful to hang people, day after tomorrow. Her journey started that morning eight years ago when I got on the train at the University . . ."

Thus she resists, and at the same time begins yielding to her growing awareness of something beyond irony in her having been forced to suffer so much, in front of the Governor, the lawyer, and her husband. The ambivalence of her attitude gives a double value to her second-act curtain-speech, "To save my soul—if I have a soul. If there is a God to save it—a God who wants it."

In the only scene of Act Three, Temple and the lawyer go to the jail on the day before Nancy is to be hanged. Temple knows what is expected of her, and yet she still resists what lies ahead:

"And now I've got to say 'I forgive you, sister' to the nigger who murdered my baby. *No:* it's worse. I've even got to transpose it, turn it around. I've got to start off my new life being forgiven again. How can I say that? Tell me. How can I?"

The lawyer makes no answer, and the jailor brings Nancy in during the silence which follows the questions. Nancy has guessed that Temple and the lawyer have tried and failed to save her; but she has not even chosen to hope for that kind of salvation because her religious belief provides an assurance beyond such hope, as she tries to explain to Temple. Her mention of being able to "get low for Jesus" strikes Temple as insinuative blasphemy, and when Nancy says, in her fumbling way, that she listens to Jesus, not for what he said but for what he is, the analogy between the sacrifice of Jesus and the sacrifice of Nancy becomes reinforced. While Nancy's faith puzzles Temple, something about it makes Temple wistful enough to try phrasing not only her confession to Nancy but also her appeal for forgiveness, in bitterly anguished phrases:

> "Then let Him talk to me. I can get low for Him too, if that's all He wants, demands, asks. I'll do anything He wants if He'll just tell me what to do. No: how to do it. I know what to do, what I must do, what I've got to do. But how? We—I thought that all I would have to do would be to come back and go to the Big Man and tell him it wasn't you who killed my baby, but I did it eight years ago that day when I slipped out the back door of that train."

The spiritual education of Temple Drake has by this time progressed far enough to make her accept the Faulknerian theme of moral continuity, but it has not yet progressed far enough to make her understand the Faulknerian theme that the individual's suffering and pentinence is a means to various kinds of salvation. When Nancy implies the latter, Temple flares into protest:

> "But why must it be suffering? He's omnipotent, or so they tell us. Why couldn't He have invented something else? Or, if it's got to be suffering, why cant it be just your own? Why cant you buy back your own sins with your own agony? Why do you and my little baby both have to suffer just because I decided to go to a baseball game eight years ago? Do you have to suffer everybody else's anguish just to believe in God? What kind of God is it that has to blackmail His customers with the whole world's grief and ruin?"

Faulkner provides Nancy with answers even for those questions, and at this final phase of the drama the themes are being discussed in general terms which are so blatant and propagandistic that Faulkner's art has become completely eclipsed. Nancy replies to Temple,

> "He dont want you to suffer. He dont like suffering neither. But he cant help Himself. He's like a man that's got too many mules. . . . He dont tell you not to sin. He just asks you not to. And He dont tell you to suffer. But He gives you the chance. He gives you the best He can think of, that you are capable of doing. And He will save you."

That precise theological point, interpreted within the larger context, would seem to mean that the individual is divinely empowered to make choices between good and evil, and then to find through mistaken choices the kind of suffering which activates the individual's capacity for penitence and regeneration and an earned salvation. By the end of the last act, Nancy has helped Temple to paraphrase the appeal of the grief-stricken parent who said to Jesus, "Lord, I believe; help thou mine unbelief." The choice, as Temple finally sees it, is between belief in a world with no continuity, no meaning for suffering, and belief in a world which must at least include something like Nancy's concept of God, and even Nancy's concept of two worlds. Temple's almost resolved and yet still struggling anguish, which implies at least the possibility that Nancy's sacrifice has not been wasted, is expressed in Temple's concluding speech about continuities between the physical and the metaphysical worlds:

> ". . . Even if there is one and somebody waiting in it to forgive me, there's still tomorrow and tomorrow. And suppose tomorrow and tomorrow, and then nobody there, nobody waiting to forgive me. . . . Anyone to save me. Anyone who wants it. If there is none, I'm sunk. We all are. Doomed. Damned."

Lawyer Stevens answers her on this point as to what makes the difference between salvation and damnation:

> "Of course we are [all damned, if ——]. Hasn't He been telling us that for going on two thousand years?"

Thus endeth the reading of *Requiem for a Nun*, wherein Faulkner-the-artist succumbs to Faulkner-the-almost-Calvinistic preacher. His viewpoint, as indirectly reflected in most of his narratives, is always intensely moral. But here the direct and overt development of themes makes it quite clear that while his double vision enables him to hold an ambivalent and at times hostile attitude toward Calvinistic Christian doctrine he occasionally slips back into attitudes which are essentially orthodox.

The major themes in *Requiem* can best be represented in terms of two inseparable patterns of continuity. In the beginning was the divine concept of cosmic continuity; but in the end the fulfillment of that divine concept depends on the individual's acceptance of God's contract or covenant with man concerning individual capacities and choices. Thus the cosmic continuity encompasses the human continuity of sinfulness and suffering and penitence and forgiveness and regeneration and salvation. Faulkner generally prefers to manipulate these themes in more poetic forms of indirection, and generally prefers to give them a more humanistic emphasis. But the roots of those themes always penetrate deeply into Faulkner's Calvinistic heritage.

It scarcely need be pointed out that the artistic weaknesses in *Requiem* are many. The three acts too largely substitute narrative recapitulations and arguments for dramatic action. The sequel-quality of the action constitutes a further artistic handicap because the various summaries of what happened in *Sanctuary* do not adequately explain Temple's immediate psychic predicament. Furthermore, the specifics of the drama do not provide enough dramatic flesh to conceal the underlying skeleton of the allegorical morality play: Temple is cast in an awkward role of Everyman; Gowan Stevens plays the role of Conscience; Nancy is an uncomfortable Christ; and the Governor only clumsily symbolizes the ultimate Judge. As for the prologues, while their symbolic pertinence to the drama can be handled by the reader, they are too heavily cluttered with verbiage and unnecessary detail to achieve the apparently intended poetic effects as backdrop for the action of the drama. Nevertheless, when *Requiem* is considered as an experimental attempt to combine narrative and drama technically while blending cosmic and individual continuities thematically, the whole can indeed be admired for "the splendor of the failure."

9

⋖⦚ THE HAMLET

I N THE three novels which comprise the Snopes trilogy—*The Ham-let, The Town,* and *The Mansion*—the subject matter alone pro-vides the most obvious factor of unification. Each of the three novels deals with a different phase of predatory encroachments made by the Snopes clan. *The Hamlet* tells how they achieved economic and social power in the little village or hamlet called Frenchman's Bend, near Jefferson, early in the 1900's. *The Town* tells how they swarmed in on Jefferson itself from 1905 to 1927. Finally, *The Mansion* tells how the most competent and the most ruthless leader in the Snopes clan brought on himself a mortal form of retribution, at the hands of a vengeful blood-relative.

In each of those novels, the narrative mode is different. But the distinguishing technical factor in *The Hamlet* is not the focus of narra-tion or style or structure; it is a curiously achieved tone. That tone is initially achieved by Faulkner's capacity to laugh at and to see something just plain funny in the grotesque and yet thoroughly human members of the Snopes clan. Taken that way, *The Hamlet* belongs with *The Reivers:* they are Faulkner's "funniest" books. Yet all the different elements of amusement in Faulkner's tone through-out *The Hamlet* serves a far more important function. Underneath the laughter, underneath the comedy, there is a very serious employ-ment of comic and ironic elements for satirical purposes.

As soon as a reader of *The Hamlet* begins to recognize the ironic and satiric quality of the narrative, this account of Snopesism begins to acquire another kind of unification which is provided by the irony of one all-pervading theme which may be summarized as follows. Many of the evils attributed to Snopesism, and of course abhorred by all the characters who align themselves against Snopesism, hap-pen to be evils which have been practised so long by so many of these other characters that they themselves afford unintentional aid and comfort to Snopesism. Although it may be granted that Faulkner's tone is only one of the technical factors which enables him to handle his narrative, here, with a fresh illusion of detachment and indifference, the unifying theme can scarcely be said to operate with particular subtlety. Nevertheless, too many readers have overlooked it, and too many critics have insisted that, ever since Faulkner created the first Snopes character in *Sartoris* (1929), he has used those two terms as allegorical types, to differentiate the goodies from the baddies. Such an egregious misreading, frequently praised and frequently quoted, was first formulated and published by George Marion O'Donnell in 1939, thus:

> In Mr. Faulkner's mythology there are two kinds of characters; they are Sartorises or Snopeses, whatever the family names may be. And in the spiritual geography of Mr. Faulkner's work there are two worlds: the Sartoris world and the Snopes world. In all of his success-ful books, he is exploring the two worlds in detail, dramatizing the inevitable conflict between them. It is a universal conflict. The Sar-torises act traditionally, that is to say, they act always with an ethi-cally responsible will. They represent vital morality, humanism. Being anti-traditional, the Snopeses do not recognize this point-of-view; acting only for self-interest, they acknowledge no ethical duty. Really, then, they are a-moral; they represent naturalism or ani-malism. And the Sartoris-Snopes conflict is fundamentally a struggle between humanism and naturalism.

That oversimplified parting of the sheep from the goats ignores Faulkner's persistently ironic unmasking of those Sartoris-like charac-ters who, blind to their own inner elements of Snopesism, strike ridiculously pathetic postures of claiming that they detest and have nothing in common with Snopesism. That oversimplification also ignores Faulkner's treatment of the Snopes family itself, or at least of such members in it as Eck Snopes and his son Wall, who are repre-sented as decent human beings struggling against other members of their own family. In short, that oversimplification ignores the con-tinuous Faulknerian preoccupation with (to use Faulkner's own familiar words) "the problems of the human heart in conflict with itself."

One mistake of the Sartorises and their like, throughout the Snopes trilogy, is their tendency to invoke ritualistic gestures of the old tradition without realizing that their hollow formalism has deprived traditional codes of whatever vital morality it once had. To equate traditionalism absolutely with "an ethically responsible will" is of course quaint. Faulkner satirizes precisely this concept by letting cer-tain characters like Flem Snopes imitate and adopt some postures of "the old tradition" to provide a palpable veneer of respectability.

It should be noticed, however, that as the Snopeses start their climb up the caste-ridden social ladder, they do not immediately come in contact with the typically Sartoris-like characters. Throughout most of *The Hamlet*, Faulkner deliberately descends to low comedy; but in *The Town*, where the antagonists are led by the Sartoris-like Stevens family, self-deceived by various forms of self-interest and yet ineffectually asserting their desire to preserve the idealism of the old tradition, Faulkner finds richer opportunities to blend compassionate satire with high and low comedy.

Structurally, the four parts of *The Hamlet* would seem to comprise such an outrageous conglomerate of gossip, anecdotes, folklore, and tall tales that no pattern could possibly emerge. Part of Faulkner's difficulty, in writing *The Hamlet*, must have been caused by his choosing to perform a scissors-and-paste job, patching together pieces or wholes of six short stories which had previously existed as unrelated units, under the following titles: "Fool About a Horse," "The Hound," "Spotted Horses," "Lizards in Jamshyd's Courtyard," "Barn Burning," and "Afternoon of a Cow." Although Faulkner revised heavily, and in some cases completely rewrote parts of these stories, even changing to Snopes the names of some non-Snopes characters, and relating them as "cousins," those revisions would seem to have been performed with a cavalier laziness which did not entirely remove certain inconsistencies of time, name, place, and distances, and certain unevenness in the style. Nevertheless, one major structural configuration does emerge from this conglomerate subject matter. At the beginning of the action, Flem Snopes, the shrewdest headman of his tribe, moves in on the established order (such as it is) of the village called Frenchman's Bend, dominated by old Will Varner; at the end of the action, Flem Snopes moves out of and beyond the village toward more attractive goals of conquest, after he has appropriated to his own uses all that he wanted out of Will Varner's store, sawmill, and cotton gin and after he has even married Will Varner's daughter Eula; in the middle, the action dramatizes the hows and whys and wherefores of Flem's very successful depredations.

Because *The Hamlet* is frequently referred to as "Faulkner's funniest book," it might be well to remember that Faulkner's kinship with Mark Twain, here quite clearly in evidence, frequently reveals itself with particular clarity in Faulkner's Twain-like combination of bland comedy and savage satire, the one on the surface and the other beneath. Like *Pudd'nhead Wilson*, *The Hamlet* is primarily a book of fools. In each there is no character who completely escapes from appearing decidedly foolish, at one time or another. In each, the author as narrator adopts a "dead pan" tone of detached indifference which merely heightens the homely wit and the devastating irony.

Because Faulkner does establish cumulative analogies between the actions of the Snopeses and the actions of their enemies, the reader needs to pay particular attention not so much to the obvious actions of the Snopeses as to the analogous actions of their enemies. The first chapter of the first book describes Frenchman's Bend in such a way as to make it vulnerable to precisely the kinds of amoralities which the Snopeses might count on using to gain an economic and social foothold. Without realizing it, Frenchman's Bend and the Varners had practiced Snopesism long before the first Snopes arrived. For example, after describing the original settlers, Faulkner continues:

> Their descendants still planted cotton in the bottom land and corn along the edge of the hills and in the secret covers in the hills made whiskey of the corn and sold what they did not drink. Federal officers went into the country and vanished. . . . County officers did not bother them at all save in the heel of election years. They supported their own churches and schools, they married and committed infrequent adulteries and more frequent homicides among themselves and were their own courts, judges and executioners. They were Protestants and Democrats and prolific; there was not one negro landowner in the entire section. Strange negroes would absolutely refuse to pass through it after dark.

The narrative tone there strikes the posture of amused unconcern, and the succeeding action is presented with the pretended detachment which is characteristic of Faulkner's comic method. The first description of old Will Varner preserves that tone of casual pleasantry, and thus subdues the ironic references to Varner as an upholder of law and order:

> Will Varner, the present owner of the Old Frenchman place, was the chief man of the country. He was the largest landholder and beat supervisor in one county and Justice of the Peace in the next and election commissioner in both, and hence the fountainhead if not of law at least of advice and suggestion to a countryside which would have repudiated the term constituency if they had ever heard it, which came to him, not in the attitude of *What must I do* but *What do you think you would like for me to do if you was able to make me do it.* He was a farmer, a usurer, a veterinarian; Judge Benbow of Jefferson once said of him that a milder-mannered man never bled a mule or stuffed a

ballot box. He owned most of the good land in the country and held mortgages on most of the rest.

The casual way in which that epithet, "usurer," is tucked between "farmer" and "veterinarian" keeps it from seeming to have any particular significance until the reader later learns that Flem Snopes also got his financial start in Frenchman's Bend by practicing Will Varner's kind of usury on Will Varner. For purposes of comedy, it is always pleasant to see two rascals posed as foils, each intent on punishing the other through shrewd horse-trading tactics. The reader can and does take a sardonic joy in watching both of them get hurt. Still other kinds of analogies between Will Varner and Flem Snopes soon accumulate. At the beginning of Book One, the first image clearly established is that of a forlorn and decaying Southern mansion, once owned by a prosperous planter remembered now as the Old Frenchman, whose abandoned treasures of money and silverware are still thought to lie buried in the weed-grown garden, now owned by Varner. Although the symbolic mansion is no longer fit to be lived in, its front lawn overlooks so many of Varner's business enterprises that he likes to sit there, in a crudely made chair which Flem Snopes will be occupying at the end of Book One. From that vantage point, even Varner can view certain kinds of people (himself excepted, of course) as fools:

> . . . His blacksmith had made the chair for him by sawing an empty flour barrel half through the middle and trimming out the sides and nailing a seat into it, and Varner would sit there chewing his tobacco or smoking his cob pipe, with a brusque word for passers cheerful enough but inviting no company, against his background of fallen baronial splendor. The people . . . all believed that he sat there planning his next mortgage foreclosure in private, since it was only to an itinerant sewing-machine agent named Ratliff—a man less than half his age—that he ever gave a reason: "I like to sit here. I'm trying to find out what it must have felt like to be the fool that would need all this . . . just to eat and sleep in."

Although V. K. Ratliff, the newsmongering sewing-machine agent who owns half of a restaurant in Jefferson, is certainly the least foolish character in *The Hamlet*, his various shrewd attempts to outsmart Flem Snopes eventually enable Flem to make a fool out of Ratliff. Far more clownish in his ineffectual self-importance is Jody Varner, the grown son and business partner of Will. Jody "emanated a quality of invincible and inviolable bachelordom." He set himself off from the overalls-clad citizenry of the village by wearing, winter

137

and summer and Sundays and weekdays, "a glazed collarless white shirt fastened at the neck with a heavy gold collar-button beneath a suit of good black broadcloth." That semirespectable garb is the one which Flem Snopes very soon tries to surpass, after he has nibbled his way into the reluctant graces of the Varners:

> . . . And the next morning he who had never been seen in the village between Saturday night and Monday morning appeared at the church, and those who saw him looked at him for an instant in incredulous astonishment. In addition to the gray cloth cap and gray trousers, he wore not only a clean white shirt but a necktie—a tiny machine-made black bow which snapped together at the back with a metal fastener. . . . a tiny viciously depthless cryptically balanced splash like an enigmatic punctuation symbol against the expanse of white shirt which gave him Jody Varner's look of ceremonial heterodoxy raised to its tenth power . . .

Fear, on the part of the Varners, gave the Snopeses their first entree—fear, compounded by the futile attempts of Jody and his father to outsmart and out-cheat the family they feared. Flem's father Ab had ominously appeared at the Varner store one day and had offered to rent an empty Varner farm on a sharecropper basis. After stupid Jody had informally closed the deal he picked up gossip that Ab Snopes had a bad reputation as a barn burner. Before his slow wits could think up defenses, Jody found out that Ab and his son Flem and two daughters and a wife and the wife's sister had moved in. Thereafter, Jody countered his father's warning to "stay clear of them folks" by insinuating his own plan to out-cheat the cheaters: "Burning barns aint right. And a man that's got habits that way will just have to suffer the disadvantages of them." Within a week, as it happened, Jody was the one who began to suffer the disadvantages: he found himself forced to take out a precarious form of fire insurance through giving Flem a clerkship in the store. Teasing Will Varner over Jody's moves, Ratliff warns Varner that "there aint but two men I know can risk fooling with them folks. And just one of them is named Varner and his front name aint Jody." Modestly, Ratliff admits that it "aint been proved yet neither" who the other man is. After his first rough encounter with Flem, Ratliff sends word to Varner that "it aint been proved yet, neither."

As Flem expands his activities, he makes bad matters worse by calling in cousin after cousin to fill positions arranged for them. Each new Snopes is presented as being ridiculously picturesque in appearance or word or deed or name (I. O. Snopes, Mink, Byron, Vergil, Wallstreet Panic, Montgomery Ward, Launcelot Snopes, Vardaman

WILLIAM FAULKNER AT HOME, 1950

139

William Faulkner

Snopes, Bilbo Snopes, and even Colonel Sartoris Snopes). The thicker they come, the more outrageous the comedy, until Ratliff wryly imagines Jody Varner cornering Flem in the store long enough to say in a trembling voice,

> "I want to make one pure and simple demand of you and I want a pure and simple Yes and No for an answer: How many more is there? How much longer is this going on? Just what is it going to cost me to protect one goddam barn full of hay?"

So long as the Snopes problem discomforts only the Varners, the other villagers who have suffered from Varner's amorality can enjoy the huge joke. Only Ratliff is shrewd enough to worry, and unintentionally to prophesy his own fall, when he warns a few of the gossips that after Flem captures Varner's homestead "he will have to fall back on you folks." Flem has already begun such a falling back, and after hearing a few funny stories of Flem's usury, Ratliff gets indignant enough to start this conversation:

> "Aint none of you folks out there done nothing about it?" he said.
> "What could we do?" Tull said. "It aint right. But it aint none of our business."
> "I believe I would think of something if I lived there," Ratliff said.
> "Yes," Bookwright said. . . . "And wind up with one of them bow ties in place of your buckboard and team. You have room to wear it."
> "Sho now," Ratliff said. "Maybe you're right."

With that equivocal "Maybe," Ratliff restrains his indignation, although he does not agree with Tull and Bookwright. In spite of his limitations and his fondness for gossip, Ratliff seems to notice two different ways for taking the fact that whatever is nobody's business turns out to be everybody's business. If that ironic twist of words can provide one definition of mere gossip it can also be taken more seriously to serve here as a working definition of moral responsibility. Variations on the phrase, "it aint none of our business," occur and recur throughout the trilogy until that refrain accumulates extremely important thematic overtones. Ratliff, more than any other character in *The Hamlet*, resents and resists the moral dodgings implicit in that recurrent refrain. To that extent, he serves as a persona for Faulkner's own moral indignation. What keeps that usage unobtrusive is the fairly consistent narrative posture of Faulkner's seemingly amused indifference.

In Book Two, entitled "Eula," that same tone of indifference prevails as Faulkner describes the storms of passion which swept the village when Will Varner's luscious, lazy, cow-like, Junoesque daughter reached sixteen, got into sexual trouble, and had to be married off prudently. The first crisis with Eula had occurred when she was eight. Through some inexplicable irony her stupid brother Jody had become "erudition's champion" by insisting that Eula should go to school, even though the lethargic girl refused to walk the half mile and had to be transported to and from school by Jody. The next crisis was precipitated by Eula's decision, when she was thirteen, that she had had enough of school. Her father's reaction was characteristic:

> "Let her stay at home then. . . . All we want anyway is to keep her out of trouble until she gets old enough to sleep with a man without getting me and him both arrested. Then you can marry her off. Maybe you can even find a husband that will keep Jody out of the poorhouse too."

In her fourteenth year, Eula increased her education when her clownish schoolteacher named Labove tried and failed to educate her in sexual matters. It did not matter to her father, "who seemed to have laid upon him already the curse of his own invincible conviction of the absolute unimportance of this or any other given moment or succession of them." In her sixteenth year, Eula had unintentionally aroused the marriageable young men of the village into a restrained frenzy, "a leashed turmoil of lust like so many lowering dogs after a scarce-fledged and apparently unawares bitch." Then warfare developed when an outlander named Hoake McCarron, who lived twelve miles away from the village, began to court Eula with considerable success, even though he had to fight off the combined force of his jealous competitors. Again her father's reaction deserves to be noticed because of its thematic importance:

> So when the word went quietly from house to house about the country that McCarron and the two others had vanished and that Eula Varner was in what everyone else but her, as it presently appeared, called trouble, the last to learn of it was the father—this man who cheerfully and robustly and undeviatingly declined to accept any such theory as female chastity other than as a myth to hoodwink young husbands with, just as some men decline to believe in free tariff or the efficacy of prayer; who, as it was well known, had spent and was still spending no inconsiderable part of his time proving to himself his own contention, who at the present moment was engaged in a liaison with the middle-fortyish wife of one of his own tenants.

Mrs. Varner's reaction is equally revealing: ". . . Turning up pregnant and yelling and cursing here in the house when I am trying to take a nap!" Jody of course was different; he struck the "traditional" Sartoris posture when he protested to his parents, "Maybe you dont give a damn about your name, but I do. I got to hold my head up before folks even if you aint." (The Snopeses use precisely the same protest.) Jody's father tries to calm Jody by explaining the facts of life: "Hell and damnation, all this hullabaloo and uproar because one confounded running bitch finally foxed herself. What did you expect—that she would spend the rest of her life just running water through it?" To Will Varner, the situation merely calls for a practical move which he immediately begins to make. Bribed with money, and with a deed to the seemingly worthless Old Frenchman place, Flem Snopes finds ample profit in assuming the responsibilities of husband and father. He marries the girl and takes her off to Texas, for a honeymoon which lasts until after the baby is born. Ratliff, acquiring this gossip, is not surprised. It seems to him that Flem could outsmart the Devil and take over Hell itself.

Book Three, entitled "The Long Summer," interweaves three other ironically contrasted love stories; the loves of Mink Snopes, of Jack Houston, and of an idiot Snopes boy named Ike. It all begins with the ironically symbolic tableau of old Will Varner holding court in his store and serving as a Justice of the Peace to preserve law and order in an argument between Mink Snopes and Houston over the possession of a yearling bull—possession maintained by Houston during a full year without protest from Mink. When Ratliff hears that Varner has settled the case in favor of Snopes, he stands on the porch of the store sarcastically parroting the proverb-mixing gifts of the weasel-faced hypocrite schoolteacher named I. O. Snopes:

". . . Snopes can come and Snopes can go, but Will Varner looks like he is fixing to snopes forever. Or Varner will Snopes forever—take your pick. What is it the fellow says? off with the old and on with the new; the old job at the old stand, maybe a new fellow doing the jobbing but it's the same old stern getting reamed out." Bookwright was looking at him.

"If you would stand closer to the door, he could hear you a heap better," he said.

"Sholy," Ratliff said. "Big ears have little pitchers, the world beats a path to the rich man's hog-pen but it aint every family has a new lawyer, not to mention a prophet. Waste not want not, except that a full waist dont need no prophet to prophesy a profit and just whose." Now they were all watching him—the smooth, impenetrable face with something about the eyes and the lines beside the mouth which they could not read.

"Look here," Bookwright said. "What's the matter with you?"

"Why, nothing," Ratliff said. "What could be wrong with nothing nowhere nohow in this here best of all possible worlds?"

Ratliff, there serving once again as an equivocal persona for Faulkner, is interrupted by the appearance of the new store clerk, Launcelot (Lump) Snopes, who announces that the show is on and the men had better hurry: the idiot Ike is again making love to the cow in Mrs. Littlejohn's neighboring barn. The loungers and gossipers know that they can enjoy the peepshow from the rear of the barn. Throughout the long summer they continue to enjoy Ike until the day when they are interrupted by the voice of Ratliff, behind them, cursing. When one of them protests that even Ratliff has come to have his look, along with them, Ratliff replies, "Sholy. I aint cussing you folks. I'm cussing all of us." Then he lifts the plank and nails it back into place, concluding, "That's all. It's over. This here engagement is completed." When he tells Mrs. Littlejohn what he has done, she approves and strikes the injured posture of a Sartoris:

"What do you think I think when I look out that window and watch them sneaking up along that fence?" she said.

"Only all you done was think," he said.

As Ratliff goes on to rage against Snopesism, and to vent his suspicion that Lump Snopes must have had ulterior motives in letting this show continue without charging admission, Mrs. Littlejohn taunts him:

"So that's it," she said. "It aint that it is, that itches you. It's that somebody named Snopes, or that particular Snopes, is making something out of it and you dont know what it is. Or is it because folks come and watch? It's all right for it to be, but folks mustn't know it, see it."

"Was," he said. "Because it's finished now. I aint never disputed I'm a pharisee. . . . You dont need to tell me he aint got nothing else. I know that. Or that besides, it aint any of my business. I know that too, just as I know that the reason I aint going to leave him have what he does have is simply because I am strong enough to keep him from it. I am stronger than him. Not righter. Not any better, maybe. But just stronger."

"How are you going to stop it?"

"I dont know. Maybe I even cant. Maybe I dont even want to. Maybe all I want is just to have been righteouser, so I can tell myself I done the right thing and my conscience is clear now and at least I can go to sleep tonight."

Ratliff does stop it, even though I. O. Snopes protests with a varia-tion on the recurrent refrain: "If anything, Lump is going to be put out considerable with what after all wasn't a whole heap of your business." Without answering, Ratliff continues to make it his busi-ness, thus further strengthening this very central facet of theme. Faulkner invites the reader to differentiate, however, between the degree of accountability, or moral responsibility, which might have been expected of the average citizenry, in their attitude toward the idiot Ike, and the contrasting degree of doom, fate, victimization which predominantly controls the lives of the three lovers juxtaposed in Book Three: Mink Snopes, Ike, and Jack Houston. The tone of compassion which dominates Book Three provides a striking contrast to the persistently sardonic and satiric tone of the first two books. Pity is heightened by means of flashbacks which implicitly illuminate the circumstances that have shaped the predicament encompassing all three of these characters.

The essential factor in Houston's story is his heritage of ignorant fanaticism—a fanaticism which he never understands even while all of his actions dramatize it. His marriage to a woman he has known since childhood, a woman accidentally killed by a horse six months after their marriage, was a marriage scarcely leavened by love, or even passion, on either side. What bound them in a compulsive at-traction amounted to a kind of slavery which neither one of them could comprehend. But her death increased his harsh bitterness. Analogously, the story of Mink Snopes's love and marriage is repre-sented as another pattern of compulsions, ignorance, and fanaticism. After he has settled the altercation with Houston by killing him from ambush with a shotgun, Mink returns home and notices his two young children "looking at him with the same quality which he himself possessed: not abject but just still, with an old tired wisdom, acceptance of the immitigable discrepancy between will and capa-bility due to that handicap of physical size in which none of the three of them had had any choice . . ." After describing how Mink's wife and children have left him and how his cousin Lump Snopes has pestered him with threats and pleas and cajoleries calculated to make Mink lead Lump to the dead man for the purpose of stealing what-ever money they might find in his pockets, Faulkner could be refer-ring to either cousin when he says that one of them possessed "an incorrigible dishonesty long since become pure reflex and probably now beyond his control." Thus the reader is invited to notice quali-ties, even in such Snopeses, which lie beyond immediate moral censure.

Faulkner's celebrated treatment of the idiot Isaac Snopes's love for Houston's cow constitutes an interesting change in stylistic pace. In this book of fools, the idiot Ike is an innocent, set apart from all the other fools, and not measurable in terms of moral codes. Yet, for these very reasons, which relate him to the idiot Benjamin Compson in *The Sound and the Fury*, Ike's actions can be interpreted poetically as providing a kind of moral mirror in which the actions of certain other characters are implicitly reflected and contrasted. As Ratliff tries to see what the men are watching through the aperture in the back of the barn, "it was as though it were himself inside the stall with the cow, himself looking out of the blasted tongueless face at the row of faces watching him who had been given wordless passions but not the specious words." All of Isaac's important motivations are provided by that "wordless passion." Even Houston, noticing how ingeniously Isaac provides food and comfort for the cow, is permitted to think "that there is perhaps something in passion too, as well as in poverty and innocence, which cares for its own." No expense of energy is too great for Isaac to make for the cow; he risks his life in saving her from the fire. His actions in tending her are selfless, his adoration makes him bring her flowers with the hay. Her presence, as she walks through the mist beside the creek in the early dawn, heightens all of Isaac's sensuous responses. He does not know what love is, and yet some of Ike's actions practically or figuratively dramatize certain meanings of love in a form far more pure and exalted than the actions of any other character in the book. So when Faulkner, in describing Isaac's love, permits his prose to ascend to a lyric intensity far greater than in any other passage in *The Hamlet*, that pastoral lyricism is not mere parody or mockery. If it mocks anything, it mocks the lack of love among the morally responsible characters. When Book Three concludes with the passage in which Eck Snopes explains to Ratliff why he has tried to provide compensation to Ike for the loss of his cow by giving the idiot a little wooden effigy, Eck's pity elevates him above all the other Snopes, and foreshadows certain actions in *The Town*, where Eck and his son turn against Snopesism, and fight it.

Book Four of *The Hamlet* returns to the comic and satiric mode while still intermingling elements of pathos, tragedy, compassion, and pity. The first section of it is devoted to the account of how Flem Snopes brought back from his Texas honeymoon a herd of wild spotted horses, along with a Texan who auctions them off to the countrypeople, and thus makes a handsome profit for Snopes, before the horses escape and run wild throughout and beyond Frenchman's

Bend. The sheer narrative power of the account is obviously heightened by Faulkner's intense delight in, and knowledge of, horse flesh. The account of the runaway horse which invades Mrs. Littlejohn's hotel and nearly frightens Ratliff out of his skin is splendidly comic. Yet Faulkner successfully dares to combine pathos with comedy by permitting Henry Armstid and his wife to become involved in the auction. The plight of the Armstids helps to throw more light on the character of Flem Snopes.

When Armstid seeks revenge against Flem, the resulting action provides a fitting close for *The Hamlet. Money-money-money*, as a symbol of self-interest, has provided a recurrent motif throughout this conglomerate of narratives. Generally considered, a Snopes is anyone who will do anything, even sell his soul (if any), for money. Now suddenly Armstid and Bookwright and Ratliff are represented as having become sufficiently Snopesian to find themselves maddened by the conviction that there must be truth in all the old stories about money buried by the Old Frenchman in the garden back of the forlorn and decaying mansion. Henry has even seen Flem Snopes digging by starlight in that garden which now belongs to Flem. Perhaps as Ratliff suggests, he has found in the old house a map of the garden which has given him the approximate location of the treasure. If Snopes can dig until midnight, then his three money-crazed enemies can dig through the rest of the night. Ratliff enlists the help of an old man who is a magician with a diviner's rod and, during one exciting secret exploration, the old man helps them locate three small bags of money in the garden. That is all the evidence needed by these prospectors. At the end of that same day, Ratliff approaches Flem Snopes and finds him willing to sell the old Frenchman's place:

> A little after six that evening, in the empty and locked store, Ratliff gave a quit-claim deed to his half of the side-street lunchroom in Jefferson. Armstid gave a mortgage on his farm . . . Bookwright paid his third in cash.

Thereafter, they are free to dig in earnest. Fearing that someone will interrupt them, they dig only at night, and for three nights they wear themselves out with frantic labors. Then it occurs to Ratliff to examine the dates on the coins, and to his chagrin he finds that Flem Snopes has fooled them with the old trick of "salting" an empty mine. A few days later, when the triumphant Flem and his wife Eula pack their belongings into their mule wagon and drive out of Frenchman's Bend toward Ratliff's restaurant in Jefferson, gossips notice that the road they are taking will make the trip three miles longer than necessary. The wits make guesses:

> "Maybe he aims to take them three miles on into town with him and swap them to Aaron Rideout for the other half of that restaurant."
> "Maybe he'll swap them to Ratliff and Bookwright and Henry Armstid for something else."
> "He'll find Henry Armstid without having to go that far."

Henry is still digging at the Old Frenchman place, the gaunt unshaven face "now completely that of a madman." Earlier, Ratliff had said of Henry, without any boomerang intention, "Just look at what even the money a man aint got yet will do to him."

10

~§   THE TOWN

IN CONSTRUCTING *The Town* as a sequel to *The Hamlet*, Faulkner did something more than continue the subject matter of Snopesism through employing a technical blend of the comic and satiric modes. He created a special and peculiar focus of narration, or way of getting the story told, and then employed that factor in such a way as to make heavier demands on the moral consciousness of his readers than he had done in any other novel, with the possible exception of *Sanctuary*. *The Town* consequently shares with *Sanctuary* a strategy which initially uses various characters in the action as targets for satirical unmasking, and then cumulatively increases the ironies in a way which enables Faulkner implicitly to make all of his readers show cause why they themselves should not serve as further targets for satirical unmasking. The following interpretation of *The Town* concentrates on this particular aspect, beginning first with an examination of the peculiar way in which Faulkner gets this story told by three characters in the action, so that he may withdraw, above or behind his creation, as though he were indifferent.

Three characters in the action take turns in telling and in trying to explain different events in this the second phase of Snopesism, and the viewpoints of these three characters are strikingly different. The first narrator, Charles Mallison, begins by admitting that he was not present when Flem Snopes moved in from Frenchman's Bend to Jefferson, back in 1905. He also admits that he himself was not even born until 1915, and so was only twelve years old when the story ended. But he had been brought up on the folklore of Snopesism because his uncle is Gavin Stevens, the Jefferson leader of the war against Snopesism. During his boyhood, Charles Mallison did stand on the fringes of certain late battles, and did serve as messenger boy, even though he had not then been old enough to understand what he saw and heard. The second narrator is Gavin Stevens himself, a modern Don Quixote and an upholder of the Old Southern Traditions of Chivalry. When he first became involved with Flem

Snopes, Gavin Stevens had just returned to Jefferson to start practicing law in his father's office, after capping his Harvard education with law school training. The third narrator is that rueful victim of Snopesistic outsmarting, the former restaurant owner and sewing-machine agent, V. K. Ratliff. Each of these three narrators tells a chapter of the story at a time. Although Charles Mallison is permitted to tell ten of them, while Gavin Stevens has only eight, and Ratliff has only six, it is Gavin Stevens who does most of the talking. According to Ratliff, Stevens does much too much talking, and the reader is eventually inclined to agree.

Faulkner gets more artistic gain from this focus of narration than might be expected. The three narrators do more than view the story from different points of view. They disagree with each other, they criticize each other, they correct each other, and they even correct themselves. Yet each has his own peculiar form of double vision. Mallison, for example, tells of his innocent boyish responses and reactions to Snopesism; but he speaks retrospectively of those responses, and from a mature viewpoint which represents the general viewpoint of Jefferson at large. Gavin Stevens, by contrast, clings poetically and romantically to his chivalric idealism; yet he acknowledges in retrospect the factors which confused and disillusioned him. Ratliff's ambiguous ways of looking and of talking are by far the most complicated of the three. He is characterized well by Stevens who says, after quoting one of Ratliff's cryptic remarks, "Between the voice and the face there were always two Ratliffs: the second one offering you a fair and open chance to divine what the first one really meant by what it was saying, provided you were smart enough." Faulkner permits Ratliff to make numerous mistakes in observation and in judgment; nevertheless, Ratliff is frequently the persona, through whose mask-like face the reader most frequently seems to hear Faulkner's own ironic voice. But as is hinted by Stevens' comment, above, Ratliff always seems to know more than he says. There are times when he speaks as though he feels the need for concealments. There are even hints that Ratliff might be the unacknowledged and unacknowledging father of that child named Linda, born to Eula Varner very shortly after she married the impotent Flem Snopes. But the reader can never be sure how to take some of Ratliff's hints.

Faulkner likes to play, thematically, with the human predicament of not being sure, and with related predicaments caused by the limits of human knowledge. Such playing occurs in all of his major novels, but particularly in *The Sound and the Fury*, in *Absalom, Absalom!* and in *Light in August*, as we have noticed. This time, the first vague suggestions of that thematic concern is revealed by the cumulative doubts, disagreements, corrections, and self-corrections of three narrators, Mallison, Stevens, and Ratliff. In scores of places the flow of narrative is interrupted by such interjections as these:

"at first we thought . . ."
"No, that's wrong . . ."
"I don't know," Ratliff said.
"So we were wondering . . ."
"Except that if we ever knowed what it was . . ."
"she didn't know herself how she done it . . ."

Such a cluster of related phrases forces the reader to be alert for whatever usage Faulkner chooses to make out of the not-knowing motif. The story is unfolded in such a way as to suggest that the picturesque psychological configurations which result from basing conclusions on fragmentary information, may be viewed as merely amusing; but those same configurations can have bearing on serious moral causes and consequences.

Underneath the comedy and even the slapstick the reader would seem invited to discover many examples of serious moral causes and consequences which stem from not knowing or from not caring. Various characters admit their "not knowing" about Snopesism, and they react differently to that admission. But one recurrent form of reaction may be viewed as a thematic continuation from *The Hamlet:* many of these characters have their own ways for saying that what you don't know won't hurt you so long as you don't make it your business to find out. They find comfort in any self-excusing form of moral laziness, and the narrative develops some ironic consequences which stem directly from such moral laziness.

Faulkner plays, and seriously plays, with another extension of this theme. It frequently happens that what a character believes he knows, from the gossip he hears, depends on what he wants to hear or believe, prior to the relaying of the gossip to him or from him. Like most human beings, most of these characters find that what they do not want to believe they can arrange not to hear.

Now it can be pointed out that the reader becomes involved in precisely these aspects of theme. After all, this is only a novel, and so the reader can relax as passively as some of the characters relax, into an attitude of laughter and amusement and moral laziness. As readers, we can tell ourselves that the predicaments of these characters are none of our business, and so we can enjoy them as jokes without permitting them to intrude painfully on our experience. Another response of the reader may be merely to laugh at the characters who use gossip as springboards and who jump to either idealistic or malicious conclusions, as their prejudices prompt them. Which way the reader jumps, in making responses to such characters, will of course depend on what the reader wants to believe about these characters.

It should be clear by this time, however, that Faulkner as literary artist is very deeply concerned with telling his narratives in such a way as to involve and even to hurt the moral consciousness of his readers. The strategy he uses could not be called propagandistic; it does not try to persuade. But it does try to move, to shock, and thus to encourage an improvement in moral perspective.

If these particular elements of Faulknerian theme, and of Faulknerian strategy, are kept in mind as we now move on to examine a few essentials of the action in *The Town*, it should be easy to demonstrate how Faulkner illuminates and extends and enriches meanings. In chapter one, Charles Mallison gives us a mixture of fact and gossip handed down to him concerning an incident which happened in Jefferson before he was born. He tells how Flem Snopes had suddenly blossomed out as the superintendent of the Jefferson power plant, apparently appointed to that newly created office by young Manfred de Spain, Mayor of Jefferson. Nobody knew why that office had been created, or why that appointment had been made. So they guessed and gossiped until it was generally agreed that Flem Snopes must have loaned or rented or traded his luscious wife Eula to Manfred, in exchange for that position. But because everyone in town admired the beautiful Mrs. Snopes and the "invincibly and irrevocably polygamous" Manfred, the prevailing attitude in Jefferson was one of approval. Mallison summarizes the Jefferson attitude:

> We were his allies, his confederates; our whole town was accessory to that cuckolding—that cuckolding which for any proof we had, we had invented ourselves out of whole cloth; that same cuckoldry in which we would watch De Spain and Snopes walking amicably together while (though we didn't know it yet) De Spain was creating, planning how to create, that office of power-plant superintendent which we didn't even know we didn't have, let alone needed, and then get Mr. Snopes into it. It was not because we were against Mr. Snopes; we had not yet read the signs and portents which should have warned, alerted, sprung us into frantic concord to defend our town from him. Nor were we really in favor of adultery, sin: we were simply in favor of simple unadulterated uninhibited immortal lust which they represented; for the two people in each of whom the other had found his single ordained fate; each to have found out of all the earth that one match for his mettle; ours the pride that Jefferson would supply their battleground.

In the sense under consideration, that passage might stand as a microcosm of the entire novel. Thus early, the reader would seem invited to notice how this moral problem involving the free people's democratic choice of Mayor is inseparable from what is simultaneously everybody's business and nobody's business. More than that, the young lawyer named Gavin Stevens is there quoted as the one who wittily crystallized the general Jefferson attitude, and thus helped to make Jefferson just as vulnerable to Snopesism as Will Varner helped Frenchman's Bend to be.

The next structural unit in chapter one works out a low comedy analogue, in the form of an amusing anecdote as to how the superintendent of the power plant, Flem Snopes, tried to improve his game of stealing brass. Figuratively speaking, he tried to blackmail two coal-heaving Negroes, until they turned the joke on Flem himself. Flem's method was to deceive the slow-witted Tom Tom into thinking that Turl was about to accuse Tom Tom of stealing a box of valuable brass fittings from the plant, and that Turl was going to make the false accusation in the hope that he could get Tom Tom fired, so that Turl could take the better position. Flem's advice to Tom Tom was that, because Turl would probably plant the box of brass where the guilt of theft would fall on Tom Tom, the best defense would be to take the box home from the power plant and hide it where even his wife couldn't find it. That would outwit Turl. But then Flem reversed the lie by telling Turl that Tom Tom had stolen the brass, for purposes of planting it on Turl, and that Turl could prevent that false accusation by going to Tom Tom's cabin, when it was safe, finding the box, and delivering it to Flem, who would hide it so that neither of them would ever find it again. Turl went, but instead of finding brass he simply found his way into bed with old Tom Tom's young wife. Harker, the engineer at the power plant, enjoyed the ridiculous situation because he knew, enviously, all about Flem's very successful processes of stealing and selling brass. For Harker, all of that hocus pocus involving the Negroes was a fine joke, and he summarized the funniest part of it in terms of analogy:

"... And when I think about Tom Tom in here wrastling them boilers in that-ere same amical cuckolry like what your uncle says Miz Snopes and Mayor de Spain walks around in, stealing brass so he can keep Turl from getting his job away from him, and all the time Turl is out yonder tending by daylight to Tom Tom's night homework, sometimes I think I will jest die."

In chapter two, Faulkner uses a favorite kind of counterpoint to heighten the next unit of action. Gavin Stevens, as narrator, recalls that when Flem Snopes marshaled various members of the Snopes family into various positions in Jefferson, he made one mistake. He placed Eck Snopes in the restaurant which Flem had vacated when Flem moved on up to the power plant. The trouble with Eck Snopes was that he happened to be a man of integrity. Ratliff had told Stevens that when Eck had worked at Varner's saw mill in Frenchman's Bend, Flem should then have seen all he needed to know about the uselessness, even the danger, of such an honest man. That was proof enough to Stevens that the father of Eck could not possibly have been a Snopes: "Indubitably and indefensibly not a Snopes; even to impugn him so was indefensible and outrageous and forever beyond all pale of pardon." Stevens goes on to explain, sarcastically, that after Eck Snopes became estalished in the restaurant he was even more of a menace to Snopesism:

"... here he was a threat to his whole family's long tradition of slow and invincible rapacity because of that same incredible and innocent assumption that all people practise courage and honesty for the simple reason that if they didn't everybody would be frightened and confused; saying one day, not even privately but right out loud where half a dozen strangers not even kin by marriage to Snopeses heard him: 'Aint we supposed to be selling beef in these here hamburgers? I don't know just what this is yet but it aint no beef.' So of course they —when I say 'they' I mean Snopeses; when you say 'Snopeses' in Jefferson you mean Flem Snopes—fired him. They had to; he was intolerable there."

The reader is thus brought back to the question implicitly raised throughout *The Hamlet:* what makes a man a Snopes, or keeps him from being a Snopes, regardless of whether his name is Eck or Stevens or Sartoris? Gavin Stevens goes on to admit, even in chapter two of *The Town*, that matters were complicated in this regard because there was another decent Snopes, Wall, who happened to be the son of Eck. Ratliff had also told Stevens the story of how cool and courageous that boy Wall had been when the spotted horses got loose in Frenchman's Bend. Now Stevens, not knowing what could happen to a Snopes boy who possessed those qualities, recalls the thoughts which crossed his mind when Ratliff told that story about Wall:

Horse boy, dog boy, cat boy, monkey boy, elephant boy: anything but Snopes boy. And then suppose, just suppose; suppose and tremble: one generation more removed from Eck Snopes and his innocence; one generation more until that innocent and outrageous belief that courage and honor are practical has had time to fade and cool so that merely the habit of courage and honor remain; add to that then that

generation's natural heritage of cold rapacity as instinctive as breath-
ing, and tremble at the prospect: the habit of courage and honor compounded by rapacity or rapacity raised to the absolute *nth* by courage
and honor: not horse boy but a lion or tiger boy: Genghis Khan or
Tamerlane or Attila in the defenseless midst of indefensible Jefferson.

As Ratliff says, Gavin talks too much, and Ratliff repeatedly
points out that Gavin's thinking is often confused. But in the pas,
sage just quoted, it would seem that Faulkner has arranged to represent Gavin's thinking as something worse than confusion. It echoes
that kind of encouragement to Snopesism which was implicit in
Sanctuary when Horace Benbow opined, "Perhaps it is upon the
instant that we realize, admit, that there is a logical pattern to evil,
that we die." But there in *Sanctuary* and here in *The Town*, Faulkner
makes no comment on the dramatic ironies, and permits the common
sense of the reader to recognize a self-blinding and self-defeating
attitude for what it is. As for what comes of it, that is the plot of the
story. In the immediate chapter under consideration, the dramatic
ironies continue to work as Gavin Stevens continues his hysterical
moaning over the plight of defenseless Jefferson, beset with Snopesism
as Flem Snopes continues to move his echelons up fast. Stevens is
even permitted to recall that there had been a Byron Snopes in
Jefferson before Flem, and that old Colonel Sartoris had not only
educated Byron Snopes but had also given him a position in the
Colonel's bank. Continuing his defeatist moanings, Stevens remembers that he himself had foreseen, well in advance, that Byron Snopes
would outwit the Sartorises, and then adds, with a sarcasm which
backfires, thematically:

> ". . . We not to know how of course since that was none of our busi-
> ness; indeed, who to say but there was not one among us but did not
> want to know: who, already realising that we would never defend Jef-
> ferson from Snopeses, let us then give, relinquish Jefferson to Snopeses,
> banker mayor aldermen church and all, so that, in defending them-
> selves from Snopeses, Snopeses must of necessity defend and shield
> us, their vassals and chattels, too."

Of course Gavin Stevens sets himself apart from the rest of Jefferson. He thinks that his sarcasm is aimed at those in Jefferson whose
actions play into the hands of Snopesism. Gavin Stevens does not
intend to include himself in such company. But the dramatic irony
of that posture is also unmasked by the unfolding of later events.

In chapter three, Charles Mallison resumes his role as narrator,
and further heightens the ironies which gather around the well-

meaning Gavin Stevens. Back in the old days, it seems, the admiration of Gavin Stevens for Mrs. Eula Varner Snopes had developed into an infatuation which was quite clear to everyone except Gavin himself. Not understanding his own motives, Gavin had decided to become a white knight and to ride to the aid of Eula, even to save her from the cruel evils and lies and gossip which had already helped to ostracize her from Jefferson society. But when he tried to enlist his sister's support, by asking her to be the first town lady to pay a social call on Eula, he discovered an ambiguous attitude in the mind of his sister (Mallison's mother):

> "You're going to save her," Mother said, not looking at Uncle Gavin now: just watching the sock she was darning.
> "Yes!" Uncle Gavin said, fast, quick: no in-breathe this time, so quick he almost said the rest of it before he could stop himself, so that all Mother had to do was say it for him:
> "—from Manfred de Spain."
> But Uncle Gavin had caught himself by now; his voice was just harsh now. "[From] you too," he said. "You and your husband too. The best people, the pure, the unimpugnable . . ."
> ". . . Just what is it about this that you can't stand? That Mrs Snopes may not be chaste, or that it looks like she picked Manfred de Spain out to be unchaste with."
> "Yes!" Uncle Gavin said. "I mean no! It's all lies—gossip. . . . But if I'm to go on this crusade . . ."

From that start, the quixotic Gavin's first crusade quickly descended into an unintentionally comic warfare over Eula, and into a series of skirmishes conducted on a sophomoric level between young Gavin and the young Mayor, Manfred. The struggle sank or rose to its mock-heroic nadir or zenith at the traditional Cotillion Club Dance, where Gavin punched Manfred because of the indecent way in which Manfred danced with Mrs. Snopes. Retrospectively, Charles Mallison points up one irony in such heroic defense of traditional codes: "What he was doing was simply defending forever with his blood the principle that chastity and virtue in women shall be defended whether they exist or not." Ratliff's shrewd comment on Gavin's predicament comes even closer to the heart of it: "He didn't want nothing from De Spain because the only thing De Spain had that he wanted, Lawyer didn't know his-self that was what he wanted . . ." After further difficulties with the Mayor, and with Eula, in which Gavin Stevens is repeatedly the loser, he decided suddenly (and for reasons which everyone understood better than he did) that his education was incomplete, and that he should follow the tradition of the old days by taking two years of study at Heidelberg. Ratliff tells, in his pleasantly crude narrative style, how he went to the station to say goodbye and had to listen and watch as the retreating white knight went through rhetorical postures without admitting, and apparently without even knowing, that he was running away:

> "Good," he says, brisk and chipper as you could want. "I was hoping to see you before I left, to pass the torch on into your active hand. You'll have to hold the fort now. You'll have to tote the load."
>
> "What fort?" I says. "What load?"
>
> "Jefferson," he says. "Snopeses. Think you can handle them till I get back?"
>
> "Not me nor a hundred of me," I says. "The only thing to do is get completely shut of them, abolish them."
>
> "No, no," he says. ". . . No, we got them now; they're ourn now: I dont know jest what Jefferson could a committed back there whenever it was, to have won this punishment, gained this right, earned this privilege. But we did. So it's for us to cope, to resist; us to endure, and (if we can) survive."

Once again, Faulkner lets the reader enjoy the ironies, without any assistance even from the narrator Ratliff. But after two years at Heidelberg, and after two more years of wartime service, spent as a YMCA secretary, Gavin Stevens returned to continue his crusade against Snopesism in Jefferson, with the same weaknesses and the same lack of success. His last great crusade, which dominates the last half of *The Town*, was to carry the torch quixotically, and again with amazing powers of self-deception, for the innocent and now blossomed and beautiful daughter of Eula and of a father whose identity only Ratliff seemed to know with certainty. Once again, the motives of the white knight were as romantic and as suspect as when he set out to save Eula herself. But Faulkner permits Gavin Stevens himself to tell what he can remember of his motives for that last crusade, and to tell it in a romantic way which raises dramatic irony to new heights:

> ". . . So that girl-child was not Flem Snopes's at all, but mine; my child and my grandchild both, since the McCarron boy who begot her (oh yes, I can even believe Ratliff when it suits me) in that lost time, was Gavin Stevens in that lost time . . ."

Even so, Gavin could never admit to himself that although the girl Linda was then approaching seventeen and he was then in his thirties, he had suddenly been swept off his feet with puppy love, or worse. He began his courtship with ice cream and poetry, explaining that he wanted to help to "form her mind." But when his own sister teased him because of his own innocence, he flared into quixotic rage: "Well, well," he said, "If that's what a mind with no more aptitude for gossip and dirt than yours is inventing and thinking, just imagine what the rest of Jefferson, the experts, have made of it by now." Then he relented, and struck a far nobler posture of knighthood, as he continued: "To save Jefferson from Snopeses is a crisis, an emergency, a duty. To save a Snopes from Snopeses is a privilege, an honor, a pride." To which his sister answered, "Especially a sixteen-year-old female one." Nothing came of all his attempts to "save" Linda, and gradually Gavin Stevens grew more and more disillusioned, as he retrospectively admits.

In chapter seventeen, Faulkner draws out the full stops of dramatic irony by permitting Gavin to rant and rave, to laugh and cry, while explaining at tedious length to the reader what he had learned about women, about the motives of Manfred de Spain, about the motives of Flem Snopes, and about his own motives. The reader, wading patiently through Gavin's rhetoric (and probably not enjoying it as much as Faulkner hoped) has by this point in the narrative progressed so far past any provisional and tentative evaluations of Gavin Stevens as to feel definitely at odds with some of his pronouncements. So after the reader has said "no" over and over again to Gavin Stevens in chapter seventeen, there is a peculiar pleasure in turning to chapter eighteen and finding that Ratliff as narrator begins, "No no, no no, no no. He was wrong." Throughout the narrative, Ratliff has been correcting Gavin Stevens, and has been reproaching him for failing to understand some of the most important motives in Snopesism. At one point, Ratliff had previously posed this conundrum: "What's the one thing in Jefferson that Flem aint got yet?" Respectability? Not exactly. All he wanted was to acquire that veneer of respectability and civic virtue which passed for integrity among the citizens of Jefferson. Poor Gavin Stevens is represented, in some of his crusades, as even helping Flem Snopes achieve some of that veneer, without meaning to help him. But ultimately, after Flem Snopes and De Spain have taken over a bank in Jefferson, after Flem Snopes has found a way of forcing De Spain out of town, and after an extremely complicated set of factors have been brought to a climax by the suicide of the beautiful Eula Varner Snopes, Ratliff is permitted to summarize matters, with an ironic-sarcastic bitterness which is not at all flattering to Gavin Stevens, for the way he has unintentionally aided Flem in his contest for respectability:

> "That's right, a contest. Not even against Linda, and last of all against Lawyer Stevens, since he had already milked out of Lawyer

Stevens all he needed from him, which was to get his wife buried all right and proper and decorous and respectable, without no uproarious elements making a unseemly spectacle in the business. His game of solitaire was against Jefferson. . . . It was like he knowed that his respectability depended completely on Jefferson not jest accepting but finally getting used to the fact that he not only had evicted Manfred de Spain from his bank but he was remodeling to move into De Spain's birthsite likewise, and that the only remaining threat now was what might happen if that-ere young gal that believed all right so far that he was her paw, might stumble onto something that would tell her different. That she might find out by accident that the man that was leastways mixed up somehow in her mother's suicide, whether he actively caused it or not, wasn't even her father, since if somebody's going to be responsible why your maw killed herself, at least let it be somebody kin to you and not jest a outright stranger."

The sting in that last sentence is sharper than anything found elsewhere in *The Town*. It is directed primarily at Gavin Stevens because he was the one who, out of "kindness," had assured the doubting Linda that Flem Snopes was her father. But Ratliff has two further ironies which he must unburden, near the end of the narrative. One of them is that Gavin Stevens, having helped Flem bury Eula respectably, entered into further collusion with Flem by helping him erect a splendid cemetery monument to Eula. The other is that Gavin helped Flem have a suitable inscription carved on that monument. Because Flem was not given to ironies, the town of Jefferson had to guess at veneer motives for Flem's choice of words for that gravestone inscription:

EULA VARNER SNOPES

1889   1927

A Virtuous Wife is a Crown to Her Husband
Her Children Rise and Call Her Blessed

To the very end of *The Town*, Faulkner remains quietly ironic, and yet quite bitter, in his treatment of that romantically idealistic, poetic, and quixotic upholder of the Southern Tradition, poor Gavin Stevens. Those readers and critics who have mistakenly viewed Faulkner himself as a romantic, wistfully yearning for the good old days of Southern chivalry, when a Snopes was always a Snopes, and a Sartoris was always a Sartoris, might easily start to correct that mistake by studying Faulkner's uses of ironies in *The Town*.

11

FAULKNER'S MORAL VISION

WILLIAM FAULKNER once said that because any author has only one story to tell he inevitably spends his art in trying to find different and better ways of telling that one story. The provocative hyperbole of that assertion invites many different responses and interpretations. But for the present purposes of summary and conclusion, it might be said that the truly unique "story" which Faulkner hinted at, and told fragments of, through all the indirections of his themes, and through all the indirections of his mythic analogies, was his own private or personal myth, his own peculiar way of looking at human experience, his own continuity of moral vision.

"Personal myth" is a term which has been variously defined. But the definition for that term which might be considered most useful, here, should not be too much at odds with the description of the term "myth" already given in chapter two. As there stated, a "myth" is a traditional and a ritualistic story which expresses the accepted beliefs of a given group of people. It conveys an immediate intuition of reality and of truth, through the vehicle of a dramatic narrative. It conveys intuitions of right and wrong relationships between the human and the divine—between the physical world and the metaphysical world. But if "myth" expresses the accepted beliefs of a group, "personal myth" might imply either the acceptance by an individual of a particular myth of a particular group, or the rejection of previously constructed myths and the substitution of a privately constructed myth. In the latter case, the first step in such construction would be an act of negation, an act of self-liberation and rebellion, followed by the expression of fresh affirmations through the form of the privately constructed myth. William Blake and William Butler Yeats might serve to illustrate. Each of them gave overt and original mythic formulations to their own private beliefs about

159

physical and metaphysical relationships. "I must create a System," said Blake, "or be enslav'd by another man's."

William Faulkner never did create a "personal myth" after the fashions of Blake or Yeats. Nevertheless, the concern of this concluding essay is to correlate, from the techniques and themes of Faulkner's narratives, and from remarks he made elsewhere, some fragments of evidence which may at least suggest the broad configuration of his moral vision, and to let that correlation stand as an incomplete figure of his personal myth. Although such an undertaking is a risky effort which must fail, it may at least resolve some of the apparent inconsistencies and paradoxes created by the themes of the novels we have considered.

❧

A few preliminary moves will be made here, initially, to point up an apparent paradox which must later be resolved—a paradox very clearly established by some of his techniques and some of his themes. In our considerations of how Faulkner got his different stories told, we noticed some peculiar recurrences. At first glance, there might seem to be no recurrences in focus of narration between *The Sound and the Fury*, *The Town*, and *Absalom, Absalom!* In each, however, Faulkner largely removes himself from the conventional role of novelist-as-narrator. Throughout the first three parts of *The Sound and the Fury*, he creates the artistic illusion that the three Compson brothers obliquely "tell" different versions of the same story. In *The Town*, he permits Charles Mallison, Gavin Stevens, and Ratliff to take turns in telling separate episodes of one story. In *Absalom, Absalom!* we are first given fragments of the Sutpen family saga, through the consciousness of Quentin Compson as he listens to and puzzles over Miss Rosa's version of that story; then we are given further fragments as Quentin listens to his father's version; then we follow Quentin as he tries to explain to Shreve; and then finally we collaborate with both of them in imagining unknown parts of the Sutpen story. In each of those novels, analogous technical processes provide the reader with contrasted approximations of the truth, concerning causes and consequences, thus requiring the reader to derive from those unsatisfactory versions of truth some higher perceptions or deeper insights of truth. As we have noticed, there is a dialectical factor operative in this technique; but at the same time one effect is the suggestion of a skeptical element in Faulkner's habits of mind. If he thus indirectly reveals his own doubts as to the validity of any single grasp of truth, he would seem to be seeking

160

more than artistic roundness of characterization when he forces the reader to examine the same pattern of actions from several different points of view.

Further insights may be gained by remembering those techniques Faulkner uses to represent so many characters as not knowing each other and as not understanding their own most obvious motives. In *The Sound and the Fury*, Ben's kind of not-knowing constitutes an extreme example; but it is ingeniously used by Faulkner. More immediate to our purpose, here, is Faulkner's way of introducing the separate characters, at the beginning of *Light in August*, as isolated by related kinds of not-knowing. Remember also that the ultimate trouble with Thomas Sutpen in *Absalom, Absalom!* is finally traced to that which he does not know about himself and about human beings in general. Some further significance is given to this recurrent motif of not-knowing, in *The Town*, through that odd technical process of making the reader scramble awkwardly through a verbal hedge created when those three narrators keep saying "I don't know" and "No, that's wrong" and "Maybe it was because" and "We didn't know" and "You don't understand" and "No no, no no, no no. He was wrong." Here again, merely through such recurrences in technical procedures and in themes, we are given hints that Faulkner's skeptical habit of mind is extended intermittently to preoccupations with agnosticism.

By contrast, Faulkner's heavy uses of Christian imagery and Christian myth can be correlated with other evidences that faith, and belief in metaphysical realities, constitute equally important factors in his habits of mind. Remember the significance of that Easter Sunday service which is attended by Dilsey and Ben in *The Sound and the Fury*. Remember Hightower's way of condemning himself, in *Light in August*, by admitting that he had preached to his congregation in Jefferson an image of a swaggering and unchastened bravo, "instead of the crucified shape of pity and love." Remember the analogies implicitly established between the self-sacrifice of Nancy Mannigoe, in *Requiem*, and the self-sacrifice of Jesus.

These reminders indicate an apparently basic inconsistency and paradox: Faulkner's techniques and themes reveal more than hints of his very skeptical and even agnostic habits of mind; yet at other times they honor certain essentials of Christian doctrine. If we are to avoid misleading conclusions about the continuities in Faulkner's moral vision, or in his personal myth, some other approach is needed to explain and resolve this basic paradox.

ぐ ۿ

In his essay entitled *After Strange Gods*, T. S. Eliot touches on an important problem which pervades the entire history of American literature—a problem which can be made pertinent to our study of Faulkner's moral vision. While discussing Hawthorne and Henry James, Eliot calls attention to the apparently inconsistent fact that both Hawthorne and James revealed, in their writings, almost obsessive preoccupations with certain aspects of their Calvinistic Puritan heritage, although neither one of them subscribed to any conventional religious belief. Eliot goes on to say that they both implemented their "exceptional awareness of spiritual reality" and their "profound sensitiveness to good and evil," by making use of certain scientific and psychological notions which happened to be new and current. He further points out that the interaction of these apparently contradictory factors helps to explain the power with which they both conveyed horror, as a means to the end of illuminating their intensely moral themes. Each observation could be applied to Faulkner.

Any attempt to resolve the apparently basic paradox in Faulkner's moral vision must come to grips with the fact that he is simultaneously fascinated and repelled by that peculiar Southern version of Calvinistic Puritanism which helped to shape his youthful habits of thought and belief. It was his rebellious negation against that aspect of his heritage which provided him with his primary motives for fashioning, independently, his own personal myth. The meaning of an asserted belief depends so much on the tension of opposition, which causes that assertion, that it is particularly important to notice how most of the tensions within Faulkner's myth are derived from his refusal to be enslaved by the Calvinistic beliefs he had innocently accepted during his youth. We need next, then, a brief summary of the apparent ways in which he liberated himself from his own sense of enslavement.

An early phase of his rebellion may be found obliquely reflected in his largely derivative poetry; but an even more explicit revelation is provided by his early prose essay entitled, *Verse Old and Nascent: A Pilgrimage*, which he wrote when he was twenty-eight years old, and published in the New Orleans *Double Dealer* in April, 1925. The following passage from that essay is pertinent:

> At the age of sixteen, I discovered Swinburne. Or rather, Swinburne discovered me, springing from some tortured undergrowth of my adolescence, like a highwayman, making me his slave. My mental life at that period was so completely and smoothly veneered with surface insincerity—obviously necessary to me at that time, to support intact my personal integrity—that I can not tell to this day exactly to what

depths he stirred me . . . It seems to me now that I found him nothing but a flexible vessel into which I might put my own vague emotional shapes without breaking them. . . . I read and employed
verse, firstly, for the purposes of furthering various philanderings in
which I was engaged; secondly, to complete a youthful gesture I was
then making of being different in a small town.

That passage adds further significance to a pair of metaphors
which Faulkner borrowed, early in his career as youthful poet. His
first published poem was entitled "L'Apres-Midi d'un Faune," perhaps with an awareness of Debussy's debt to the Symbolist move-
ment in poetry and to the Impressionist school of painting. Faulkner's
first published volume of poems was entitled *The Marble Faun*, apparently with an awareness of Hawthorne's Italian romance. But as
the above prose passage suggests, Faulkner found poetic reasons for
identifying himself, figuratively, with fauns and satyrs and other
worshipers of Dionysus, during those early years when he was sing-
ing his own pagan love songs. His particular forms of negation and
rebellion must have given him peculiar sympathy for Swinburne's
erotic poetry, Swinburne's passionate pagan admiration of Greek
mythology, Swinburne's defiant attacks against authoritative reli-
gions, and particularly Swinburne's outspoken reaction against the
rule of Puritanism. The youthful Shelley had made his own violent
negations against Calvinistic dogma, and Shelley may have led
Faulkner to the discovery of convenient pagan notions concerning
the erotic, in *The Symposium* of Plato—those different steps of ascent
from physical love to metaphysical love, as explained to Socrates by
Diotema, and those poetic explanations of the mirror principle.
But for the time being, Faulkner's erotic preoccupations were coupled
with his negations of his religious heritage in ways which must have
made him more sympathetic towards Freud and Darwin than towards
Diotema. Under the circumstances, the Freudian and Darwinian
concepts of predestination known respectively as psychological and
naturalistic determinism must have offered attractive substitutes for
the Calvinistic concept of predestination. Throughout all these early
phases of Faulkner's rebellious negation he began to make related
substitutions of belief, and thus started to reconstruct his own moral
vision, his own personal myth, by assembling attractive pieces and
fragments from the physical and metaphysical lore of Swinburne,
Shelley, Plato, Greek mythology, Freudianism, and Darwinianism.
His reactionary negations provided the tension which gave special
significance to him in affirming certain pagan and secular and humanistic beliefs that the universe is primarily man-centered.

Somewhere in this process, however, Faulkner seems to have recognized that he needed and wanted to preserve or re-establish at least a reinterpreted version of his inherited belief that the universe was planned, created, and ordered by a benevolent, if not anthropomorphic Prime Mover. Without too much difficulty he salvaged such belief by refashioning certain basic Christian assumptions, while still rejecting tenets which interfered too much with his humanistic and secular preoccupations. For example, he rejected the notion of divine grace which is the keystone of Christian doctrine— the belief that the redemption and salvation of sinful man depends on that gift of God made available through Christ's sacrifice on the cross. When he was asked, in 1958, how it happened that no character in any of his narratives is represented as being saved by divine grace, he first acknowledged the accuracy of that observation and then explained with pleasant seriousness that it must be because he himself thought of God as being in the wholesale and not in the retail business. The wit of that remark was not intended as jest. It at least implied Faulkner's persistent belief that God is still in business, although Faulkner had much earlier reinterpreted the word "salvation" to make it represent man's humanistic concern for saving the life of the race, on earth, without any interest in or belief in the possibilities of a life after death. He had thrown oblique light on much the same point, in 1951, when he had publicly said, "It is not man in the mass who can and will save Man. It is Man himself, created in the image of God so that he shall have the power and the will to choose right from wrong and so be able to save himself."

From such evidences we can more clearly understand how Faulkner's reaction against his Calvinistic heritage motivated his initial negations and then led to subsequent affirmations, and how his eclectic counterpoint of humanistic and scientific and theistic pieces became a form of harmony within his personal myth. It might seem to any dogmatist that Faulkner could never make such an odd assortment of lions and lambs lie down together. But when an acknowledged dogmatist like Randall Stewart blindly goes to the other extreme and rashly asserts that Faulkner is "one of the most profoundly Christian writers in our time," he thus misconstrues and misunderstands Faulkner's independently complicated ways of looking at human existence. Even the most restrictively theistic representation of that moral vision must make room within it for the Hellenic bias in Faulkner's very strongly humanistic and pagan beliefs.

$\prec\!\!\!\zeta\ \ \zeta\!\!\!\succ$

Now we are in a better position to review some further evidence that Faulkner's ambivalent uses of mythic analogies, throughout all his major narratives, throw further light on the configuration of his personal myth. Quite obviously, he can and does achieve thematic reinforcements from his artistic handling of Greek myths without needing to accept whatever he finds outmoded in the poetry of Greek religious beliefs. But it should also be equally obvious that he achieves thematic reinforcements from his artistic handling of Christian myths without needing to accept whatever he finds outmoded. We have seen the predominance of Christian elements in the mythic analogies. A review of his favorites, here, will help to show how he adapts and reinterprets them to make them fit his personal myth.

Many of Faulkner's narratives show his liking for the mythic metaphor that earth is a battleground for that great physical-metaphysical struggle between God and Satan, wherein man is inescapably caught. Faulkner seems further attracted by the doctrinal poetry that each individual human being is a microcosmic mirror of that larger battleground, and that man's inner psychological conflicts reflect the metaphysical battle between good and evil. In his implicit analogizings which invoke these metaphors, however, certain reservations are suggested. First of all, he quite clearly rejects the traditional Christian notion that soul and body are two separate entities, and that while the soul belongs to God the body belongs to Satan. Faulkner prefers to view soul and body as metaphorical aspects of one and the same energy; like Blake, he believes in the marriage of Heaven and Hell. Furthermore, he can make only ironic and sarcastic uses of the doctrinal poetry that there is either an immediate or ultimate parting of the sheep from the goats, among men, on earth, or between Heaven and Hell. In Faulkner's myth, as we have noticed, there is motive for discovering that not all of the Snopeses act amorally and that not all of the Sartorises act with an ethically responsible will. But remember just one further piece of narrative evidence on this point. Isaac McCaslin is eventually permitted to discover that his idealistic act of repudiating the evils in his birthright had been conducive to evil. When Faulkner says that the only subject worth writing about is the problem of the human heart in conflict with itself, that metaphor implies his own capacity for recognizing that good must be born of evil, man being man, and that evil keeps getting born of good, for the same reason. Faulkner's ambivalent and multivalent vision finds good and evil so inextricably related that they breed their opposites.

Another basic element of Christian myth which Faulkner poetically reinterprets and selectively adapts to his artistic and thematic needs, is the doctrinal extension which rests on the first chapter of Genesis. In the beginning, God created the heavens and the earth out of the original chaos; He created man in His own image; He created all geographical space, and all time, as intervals within the vastness of eternity, for purposes of permitting human beings to share with Him, in the process of advancing or retarding a divine plan, through the performance of freely willed and therefore morally responsible actions. As we have seen in *Requiem*, however, Faulkner's reinterpretation of that myth is made by grafting to it certain Darwinian and Freudian concepts, or by substituting poetically handled findings of evolution, geology, biology, anthropology, and psychoanalysis. We have noticed that his imagination, in fine frenzy rolling, seems to experience no difficulty in perceiving that man was created, in the image of God, through a very tedious process of evolutionary and geological development, across the centuries. Many of his narratives provide hints that he particularly likes the poetry of scientific notions concerning how it happens that man is still born animal, with instinctive motivations which have ambivalent possibilities. With such assistance, Faulkner rejects and discards the Hebraic-Christian myth that paradisiacal perfection was man's first state, lost through an act of original sin, but regainable. Not included among Faulkner's mythic analogizings is the Adam and Eve fable—perhaps because even the poetry of it was spoiled for him, during his youth, by Calvinistic correlations of the First and the Second Adam to explain the wonders of divine grace.

As so many of Faulkner's narratives figuratively reveal, the substitutions for the Adam and Eve story which he made in his own personal myth were apparently drawn from anthropologists like Sir James Frazer. Faulkner's analogizings imply that he finds evidence, congenial to his reactionary needs, that even in the earliest evolutionary phases of the primitive human family the savage formulated from practical and superstitious experience those rituals of totem and taboo which indicated the first fumbling attempts to differentiate between those forces in nature and in human nature which are life-creating and life-encouraging, as opposed to those forces which are life-injuring and life-destroying. Poetically considered, those aspirations of primitive man could be said to represent man's earliest attempts to place himself in accord with the divine, and even to identify himself with the divine plan, or the image of God.

Faulkner's narratives indirectly suggest further reasons why he does not make elaborate uses of the Adam and Eve fable, either in his own personal myth, or in his art. On that fable rests the doctrina elaborations of predestination and free will, so variously interpreted within the truths of Christian theology. His own partial and flexible substitutions of Darwinian and Freudian notions seemed to make him particularly scornful of the Calvinistic view concerning pre-destination. Remember the dramatic irony in Faulkner's permitting so many of his characters to justify their most vicious mistakes by falling back on the notion that God has commanded, guided, deter-mined and thus sanctified whatever they did. Remember that ironic procession of predestinating characters who shape the life of Joe Christmas, starting with old Doc Hines and ending with young Percy Grimm. Remember Joe Christmas himself, trying to explain why he must kill Joanna Burden: "I had to do it." Remember Faulk-ner's ironic comment, "He believed with calm paradox that he was the volitionless servant of the fatality in which he believed that he did not believe." Remember how Mr. Compson pessimistically ex-cuses all human failures, including his own, by negatively scrambling Hellenic and Hebraic-Christian notions about "fate, destiny, retribu-tion, irony, the stage manager—call him what you will."

Faulkner said that he reread parts of *Don Quixote*, each year, and so there is reason for noticing that he shares with Cervantes a sense of amusement and sadness over one particular form of self-deception, here pertinent. It is the chronic human tendency to create psycho-logical or subjective illusions, and then to believe in them as objec-tive truths, just so long as the believer can derive any sense of comfort or profit from such illusory beliefs. Faulkner stresses the comfort; but Cervantes stresses the profit motive. In Faulkner's works, all those ironies he builds around Calvinistic predestination are capped by Hightower's very seriously sarcastic observation, "After all, there must be some things for which God cannot be accused by man and held responsible."

∽§ §∾

Because Faulkner's multivalent handling of tragedy provides an important reflection of his views concerning free will and predestina-tion, there may be justification for digressing here to consider the Faulknerian concepts of tragedy. Many critics and interpreters have suggested that Faulkner likes to cast his narratives in forms which reveal that his concept of tragedy is at one with the Greek concept. But which Greek concept? Even in the plays of Aeschylus, Sophocles, and Euripides, interpreters have found at least three different con-cepts of tragedy. According to one concept, the protagonist may be

167

represented as overwhelmed by outer and inner forces which he does not understand and which he can not control; hence he becomes a tragic victim of meaningless Fate, no matter how much he struggles. According to an opposed concept, the protagonist may be represented as brought low through his own errors in judgment—through some shortcoming or lack of insight. Then the consequence is a tragedy of character. Between these two extremes, we are told, some Greek tragedies represent the protagonist as caught in a web of events which are caused in part by fate and in part by his own freely willed actions; but the two factors are inextricably combined. The Christian concept of tragedy is at least analogous to the second of those three Greek concepts; it is essentially tragedy of character, in which the hero is viewed as morally responsible for what happens to him. Within the Christian premises, of course, if the doomed man comes to himself and repents of his own sinful choices, or errors in judgment, during the action, he can thus presumably make his repentance the first step toward the achievement of divine forgiveness, redemption, salvation, and life everlasting. One essence of tragedy is thus removed and we may notice that Faulkner rarely permits his tragic characters to arrive at such self-recognition scenes. But in what sense are Faulkner's tragedies at one with Greek concepts of tragedy?

Faulkner has said that "man's free will functions against a Greek background of fate," and that remark suggests that he consciously interweaves at least two concepts of tragedy throughout his narratives. At times he represents some of his characters purely as victims of fate, or of deterministic forces. He represents such predicaments as tragic, although with complete awareness that more restrictive definitions might classify the same predicaments as merely pathetic. At other times, he represents an individual as making an error in judgment, before or during the narrative, so that this error precipitates a "tragedy of character." Most of the time, however, he prefers to create narrative situations in which there is a decidedly ambivalent relationship between the contrasting forces of fate and free will.

With those generalized possibilities again in mind, we may now briefly recall some restricted aspects of evidences already considered. In *The Sound and the Fury*, as we have seen, the claim can at least be made that all the Compsons are inexorably fated or doomed. Mr. Compson prefers that view, and Quentin shares it. With his father's help, Quentin finds masochistic consolation in the assurance that he is the victim of circumstance. Unconsciously, however, he is permitted to reveal through his own stream-of-consciousness analogizings that he is at least partially responsible for what has happened to Caddy, and for what is ironically "happening" to himself. Although Jason agrees with Quentin that Caddy must be blamed for her own predicament and also for the disgrace she has brought on the entire family, it would seem that in Faulkner's eyes Caddy is the best of all the Compsons, and that she is the one who is truly victimized, by a variety of interpenetrative circumstances. Faulkner's comment on Caddy in his "Appendix" to *The Sound and The Fury* is worth remembering: "Doomed and knew it, accepted the doom without either seeking or fleeing it." That suggests a variant from the conventional concept about the tragedy of fate. But the point to notice, here, is that Faulkner handles events involving Quentin and Caddy in ways which build tensions around at least three opposed concepts of tragedy. Then Faulkner lets the reader decide which is most applicable.

Considered within this framework of variable possibilities, *Absalom, Absalom!* contains three tragically related characters: Thomas Sutpen and his two sons. The predicament of Thomas Sutpen, who in effect loses both of those sons, takes on deeper meanings if no single concept of tragedy is applied to him. Mr. Compson is "in character," of course, when he explains to Quentin that Sutpen is a mere plaything of Fate. Quentin's grandfather had previously excused Sutpen by saying his trouble stemmed from his peculiar form of innocence. Although Faulkner encourages the reader to resist and challenge both of those oversimplifications, notice that up to a certain point in his life Sutpen is represented as having been conditioned and thus blinded by the interaction of certain social and religious assumptions which provided him with part of his self-justification. Then the question arises, when does Sutpen come of age, figuratively speaking, to the extent that he has to assume his moral responsibilities for what happens to him, if he has to assume them, in spite of that conditioning? In the middle portion of the Sutpen saga, there may be an interplay of the two extreme concepts of tragedy. But as the later phases of his story are presented, Sutpen's inhumanities become increasingly inexcusable. By the time he earns his doom, at the hands of Wash Jones, his character becomes his fate. Much the same pattern of tragic developments is applicable to Henry Sutpen: like father like son. Charles Bon is different. He is represented as deliberately choosing to effect a tragedy of revenge, and he spends his life willingly to achieve that effect. Thus in *Absalom, Absalom!* Faulkner brings three or four concepts of tragedy to bear, and again lets the reader apply them.

Light in August counterbalances two tragic characters, Joe Christmas and the Reverend Gail Hightower. Throughout his childhood and youth, Joe Christmas is so rigorously molded by so many self-justified

Calvinists that the reader can sympathetically call him either a "fated" or a "predestinated" victim. Such an interpretation is intensified by the tragic irony of his being forced to serve as a scapegoat for that society which creates him in its own image, heaps its own sins on him, and then crucifies him. Up to a certain point in his life, Joe Christmas is given very little freedom of choice. Yet Faulkner is manipulating more than ironies when he interweaves evidences to support Joe's conviction that "I have lived to make me what I chose to be." The reader may be left in doubt, at the end of the story, whether to call his a tragedy of fate, or a tragedy which combines fate and choice, or finally a tragedy of character. But if the conclusion is reached that Joe Christmas can not be held morally responsible for what happens to him, we are not left in doubt about the guilt of that society which helped to shape him. That guilt is glossed by Hightower. With ironic pertinence, then, Faulkner ambivalently reduces Hightower's tragedy to the base concept of Christian tragedy. Byron Bunch is permitted to sharpen that focus by refuting Hightower's claim that he has achieved immunity from the present, and through no choice of his own. In his self-recognition scene, Hightower implicitly acknowledges that Bunch had been correct in holding him morally responsible for his own fate, and for the fate of at least part of his society. As we noticed, the major failures of the individuals and of society, in *Light in August*, are thematically ascribed by Faulkner to the failures of Christian preachments and practices. But once again, the immediate point is that Faulkner invokes and manipulates several different concepts of tragedy.

Quite distinct from all the others is the tragedy of Isaac McCaslin in *Go Down, Moses*. His predicament has little enough to do with Cordelia's, and yet the previously mentioned analogy is worth keeping in mind: "We are not the first who, with best meaning, have incurred the worst." The reader shares with Isaac the awareness that his carefully calculated attempt to free himself from his evil birthright was nobly and idealistically motivated; but that fact only intensifies the tragic irony of the consequences. This time, there is no sense in saying that fate and free will are here intermixed, and that Isaac is represented as having become victimized in part by the pagan Sam Fathers and in part by his Christian heritage. Isaac ultimately blames himself, and although Faulkner is obviously compassionate in his attitude towards Isaac, Faulkner seems to agree. What concept of tragedy is most applicable here? The Christian concept, with a Faulknerian twist: evil is here born of good.

Sanctuary offers a counterpoint of tragic predicaments in which

Lee Goodwin serves variously as a foil for Temple Drake. In the sense that Lee Goodwin was lynched for two crimes he did not commit, he is clearly a victim of circumstance, and Temple Drake is partially responsible for his death because she bore false witness against him in court. Yet Faulkner endows with thematic pertinence the fact that Lee Goodwin, out of moral cowardice, refused to name Popeye as murderer. In the plight of Temple Drake, her thoughts on the "circumstances in which she had become involved" are not very persuasive. Nor is the reader moved by her lawyer's plea, in court, for "this ruined, defenseless child." If anyone is left in doubt concerning Faulkner's attitude towards Temple Drake in *Sanctuary*, the total action of *Requiem* should resolve that doubt. Nevertheless, the pairing of Temple Drake and Lee Goodwin enables Faulkner to work ambivalently with at least two concepts of tragedy in *Sanctuary*.

It could be argued that there is a dialectical factor reflected in Faulkner's frequent way of establishing two extreme concepts of tragedy, in a narrative, and then his gradual intermingling of those two extremes. But here once again the indelible effect of his Christian heritage is apparent, because his primary concern is with those aspects of tragedy in which man's own actions bring on him his own fate. Faulkner grieves repeatedly over disasters and miseries which are unavoidable; but he grieves most over those for which human shortcomings are to blame. If one is trying to decide just how truly Greek his concept of tragedy may be, one final factor of measurement may be helpful. In most of Greek tragedy, the ultimate effect on the audience is one of dark conclusions concerning events which were, in the premises, inevitable. By contrast, in much of Christian tragedy, the development and the denouement frequently imply that the outcome is particularly pitiful because the crisis could and should have been averted. That latter quality is generally found in Faulkner's tragic narratives. He reminds his readers, in various ways, that man usually does have the power and the opportunity to assert significant moral force through freely willed actions, and that such actions can help to correct many of those tragic mistakes which have darkened man's past. To that extent, he further implies, man has demonstrated his capacity to change and improve the human condition, even though man has always had, and will always have, the power to obliterate himself. Unmistakably, then, beneath the surface of Faulkner's tragic narratives there is always a moral earnestness which is calculated to evoke something more than pity and terror.

This digression on tragedy may justifiably end with a brief mention of Faulkner's handling of the comic in ways which have further dialectical overtones. At times, of course, his very strong sense of what is amusing and ridiculous expresses itself through dramatizations of harmless inconsistencies which cause laughter, as an end in itself. But when the comic protagonist is motivated by fallibilities of hypocritical deception and self-deception, involving moral consequences, satiric elements become combined with the comic elements, for purposes of implying moral judgments. Then the ultimate synthesis between the Faulknerian forms of the comic and the tragic becomes available. In *The Town* and in *Sanctuary*, for example, we saw the intermixture of the comic, the satiric, and the tragic.

୶ঌ ঌ৶

Those digressions on restricted aspects of tragedy and comedy grew out of our considering Faulkner's reactionary and reinterpretative responses to aspects of Christian myth which involve the doctrines of free will and predestination. Now we can return to examine Faulkner's way of adapting to his own moral vision, to his own personal myth, another basic factor in Christian myth: the crucifixion story. We have noticed his elaborate uses of that story in his techniques and in his themes. Those uses include his comically ironic arranging to let Jason's day fall on Good Friday, in *The Sound and the Fury*. There is even a bitterly satiric element in his establishing an implicitly inverted analogy, in *Light in August*, by letting Joe Christmas be crucified as a scapegoat. Yet there is nothing satiric or inverted in Faulkner's use of the crucifixion story to reinforce positive elements of theme, in *The Sound and the Fury*, by representing Dilsey and Ben as attending the Easter service to watch the Negro preacher act out an important meaning in that story. Nor is there anything ambiguous in Hightower's self-condemnatory remembrance of what he had preached "instead of the crucified shape of pity and love." Furthermore, Faulkner implies no irony or ambiguity in the establishment of implicit analogies between the self-sacrifice of Nancy Mannigoe and the self-sacrifice of Jesus.

Yet Faulkner once very pointedly said, "That Christ story is one of the best stories that man has invented, assuming that he did invent that story." If he viewed it as a mere fiction, why did he cherish it so highly, and make so many different artistic uses of it? Apparently because it still retained, as such, a very important mythic value. In his reactionary fashioning of his own moral vision, he has chosen to assign pagan or secular significance to the life-giving, life-encouraging, life-transforming, and (in a Faulknerian sense) redeeming and saving power of love, as expressed by man and woman on earth, and

172

as affecting life on earth. But he has been forced to reinterpret and restrict even the mythic value of "that Christ story," in order to possess it. That which seems to interest Faulkner not at all is the notion that Jesus was God, or was at least a divinely sent avatar whose love afforded mankind the possibility of eternal bliss in a life after death. But, as Faulkner demonstrated in so many ways, a successfully figurative usage of mythological imagery and assumptions (Christian, Greek, pagan) does not require of the artist a literal or dogmatic belief in any of these myths.

It is possible that Faulkner adapted the Christian myth of love to his own needs by combining it with Freudian and Platonic reinterpretations, within his own moral vision. The initial conflict over the meaning of the term "love" must have begun for him at about the age when he began to admire Swinburne—the age when he began to explore, physically, and poetically, the pagan realms of fauns, satyrs, and worshippers of Dionysus. Up until that time, he had been taught, from Christian doctrine, that there are only two categories of love; that one is good, and the other is evil; that only the love which is sanctified by the spirit is good; and that the love which is sanctified merely by the body is evil. But his Dionysiac leanings and his personal experiences could have persuaded him without benefit of either Nietzsche or Freud that the notion of any such duality between the spiritual and the carnal, or between the soul and the body, insults and degrades the primary forms of love and life. Many of Faulkner's narratives represent the erotic drives as containing inseparable potentials, both for physical and spiritual good and evil. But he seems particularly interested in dramatizing evidences that even the most unconventional and pagan expressions of genuine love can have their validity. Lena Grove, in *Light in August*, is represented as one such unconventional pagan, whose love is honored by Faulkner as an inspiring affirmation of life. Ruby Lamarr, in *Sanctuary*, comes as near to being the tragic heroine as is possible in that peculiar novel. Even the prostitute Nancy Mannigoe, in *Requiem*, is honored because of her capacity for self-sacrificial love. Whatever the limitations, perversions, distortions, or loftiest possibilities of love, Faulkner consistently represents it as having its source in the animal instincts of the body, and as having its various forms of fulfillment at different levels of experience which ascend until they bring the human integer nearest the divine. Thus it would seem that in his reactionary fashioning of his moral vision and of his private myth, his own personal experiences enabled him to give a somewhat Freudian interpretation to that Platonic encomium of love in *The*

Symposium, where Socrates paraphrases Diotema's progression: Anyone who starts learning of love through the lowliest human forms, and then progresses to the love of beauty in all earthly things, may mount upward by using these perceptions as steps, until that ascent serves as a means to his becoming "the friend of God" and also as a means of becoming immortal, "if mortal man may be."

As already implied Faulkner found that he needed to reinterpret the conventional meaning of the term "immortality" before he could make it useful within the framework of his reactionary moral vision. Here again Diotema's preliminary uses of the term could have proved helpful to him. Faulkner makes "immortality" refer only to the continuation of life on earth, through generation after genera- tion. He finds in the human race a seemingly unquenchable capacity for clinging to earth, and feels that the race has achieved success in it, so far, only through conscientious expressions of moral truth, and in spite of man's own self-destructive brutality. In that context, "truth" has a particular meaning for Faulkner. "Truth" is the quality of being in accordance with those facts or realities of experience which have thus far enabled man to achieve and preserve his "im- mortality." Thus the human perception of "truth" is the conscien- tious awareness of the individual, and then of the social group, concerning that which must be done to assert and thus renew the via- bility of valid and constructive human experience. The Faulknerian ethic which is seen as implementing this concept of "truth" stresses certain cardinal forms of response which are called virtues within Christian doctrine. Seeming to dislike the term "virtues," perhaps because it had become soiled for him by unpleasant Christian asso- ciations, Faulkner prefers to call his selection of fundamentally right attitudes or responses which conform to truth, "the verities of the human heart." Man's conscience, or his instinctive reaction against the falsehood of evil, motivates the protesting expression of those attitudes and responses. In such reactions, man's purpose is not to attempt the attainment of lofty goals, and not to advance the im- possible ideal of achieving human perfection, but rather the practical end of helping to effect decent human survival on earth. For Faulk- ner, these right attitudes or responses, these "verities of the human heart," include compassion, aspiration, courage, endurance, self- sacrifice, and love.

Within the Faulknerian vision human beings express their reac- tionary protests against whatever falsehoods or evils injure "truth," by making innumerable kinds of response which may be arranged within three categories. One category includes any courageous and yet mistaken form of protest which asserts that life has been made unbearable by man's inhumanity to man, and that death is therefore preferable to life. (In *The Sound and the Fury*, Quentin Compson is represented as making that mistaken response.) A second category includes any well-intentioned attempt to honor "truth" through the performance of some compassionately self-sacrificial act of protesting withdrawal from an immediately perceived falsehood, or evil. (In *Go Down, Moses*, Isaac McCaslin is represented as making that mistaken response.) A third category includes any attempt to remove, or to correct, or to defend someone from any immediate manifestation of falsehood or evil, be it large or small. (In her humble way, Dilsey repeatedly performs such protesting actions, in ways which express her courage, compassion, aspiration, self-sacrifice, love, and endurance.)

Mankind fails, and fails repeatedly, because each human being has only a limited and partial perception of "truth." The "human heart in conflict with itself," stands in its own way and thus blinds itself to what the heart or conscience or spirit or soul could otherwise know as "truth." But these tragic facts do not discourage Faulkner's persistent belief that the odds are always in man's favor, and that the power is within man's capacity to endure, survive, and prevail. All the right attitudes or responses are seen by Faulkner as imitations, or mirrorings, of elements in the divine Idea, the initial Source, from which comes the inspiration and the aspiration.

❧　☙

These attempts to correlate from Faulkner's own utterances, at least the broad configuration of his moral vision, are calculated to remove some of the apparent paradoxes and inconsistencies which are so often found troublesome in his themes and techniques. There is consistency in that "one story" which he has tried to tell even while he has been fashioning it out of the many pieces he has drawn from earlier myths. There is no actual paradox or inconsistency in his position: His intricate rearrangements and adaptations have provided him with a firm theistic base for one foot, and a firm humanistic base for the other foot. His reason for keeping the greater part of his weight on the humanistic base should now be clear. He sees a mistake in man's tendency to reduce his own need for endeavor, and to alleviate his own responsibilities, by appealing to God for help. He also sees a mistake in man's consequent tendency to hold God responsible, sooner or later, for man's own failures.

There remains one final aspect of Faulkner's moral vision—one final piece which needs to be fitted into this representation of his personal myth. It is Faulkner's conviction concerning the part which the artist must play in the moral scheme of things. A suggestion was made, earlier, that Faulkner may have formulated some of his aesthetic by making reinterpretative adaptations from Shelley's "Defence of Poetry"; but one major exception must be made there. The purely Platonistic separation of body from spirit, as approved by Shelley, seems to have caused Shelley to hedge on the question as to whether the artist should portray the worst horrors of vice, evil, and suffering. Faulkner does not hedge on this point, perhaps because of his belief in the inseparability of body and spirit, the inseparability of positives and negatives. He insists that the artist should exercise his capacities for describing horror and evil as a means of measuring the distance between certain actualities and certain possibilities. His entire career as a writer consistently illustrated that conviction, and has caused many misunderstandings. So his own words are needed, here, to explain how the portrayal of horror and evil fits into the part which the artist must play in the moral scheme of things. When he was in Japan in 1955, and was asked by an interviewer to explain, he answered:

> Yes—never to use the evil for the sake of the evil—you must use the evil to try to tell some truth which you think is important. There are times when man needs to be reminded of evil, to correct it, to change it. He should not be reminded always only of the good and the beautiful. I think the writer or the poet or the novelist should not be just a "recorder" of man—he should give man some reason to believe that man can be better than he is. If the writer is to accomplish anything, it is to make the world a little better than he found it, to do what he can, in whatever way he can, to get rid of the evils . . . that's his job. And not to do this by describing merely the pleasant things—he must show the base, the evil things that man can do and still hate himself for doing it, to still prevail and endure and last; to believe always that he can be better than he probably will.

That puts the last piece in place. For Faulkner, the literary artist plays his part in the moral scheme of things by letting the indirections of his art create in his readers an awareness not only of conflicts but also of the possibilities for greater harmony through reconciliations of opposed drives in the human heart. In that way, Faulkner is convinced that all artists may serve as "the mirrors of the gigantic shadows which futurity casts upon the present," to use Shelley's words, and as the "unacknowledged legislators of the world."

SELECTED BIBLIOGRAPHY

Note: (P) indicates works available in paperbound editions.

FAULKNER'S NOVELS

Soldiers' Pay. New York: Boni and Liveright, 1926. (P)
Mosquitoes. New York: Boni and Liveright, 1927. (P)
Sartoris. New York: Harcourt, Brace, 1929. (P)
The Sound and the Fury. New York: Cape and Smith, 1929. (P)
As I Lay Dying. New York: Cape and Smith, 1930. (P)
Sanctuary. New York: Cape and Smith, 1931. (P)
Light in August. New York: Smith and Haas, 1932. (P)
Pylon. New York: Smith and Haas, 1935. (P)
Absalom, Absalom! New York: Random House, 1936.
The Unvanquished. New York: Random House, 1938. (P)
The Wild Palms. New York: Random House, 1939. (P)
The Hamlet. New York: Random House, 1940. (P)
Intruder in the Dust. New York: Random House, 1948. (P)
A Fable. New York: Random House, 1954.
The Town. New York: Random House, 1957. (P)
The Mansion. New York: Random House, 1959.
The Reivers. New York: Random House, 1962.

COLLECTED SHORT STORIES

These Thirteen. New York: Cape and Smith, 1931.
Doctor Martino and Other Stories. New York: Smith and Haas, 1934.
Go Down, Moses and Other Stories. New York: Random House, 1942.
Knight's Gambit. New York: Random House, 1949. (P)
Collected Stories of William Faulkner. New York: Random House, 1950.
Big Woods. New York: Random House, 1955.

PLAY

Requiem for a Nun. New York: Random House, 1951. (P)

COLLECTED POEMS

The Marble Faun. Boston: The Four Seas, 1924.
A Green Bough. New York: Smith and Haas, 1933.

COLLECTED SELECTIONS

The Portable Faulkner, ed. Malcolm Cowley. New York: Viking Press,
1946. (P). [For this volume, Faulkner wrote an "Appendix" for *The*

Sound and the Fury entitled "Compson: 1699–1945," pp. 737–58; it was reprinted in *The Sound and the Fury* (Modern Library, 1946), pp. 3–22.]

The Faulkner Reader, with a foreword by William Faulkner. New York: Random House, 1954. (P) [Contains "The Nobel Prize Address," complete text of *The Sound and the Fury* (with "Appendix"), selections from several novels, and short stories.]

Early Prose and Poetry, ed. Carvel Collins. Boston: Little, Brown, 1962. (P)

ADDITIONAL WORKS

Salmagundi, ed. with Introduction by Paul Romaine. Milwaukee: Casanova Press, 1932. [Contains three essays (including *Verse Old and Nascent: a Pilgrimage*) and five poems, reprinted from the (New Orleans) *Double Dealer*, 1925.]

Mirrors of Chartres Street, ed. with Introduction by William Van O'Connor. Minneapolis: Faulkner Studies, 1953. [Contains eleven sketches reprinted from the (New Orleans) *Times-Picayune*, 1925.]

New Orleans Sketches, ed. with Introduction and notes by Ichiro Nishizaki. Tokyo: Hokuseido Press, 1955. (P) [Contains thirteen sketches reprinted from the (New Orleans) *Times-Picayune*, 1925.]

Jealousy and Episode: Two Stories. Minneapolis: Faulkner Studies, 1955. [Contains two sketches reprinted from the (New Orleans) *Times-Picayune*, 1925.]

Idyll in the Desert. New York: Random House, 1931. [Short story]

Miss Zilphia Gant. Dallas: Book Club of Texas, 1932. [Short story]

This Earth, A Poem. New York: Equinox Cooperative Press, 1932.

INTERVIEWS (RECORDED)

Cowley, Malcolm (ed.). *Writers at Work*. New York: Viking Press, 1958. [See Jean Stein, "William Faulkner" (pp. 119–41), reprinted from *Paris Review*, IV (Spring, 1956).]

Gwynn, Frederick L., and Blotner, Joseph L. (eds.). *Faulkner in the University*. Charlottesville: University of Virginia Press, 1959.

Jelliffe, Robert A. (ed.). *Faulkner at Nagano*. Tokyo: Kenkyusha Ltd., 1956.

BIBLIOGRAPHY

Beebe, Maurice. "Criticism of William Faulkner: A Selected Checklist with an Index to Studies of Separate Works," *Modern Fiction Studies,* II (Autumn, 1956), 150–64.

Hoffman, Frederick J., and Vickery, Olga W. *William Faulkner: Three Decades of Criticism*. East Lansing: Michigan State University Press, 1960. [Bibliography, pp. 393–427.]

Meriwether, James B. "William Faulkner: A Check List," *Princeton University Library Chronicle,* XVIII (Spring, 1957), 136–58.

BIOGRAPHICAL ESSAYS

Cantwell, Robert. "The Faulkners: Recollections of a Gifted Family," *New World Writing,* II (November, 1952), 300–15.

Carter, Hodding. "Faulkner and His Folk," *Princeton University Library Chronicle,* XVIII (Spring, 1957), 95–107.

Smith, Marshall J. "Faulkner of Mississippi," *The Bookman,* LXXIV (December, 1931), 411–17.

Stone, Phil. "William Faulkner, the Man and His Work," *Oxford Magazine* (Oxford, Mississippi), I (1934), 13–14.

CRITICAL AND INTERPRETATIVE STUDIES

Hoffman, Frederick J. *William Faulkner.* Twayne's United States Authors Series #1. New Haven: College and University Press, 1961.

Hoffman, Frederick J., and Vickery, Olga W. *William Faulkner: Three Decades of Criticism.* East Lansing: Michigan State University Press, 1960. [Twenty-three essays, including George Marion O'Donnell, "Faulkner's Mythology," pp. 82–93.]

Howe, Irving. *William Faulkner: A Critical Study.* New York: Random House, 1952.

Malin, Irving. *William Faulkner: An Interpretation.* Stanford: Stanford University Press, 1957.

Miner, Ward L. *The World of William Faulkner.* Durham: Duke University Press, 1952.

O'Connor, William Van. *The Tangled Fire of William Faulkner.* Minneapolis: University of Minnesota Press, 1959.

Vickery, Olga W. *The Novels of William Faulkner: A Critical Interpretation.* Baton Rouge: Louisiana State University Press, 1959.

INDEX

Note: Characters and other fictional subjects from Faulkner's works are entered in small capital letters.

Index

182

Index

❧ ❧

This book is an original work (No. 10) in the American Authors & Critics Series. It was written by a distinguished educator, carefully edited, and produced in accordance with the highest standards of publishing. The text was set on the Linotype in Old Style No. 7 by Plimpton Press (Norwood, Mass.). The paper for this edition was manufactured by the S. D. Warren Company (Boston, Mass.) and supplied by the Canfield Paper Company (New York, N. Y.). This edition was printed by the Plimpton Press (Norwood, Mass.) and bound by Sendor Bindery (New York, N. Y.). The cover was designed by Rod Lopez-Fabrega.

G45937   OCLC

3.50

PS3511 Thompson, Lawrance Roger, 1906–
A86Z977   William Faulkner; an introduction and interpretation
New York, Barnes & Noble ₁1963₎

    184 p. illus. 22 cm. (American authors and critics series, no. 10

    Includes bibliography.

3 11/93
5 - 4/95
5 - 2/08

   1. Faulkner, William, 1897–1962.